ETERNAL HOPE

Books by
EMIL BRUNNER
Published by The Westminster Press

Eternal Hope

The Misunderstanding of the Church

The Christian Doctrine of Creation and Redemption, Dogmatics, Vol. II

The Scandal of Christianity

The Christian Doctrine of God, Dogmatics, Vol. I

Man in Revolt

The Mediator

The Divine Imperative

Revelation and Reason

The Divine-Human Encounter

Emil Brunner

ETERNAL HOPE

Translated by
HAROLD KNIGHT

Philadelphia
THE WESTMINSTER PRESS

First Published in Great Britain in 1954
by Lutterworth Press, London

PRINTED IN THE UNITED STATES OF AMERICA

To the memory of my sons
Peter
1919—1942
and
Thomas
1926—1952

CONTENTS

Chapter One

THE SIGNIFICANCE OF HOPE IN HUMAN LIFE

WHAT oxygen is for the lungs, such is hope for the meaning of human life. Take oxygen away and death occurs through suffocation, take hope away and humanity is constricted through lack of breath; despair supervenes, spelling the paralysis of intellectual and spiritual powers by a feeling of the senselessness and purposelessness of existence. As the fate of the human organism is dependent on the supply of oxygen, so the fate of humanity is dependent on its supply of hope.

It is scarcely necessary to prove that Western humanity of to-day, at least in Europe, has entered a phase when it is feeling an acute and distressing need of breath through the disappearance of hope. Everyone is becoming aware of this, to a greater or less degree, and if anyone is not aware of it he can find the proof of it in contemporary literature and philosophy. Why this is so, and how this situation has come about, and whether it is inevitable or whether there exists any way of escape from this pervading sense of hopelessness, is the object of this book.

Hope means the presence of the future, or more precisely it is one of the ways in which what is merely future and potential is made vividly present and actual to us. Hope is the positive, as anxiety is the negative, mode of awaiting the future. Through anxiety and hope man relates himself to the future in passive expectation. But he may also have an active rather than a passive attitude towards the future. He may make plans and projects in order to shape the future according to his wishes. Through such an active attitude man imagines himself to be the architect of his own destiny. In that case the future ceases in some measure to be mere futurity. It does not come upon man from without, but he goes towards it, anticipating it and controlling it. The life and thought of modern Western European man is plainly distinguished from that of man in other epochs and other culture cycles by the fact that this active attitude through which man seeks to control his future emerges ever more predominantly into the foreground. But in proportion as man has the feeling that he has power over his future and can plan and determine it, those passive modes of realizing the future through anxiety and hope recede into the background. He who creates his future need neither hope nor fear.

At some point in the course of modern history—it was most probably at the time of the Renaissance—Western European man began to experience this strange confidence in his own powers of controlling and constructing his future. From that time onwards hope loses significance in proportion as self-confidence grows. If man had his future entirely in his own hands, he would no longer either hope or fear. Instead of waiting in expectancy of what the future might bring, he would sit, so to speak, at the switchboard which regulates it, certain at every moment which lever to pull, which button to press. He would indeed be the master and controller of his future. He would even feel that the expression "master of his fate" was no longer relevant, was unworthy, since "fate" would still be reminiscent of the idea that his future was something sent to him, that he did not shape it as its author and determiner. Western man has not yet reached this stage of development, but his mental picture of himself increasingly resembles that of the man at the switchboard.

But no one can altogether conceal from himself the fact that man is very far from being the unqualified arbiter of his future. He cannot remain unaware that his power and freedom to shape the future is limited because dependent on factors over which he has no control. One such is nature; a second is the other, the not-self.

It is obvious that man is dependent on nature. The attempt to eliminate or at least to reduce this dependence more and more is what we call technology. In the structure of modern Western life technology forms the characteristically predominant feature. But that even this is dependent on the other is equally unmistakable. The most self-confident planner realizes that when, for example, he is drugged or becomes slipshod and reckless the counter-action of the other may become perilous to him. He must therefore try to eliminate as far as possible the danger which threatens him from the other, either by adopting compelling rules or by including the other in the pattern of his own planning, by organization. Hence we find that both these measures—directives and organization—designed to counter the factor of insecurity in human life, belong to the characteristically predominant traits in modern Western human life.

Since the degree of his control over the future depends on the success of these man-made means, the hope of modern Western man assumes a new form; it becomes hope in the increase of the means whereby his dependence and insecurity are progressively diminished and his power to determine the future correspondingly increased. It becomes therefore hope which is at the same time self-confidence, a middle term as it were between hope and self-assurance. We might describe it as hope in the basis of self-confidence. Its more familiar name is belief in progress. This belief in progress is the typical modern Western form of hope.

This hope that man will be able more and more to fashion and control his future is obviously something characteristic of modern Western humanity. Modern man is well aware of the fact that it is characteristic of him. But that it is something which distinguishes him, the modern Western human being, from the human beings of other epochs and other cultures, is a fact which he does not immediately realize but which is first brought to his notice by acquaintance with those other types of humanity, whether through historical study or through travel to other continents. The last few centuries of Western European and American history will come to be defined as the epoch of the belief in progress. This qualifying and characteristic description urges itself upon our attention so much the more because we are already in a position to look back upon the phenomenon as a fact of past history. For as clearly as the nineteenth century marks the climax of this belief in progress, so clearly is the twentieth century the time of its rapid decline. Indeed, so far as Europe is concerned, one must perhaps already say that the belief in progress was, but no longer is, the hope of humanity in our time. The two world wars and the rise of the totalitarian state have destroyed it. They have shattered the two main pillars on which it rested, belief in technics and belief in the state and organization as the means of guaranteeing man's progressive control of his future, and in the process the belief itself has been shattered too.

There is in fact no doubt that this hope, hope based upon self-confidence, as we can only now in retrospect quite clearly perceive, was both historically and objectively a strange and unusual thing.

Historically. In no other moment of culture or epoch of history has it existed. Only in Western Europe could it arise, because there the Christian faith afforded the presupposition for its existence. And yet belief in progress as hope resting upon self-confidence is the opposite of the Christian hope, which is hope founded upon trust in God. Belief in progress was only possible in Christian Western Europe, but only because in proportion as Christian faith declined the former arose as its distortion and substitute, its parasite. For it lived on the very powers which it destroyed. And just as belief in progress replaced and inherited the Christian hope which had once prevailed in Western Europe, so now, at a time when this belief itself which had become the hope of Western Europe is dying, we are witnessing the emergence of sheer hopelessness in the form of a philosophy of despair, of the nihilistic meaninglessness of life.

But what history is thus disclosing should not in fact surprise us. For what a curious type of hope was this mixture of self-confidence and expectation! Whose hope was it in reality—this hope in progress? For whom was this progress to avail? Whose future was here anticipated by hope and expectation? How can it irradiate my present situation, inspire my deeds, or satisfy my aspirations—the thought that at some distant date generations of mankind who are as alien to me as the ghostly inhabitants of the past will be sitting at that imaginary switchboard which will enable them to control their future? What a strange absence of mind were needed to ignore the fundamental fact which must ruin all such self-security, whether for the present or the future—the fact, namely, that all men must die! Hence was not this hope essentially only a slightly concealed hopelessness?

Or may we not perhaps have been deceiving ourselves in asserting the utter necessity and the fundamental significance of hope? Hope has not always been spoken of in favourable terms. Was it not Goethe who described the wretchedly contemptible man, the Philistine, as a useless compound of fear and hope? Does not the wisdom of the common man proclaim that he who lives on hope dies of hunger? Would it not perhaps be truer to describe hope as a form of indulgence which the really efficient man renounces because his mind is so occupied by the exigencies of the present that he has no time or interest for thoughts of the future?

In fact there are many men, and among them certainly some of the best, who are not much preoccupied with thoughts of the future, who rather take things as they come and do their duty day by day without bothering much about the shape of things to come; and again there are others who understand how to practise the *carpe diem* and thus preserve a fine humanity; and others again who, though on a higher level, take the lazzarone as their model, who lives from hand to mouth and finds his happiness in so doing. Was it not the longing for this elemental simplicity of life which drove a Gauguin to seek refuge among the primitives of the South Sea and which lies behind the noticeable leaning towards the primitive in contemporary art and literature?

But let us make no mistake! The attempt to sunder the present from the future, and to live happily in the passing moment, failed not only with Dr. Faustus. The artistic "Robinson Crusoes" of the Western European, who has grown weary of culture, are quite understandable and often impressive as attempts to effect a return to nature, but are yet essentially only an expression of an unconfessed despair of life. The fact is that man is not so constructed as to succeed in achieving happily this return to nature, since it brings him into conflict with the deeper aspect of his humanity, which also requires realization. The gaze directed towards the future, giving birth either to longing or aim, is an essential part of the properties of this humanity. The man who in the bitterness of his disillusionment thinks he is entitled to renounce all forward-looking thoughts becomes, whether he wills it or not, whether he is aware of it or not, a traitor to the cultured humanity of Western Europe and its mission. For the truly human arises always through the process of transcendence from the given away into the non-given, from the present away into the future. We cannot revoke what we said originally about hope.

Perhaps we should distinguish between different kinds of hope. No work of man, not even the plainest, can be successfully performed without hope. The farmer sows, the mother nurses and rears her child, the responsible statesman guides and achieves—on the foundations of hope. Over all human action hovers the thought that thereby—through the performance of this particular deed—things are bettered, that it is rewarding to do the right, that the *character indelebilis* of the human is to realize the ideal. No spade, no needle, no chisel, no saw would be taken in hand if it were not permissible to believe that something good would come out of it. The picture of the future sets in motion the powers of the present, but can have this effect only through hope.

Let us then make a distinction between two kinds of hope: hope in the more sober and limited sense, implying a future so imminent and closely bound up with the present as to be hardly distinguishable from it, and, further, hope in the sense of something universal and all-embracing, gathering up the whole of life and the life of all far-reaching aims! There are small and great hopes, partial and total hopes, individual hopes and hopes which include in their range humanity itself. But only in the former sense does hope appear to be a necessary and integral part of human existence. Hence it is that even in a time like our own, when hope in the total, comprehensive, sense is on the decline or has even utterly vanished, life nevertheless goes on its way. Peasants till their fields, workers in factories and offices, heads of departments, teachers, professors and doctors perform their tasks, the machinery of civilization continues to run; each man works energetically and with enjoyment in his particular sphere, actuated by his tiny personal hopes and ambitions, though for the most part without feeling the inspiration of any great hope, such as would embrace the future of humanity or his own individual life in its totality. We can muddle through without the help of the latter.

Yes, or can we? We must not take the answer too lightly from a casually chosen and limited sector of present human experience. By reason of the very structure of human existence it is not possible in the long run to limit our inquiries to partial aims any more than to partial causes. In the mind of man there lives a need to see things as a whole—a feature of the human consciousness which cannot be ignored. Just as an inquiry into causes cannot stop until it fathoms the ultimate, so it is with an inquiry into meaning and purpose. The question of the whither is as radical as that of the whence. Of course the individual can resign and wean himself from this pursuit of totalities and systems. But what is implied in this surrender? Does not something happen to a man who gives up what is so vital? Can humanity as a whole do what the individual can do? Can partial aims really be in the end distinctly maintained and affirmed in their partiality; do they continue to exercise their dynamic power when the sense of the totality, the universal, is lost, and are those tiny personal hopes to be properly and permanently nourished in an atmosphere of general hopelessness?

For a century now positivistic philosophy has not only expounded, but expounded with paradoxical zeal, the thesis that to renounce inquiry into ends is the mark of a culturally mature mind. With the arrogance of the learned, it has preached to humanity metaphysical and religious abstinence. It has forgotten in the process that it was resigning only one of the two questions, that concerning ends, whereas it was urging the erudite world to pursue the inquiry into causes without setting any limits. But positivism lived in this matter —without being aware of the fact—on a rich inheritance of Christian humanistic values and meanings which deceived it as to its own poverty so long as the source lasted. In particular, positivistic philosophy was one of the main supports of an optimistic conception of progress, hence of a universal hope. In proportion as this secret Christian inheritance has become exhausted and the optimism of the idea of progress has been subjected to complete disillusionment, it has grown more and more pertinent to ask whether a life without hope is possible, whether the elimination of metaphysical and religious inquiries can be permanently maintained without surrendering life to a process of inner decadence.

In order to be able to answer the question negatively, it has been usual to refer to pre-Christian antiquity and extra-Christian cultures where it was possible to develop a high degree of enlightenment in spite of the fact that a comprehensive hope, embracing humanity as a whole and the life of the individual equally, was obviously lacking. But in this answer it is forgotten that Western man, through more than a thousand years of Christian nurture, has been accustomed to see his present existence set in the light of the future, and that, on the other hand, Christianity has destroyed mythical-metaphysical depths of meaning which can no longer be restored by a modern type of thought supposedly emancipated from the Christian faith. Hence the menace of nihilism to-day, of a despairing philosophy affirming the meaninglessness of life, is a new phenomenon in world history making the inquiry into the basis for some vital hope appear as a matter of the most immediate urgency.

Chapter Two

BELIEF IN THE PROGRESS OF HUMANITY

IN a certain limited sense belief in progress is a presupposition of all human action. Whosoever does something that goes beyond instinctive reaction, does it in the conviction that thus something or other is improved. He who tills the soil, or fabricates from raw material an object of utility, he who builds or makes something, does so because he expects that thereby a value will be realized which will enrich, render secure, or improve his own life or that of other human beings. The motive of his deed is the difference in quality between what follows it and what precedes it. There is sense or purpose in doing this or that, just because of the possibility of realizing this progress.

Thus men have thought at all times, ever since they began to rise above the merely instinctive and impulsive modes of action; that is, ever since they began to become men. The thought, however, that humanity as a whole is implicated in a continuous movement of progress and amelioration, that later generations will be better equipped or stand on a higher level than former, that therefore history in its totality is moving towards a goal which is more worthwhile, "higher", more human or better, is a thought which was just as foreign to the men of classical antiquity as to the great cultural peoples of Asia to-day (1). Since they regarded themselves and the whole of human existence as conditioned primarily by the process of nature and looked upon human history as a form in which nature was manifested, human life was for them caught up in the cyclical movement of natural phenomena—the rhythm of day and night, summer and winter, birth and death, and the changelessness of this cyclical movement was for them especially apparent in the circular motion of the stars, which remained the same from year to year, from century to century. Whether one had in view the nearer cycles of the vegetable and animal worlds or directed one's gaze upwards towards the constant motions of the planets, the fact remained that man and his destiny, man and his history, were enclosed within these ever-recurrent rhythms of nature. Just as the circle has neither beginning nor ending, so it is with the history of humanity, and as a circular movement leads nowhere but constantly turns back upon itself, hence representing a ceaseless repetition of the same thing, so too for those men human history was an everlasting self-repetition. What man experiences in all intelligent action, namely, that through the exercise of his freedom something is vitally changed, that something new arises, that something is bettered—this specifically human awareness could not gain universal acceptance because man did not dare to free himself from the circular repetitions of nature: his tiny progresses and creative achievements became lost in the eternal cycle.

Of course the thinkers and poets of later classical antiquity made the discovery that the Greeks and Romans were superior to the barbarians, that with them something higher or better had come into the world which had not existed before, and they did not fail to connect this new and better thing with the superior gift of intelligence and the disciplined and cultivated use of it characteristic of the Greeks and Romans (2). Somehow they grasped the inner coherence of reason, freedom and culture. But that insight was not sufficient to enable them to break the charm of the circular conception, the idea of eternal recurrence. In spite of the fact that they had such great historians as Herodotus, Thucydides, Polybius and Tacitus, history in its peculiar characteristics as opposed to the non-historical cycles of nature never became a clear object of their thought. Obviously some greater power was needed than that of Græco-Roman intelligence and culture if the fatal charm of the idea of cosmic recurrence was to be shaken off.

This power was found in the revelational faith of the Israelite-Christian tradition. The world is created by God;

it has a beginning. But this divine Creator is also the Redeemer who is guiding the world to the attainment of some goal. This cosmic goal, however, is not simply the return to the cosmic beginning but, in contradistinction to the latter, is something essentially new—consummation in eternity. Between the beginning and the end, world-history stretches as a straight line; that is to say, a line which does not return to its point of departure (3). The conception of the circle, of the everlasting return, has been shattered, and that not indeed through the free exercise of human intelligence, but through the transcendent freedom of the God of revelation. The man of faith certainly looks back to the beginning also, to the event of creation, but above all he looks forward to the end, when redemption will be consummated. For the first time in history there are men who live their lives through the inspiration of hope, men who are distinguished from all their predecessors by the fact that they are able to look forward. This hope, this forward-looking attitude, is to be the theme of this book.

But it was first necessary to draw attention to the fact that the faith in progress characteristic of modern times became possible solely through liberation from the thought of history as a circular movement, and that this liberation is due to Christianity alone (4). For a millennium and a half the Christian church has been educating the peoples of the West in this faith in God the Creator and Redeemer, the God who launches the process of saving, redemptive, history which enables man to look forward. And yet this Christian faith is no mere belief in progress. It is hope based upon faith in the activity of God, not, however, hope based upon the self-confidence and self-security of man. In the middle of the second millennium began the movement of severance from this Christian faith, taking place simultaneously with the movement which gave birth to a revival of Christianity through fresh contact with the original sources of Holy Scripture. The movement of severance is called the Renaissance, the movement of revival, the Reformation. The severance took place—at first hardly discernible as such—in the self-affirmation of the free man, rejoicing in his powers of creative action and rational thought. This self-certitude—formulated most sharply in Descartes' *Cogito ergo sum*—replaced the certitude of faith in God, the self-reliance of the resourceful man supplanted trust in the God of grace.

Fully two centuries were to pass, however, before this self-confidence took the form of belief in progress. The Abbé de Saint Pierre and Fontenelle seem to be the first in whom this new idea is found (5). One of the works of Saint Pierre bears the significant title: *Observations sur le progrès de la raison universelle* (1737). His main thesis is that two features characterize the essence of reason: firstly, that it is universally, for all men and at every time, the same, and secondly that it spreads, overcoming the forces opposing it, and in course of time gaining undisputed mastery. Hence necessarily there is progress: for the sway of reason is what unites mankind, freeing them from their one-sided persuasions and prejudices, holding in check the irrational impulses of human nature, and making men virtuous and just. To man's reasoning ability belongs—as Rousseau somewhat later was to emphasize—*la faculté de se perfectionner*. Thus hope in progress is in fact, as we suggested, hope based upon the self-certitude of man.

If this belief in progress is the child of the enlightenment of the early eighteenth century, in the nineteenth century it received firstly (*a*) a deepening, then (*b*) an extension, but especially (*c*) an effective practical demonstration.

(*a*) German idealism gave to the idea of progress a new metaphysical basis and explanation by interpreting reason itself in theological terms as divine, and at the same time transmuting the homely conception of progress into the loftier idea of development. The history of humanity is the history of the unfolding of the divine spirit immanent in the human spirit, the history of the cultural development of man through the expansion within him of the divinely implanted power of reason (6).

This idea of development which sprang from idealism was then taken over about the turn of the century by the natural sciences, and in the process utterly alienated from its original sense. If already Lessing in his *Education of the Human Race* had theologically underpinned the faith in reason typical of the enlightenment, with Herder's *Ideas for a History of Humanity* there takes its rise that splendid philosophical interpretation of history which reaches its term and crown in the system of Hegel, and the foundation of which is the thought of the divine spirit flowering within the human spirit. The history of humanity—with Schleiermacher the history of the world in general (7)—is explained in terms of the continuous expansion of the human mind, a process which has its roots in the divine source of mind.

(*b*) Whereas here in idealism the concept *evolutio* may be understood in its literal sense as an unfolding of what is initially latent, the idea of evolution or development became susceptible of quite a different meaning from the moment when it was taken over by the natural sciences and, received in this Darwinian sense, became in the second half of the nineteenth century the chief fulcrum for the optimistic philosophy of progress (8). Through Lamarck and Darwin it was transplanted from the sphere of metaphysical speculation into that of the experimental sciences and at the same time transformed from an essentially teleological into an essentially causal principle. The observation of natural phenomena teaches us that all the existing forms of life are the resultants of quite other species and classes, and that the temporal sequence of these successive transformations follows an upward curve from the undifferentiated to the differentiated, from the rudimentary to the higher. The last and highest and the most richly endowed shoot on the tree of evolution is that of *homo sapiens*. Humanity therefore can look back on an evolutionary process spanning many millions of years, and the course of this development would seem to make justifiable and probable very optimistic expectations for the future. The emergence of the higher from the lower can hardly have reached its final term with man as he is in his present phase of development. To survey only the last, to some extent visible, stages: the evolution from *homo primi-*

genius or indeed from *sinanthropus pekinensis* to *homo sapiens recens* suggests the thought that in the next five hundred millenniums the continued higher development of the human race will not remain behind what has been attained in the past, and that therefore humanity can look forward to an unimaginable further increase in the range of its potentialities.

(*c*) While the future of humanity was thus prognosticated optimistically on the basis of scientific research, there took place at the same time in the more immediate sphere of human civilization developments which conveyed good and apparently conclusive intimations in favour of the same optimistic picture of the future. For was there not to be noted in the last few centuries a phenomenal progress in scientific knowledge and had there not taken place in parallelism with it—and partly, but only partly, in consequence of it—a technological revolution which seemed to justify the proud confidence of man that in future ages nothing would be impossible to him? A third historical fact pointed in the same direction. Since the time of the French Revolution the nations had been involved in a movement whose unequivocal meaning and equally—as it appeared—unequivocal result must be the increasing political freedom and maturity of the human race. Closely connected with this but equally with the first two factors was a fourth factor, which perhaps in the long run was the most effective, the most calculated to rouse the highest hopes of the future. This was the spread of knowledge and education through state responsibility for schools of every grade. The aim—a humanity without illiterates—seemed capable of realization at no great distance of time. What will humanity become when every man of any education is in a position to realize his capacities! Truly the nineteenth century belief in progress and the inspiration of that belief could boast of being no daydream, but of resting upon a solid foundation of fact!

But from the end of the century onwards the voices of doubt grew ever louder, and in the first decades of the new twentieth century this creed of modern man collapsed under the shock of the terrible new eventuality of the world war and totalitarian revolution, and now for the first time the arguments of those who had never believed in this apparently so illuminating theory could gain a hearing (9).

1. Of course it is not to be disputed that in certain areas of human life, notably those of technics and social-technical organization, there has actually taken place an increase of cultural resources and thus a continuous expansion of human freedom. In regard to knowledge too, and especially the natural sciences, we may speak of constant progress, inasmuch as later generations have been able to assimilate and develop further what they have gained from their predecessors. But in other spheres the use of the idea of progress is of doubtful validity, and yet again in others the affirmation of actual progress is quite simply contradicted by facts.

2. If we seek to discover the reason for this complicated state of affairs, there emerges a sort of law—I have elsewhere (10) termed it the law of the relation to the personal centre, implying that the more it is a question of man in himself, the less is there to be discerned any real degree of progress in the course of history.

There is plainly progress in regard to means, but hardly any is discoverable in regard to the ends of man. For here there are no secure traditional values, no storehouse of good that could be inherited or quite simply conveyed from one generation to another. Progress, by means of which man's liberation from nature is being continuously increased, finds its limit precisely in man's freedom to use as he wills the resources in regard to which progress is possible. Education of course attempts to overstep this limit and to secure a transmissible set of values even in the sphere of freedom. So far as pure knowledge is in question, such a transmission and therefore accumulation of values is no doubt possible: a secondary schoolboy of to-day knows more than the greatest scholar of antiquity. Where, however, it is a question of what is properly human and personal, for example, in the direction of life and the setting of aims, and hence the subordination of means to ends, then, while the transmission of culture through education does not necessarily fail, the guarantee of its continuity becomes impossible. Again and again it happens in the history of humanity that an intellectual cultural inheritance, which the generation of fathers considered secure, is not prized by the sons and thus not taken over. Continuity, hence accumulation and increase of value, finds, as we said, its limit in the freedom of the person. For this reason recently the planners of state education have reached the point when they seek to eliminate the uncertainty springing from the factor of freedom by effacing the personal element. In so far as they have succeeded, the result is the very opposite of progress: it is the dehumanized man.

3. This already implies that the development of democratic freedoms and the extension of education by state schooling are very dubious instruments of progress. Democracy in the sense of the sovereignty of the people may—as recent history teaches and as Aristotle already knew from bitter experience in Athens—degenerate into the rule of the masses, and dictatorship and the spread of state education may lead to a levelling of personalities, a subordination of man to a particular political social cultural programme, and the consequent elimination of personal freedom. Whether these methods will prove effective in the long run only the future can decide: but one thing is certain, in so far as they are effective they can lead only to the destruction of the specifically human in man, hence to the exact opposite of what the authors of the belief in progress understood by that creed. Either the control of the future is shipwrecked on man's freedom or this control results in the destruction of that freedom.

4. Belief in progress, as we saw, arose out of the faith in reason and the self-assurance it conveyed. But in this connexion the ambiguity of the idea of reason was overlooked. Reason may imply something formal but also something substantial. Reason in the formal sense—the capacity or the power of man to recognize truth, and to set himself aims to pursue—is the natural basis of his freedom; it is the source of his power to create culture, what is new, what has never

before existed. But reason may also be understood in the substantial sense as the right recognition, the right purposes, the life in accordance with reason. The mere fact that reason is increased in the formal sense, that the sphere of man's freedom is broadened, is no guarantee that this heightened freedom will be used in the right and reasonable way. The increased spiritual and intellectual capacities of man by no means necessarily imply a right, a good, and an ethical use of reason. In replacing the Christian dogma of the radical sinfulness of man by that of his rational freedom and innate goodness, the enlightenment overlooked the truth of the Christian recognition that the more spiritually developed man is, the more strongly and dangerously will he be able to express that sinfulness. Indeed, the more man trusts in and affirms his freedom the more likely he is to misuse the freedom which he confuses with absolute, i.e. divine, freedom.

Modern man, who, for the sake of his freedom, emancipated himself from God and became godless, thus became inevitably the destroyer of the divine order of creation, the destroyer of life and finally the destroyer of himself. The greater the resources which progress places in his hands, the more dreadful must be his work of destruction. This is the lesson which humanity has had to learn in recent decades, and in awful contemplation of the nothingness of its optimistic hopes of progress. The monstrous increases in the scientific means of conquering nature have been exposed as dangerous possibilities of universal suicide. Science and technics in the atom bomb, social political organization in the totalitarian state, and state education in totalitarian uniformity have seen the dreadful unfolding of their truly dæmonic potentialities. And at the same time the charm of the idea of progress has vanished and humanity, in the full flower of its development, has fallen a prey to the panic of nihilism.

5. Even the glow of the idea of natural scientific evolution has faded in the realization that with the evolution of humanity a new level has been reached, upon which we have to reckon with the operation of other than merely natural factors. The

history of man follows other laws than those of natural evolution; for history is the sphere of freedom which permits man, for example, to transcend the laws of natural selection. Man is that animal who is capable of discovering and using the means of his self-destruction. Furthermore, since we have heard of Nietzsche's theory of the mastery of the superman and have witnessed its outcome and perversion in National-Socialism, scarcely anyone will now have the courage to expect a better future for humanity from the regimentation of man, whether through natural leadership or by tyranny. Darwin in his time gained the idea of a natural hierarchy of power from his observation of human leadership. We can now see with terror what can be the result of that theory when it is wielded by a totalitarian dictator (11).

Belief in the progress of humanity has therefore had a short life for the reason that it rested on a *quid pro quo*, namely, the confusion between formal reason, i.e. freedom of control, and substantial reason or the objectively good life. In the ecstasy of its enthusiasm about the stupendous success of science and technics and its emancipation from the fetters of feudal authoritarianism, Western humanity has deified formal freedom based upon man's natural reason and has confidently expected this combination of freedom and reason to usher in the millennium. But only a few decades have been required to shake it free from this stupor and to qualify and moderate its hopes. But will it be able to extricate itself from the opposite of these illusions—from defeatist pessimism and nihilism, which are already beginning to take hold of it, and to win through to a new and different hope?

Chapter Three

THE GROUND OF THE CHRISTIAN HOPE

BELIEF in progress, hope in a better future, was an illegitimate child of Christianity. For the first time in the history of humanity, through the instrumentality of Israel, and then through the Christian heirs of the Israelite religion of revelation, it happened that the attention of man was directed towards the future through the hope, springing from faith in Christ, that the true end of man's being would find ultimate fulfilment in the kingdom of God. For 1,500 years such was the hope of Western humanity. In fact the "future" itself, as also its Latin equivalents *avenir*, *avenire*, etc., are of Christian origin (1). Humanity has a future because it awaits the coming of the kingdom of God in the future coming of its Lord. The life of the world to come as distinct from *futurum* is an eschatological concept; it suggests the realization of hope through an event which springs from the beyond, from the transcendent; not like *futurum*, something which grows out of what already exists.

The dissolution of this faith in the life that is to come and its replacement by the modern belief in progress could not take place without far-reaching and intensive criticism of the Biblical foundations and theological formulations of the Christian hope. But it is not the case, as theologians often suppose, that the Christian faith in revelation was wantonly thrown away through the blind arrogance of generations intoxicated by the success of increasing scientific knowledge, that is, through an act of *hybris* on the part of man in revolt against God the Creator.

Just as the French Revolution is to be explained as a necessary and inevitable reaction against the unbearable conditions of a feudal and absolutist order of society, so the intellectual movement of the enlightenment which preceded it has its intrinsic necessity and its good and moral justification. What had risen out of the Christian revelation in the hands of Western man, and especially in the hands of the church and its theology, could no longer satisfy men who valued truth and intellectual freedom. If the Christian hope is once again to be the hope of humanity, it can only come about in so far as the criticism of recent centuries is sincerely met and appreciated and not simply by a return to the faith of the Middle Ages or of the Reformation.

The necessity of this critique is seen already in regard to the question which is central to the Christian hope. The traditional answer of the church—both in the Middle Ages and at the Reformation—runs: the basis of the hope lies in divine revelation, given in Holy Scripture. Our answer runs: the basis of Christian hope lies in the revelation of God given in Jesus Christ. Divine revelation is not a book, not a dogma, but a history, the history of the Christ. Of course, we know this history only through the witness of Scripture; but not this but what is attested by it is the real revelation. This disposes at once of a whole host of objections which, since Biblical criticism has existed, have been raised against the supposed infallible authority of Scripture, precisely in regard to questions which concern the Christian hope. It is in fact not to be disputed that in the Bible we find a world-view which is not and can no longer be that of the modern man. It is equally indisputable that the statements of the Bible concerning the future are not only to some extent contradictory but are laden with mythological ideas which have become alien and partly even meaningless to us. Reflection on the distinction between the fact of revelation itself and the scriptural testimony to it frees us from much ballast, which not only has nothing to do with the essence of the Christian hope but on the contrary obscures it. But only in contemplation of the future as revealed in Jesus Christ will it be possible to make this distinction between what is conditioned by time and what is eternally valid.

To begin with, we must ask fundamentally what is meant

by the statement that the ground of our hope is laid in the revelation of Christ and nowhere else. First, this has the negative implication that the Christian hope is based not on anything immanent in the structure of man's being itself. When for example Schleiermacher (2) says concerning the doctrine of the last things that "it has only the utility of a symbol to which we must approximate", or "the Christian has the tendency to picture to himself conditions after death", such a radical statement makes clear at once that what is here in question is not the Christian hope but more or less intelligent speculations which offer no firm foundation for a really living hope. Or, to take another famous example, when Kant in the *Critique of Practical Reason* speaks of "the immortality of the soul as a postulate of the purely practical reason" (3), whatever that may mean, it is not the Christian hope, for the latter does not rest upon postulates. Again, various kinds of occult experiences of the type of those of Nostradamus or the spiritualists may lead to specific statements about the future destiny of man or of humanity, but they have as little to do with the Christian hope as the wish fantasies which Siegmund Freud in his *Future of an Illusion* dissects psycho-analytically.

We should proceed rather from the presupposition, which sober reason suggests, that the future is the sphere of the radically unknowable. This statement of course must be qualified to the extent that it is possible on the basis of established regularities or laws of nature to foretell certain events with a high degree of probability which borders on certainty. This has been recognized in the dictum "*savoir, c'est prévoir*". But these reservations affect only a very limited area which is meaningless for the questions with which we are here concerned. In these matters the vital principle is: we do not know the future, but as Christians we confidently affirm it.

But this negative statement must be completed by its positive counterpart: namely, that the future is revealed to us and that revelation in the New Testament sense and revelation of the future is one and the same thing. Hence the

Christian faith, which lives entirely in the power of revelation, is also and in every part expectation of the future, hope of the future. Teaching concerning the last things, eschatology, is not merely an appendix to Christian doctrine. Rather faith makes no affirmations but such as ever imply the Christian hope of the future (4). When we speak of God we mean the God of revelation, the God of the Covenant, the God whose world-plan is disclosed to us in Jesus Christ. When we say that man is made in the image of God we mean man's eternal destiny, which in the aspect of divine predestination is our beginning, and in that of its future consummation, our eternal goal. When we speak of the "ecclesia" we mean the communion of those who are one in Christ and the end of which, the Kingdom of God, is the object of our hope in the future. Christian faith is so closely bound up with the Christian hope of the future that faith and hope can be regarded as two aspects of one and the same thing: the revelation of the Christ. In one point Schleiermacher might well have been right, viz. that the Christian faith is teleological (5); this is in fact absolutely right in the sense that the whole content of the Christian faith is orientated towards the *telos*, the end. The Christian faith is distinguished from all other religions in that in it faith and hope are inseparably, indeed almost inextricably, one. Faith is the foundation of hope, hope is that which gives content to faith. But both faith and hope are rooted in the revelation of God in Jesus Christ.

Through this unity of faith and hope the revelation of the inscrutable Will of God in Jesus Christ becomes the answer to man's deeply felt question as to the meaning of his existence; an answer which he himself is not capable of providing. For all man's questions imply in the last resort the one question as to the *telos*, the final goal and meaning of life. As we saw, there is always the possibility of assimilating and expressing partial meanings. One can live on that level and even live humanly thus. And yet the partial meaning, just because it is only a partial meaning, is always at the same time a partial lack of meaning; he who cherishes merely partial purposes and never succeeds in believing them to be rooted and completed in an ultimate meaning must find his life as a whole infected with meaninglessness. These partial purposes may be never so highly valued, they may be called culture, humanity, world peace or world justice: the mere fact that they do not reckon with the phenomenon of death suggests behind the fulfilment of meaning a certain void. There are meaningful ends which open up to the individual man the vistas of eternity; but the mere fact that this fulfilment of meaning is only possible at the expense of solidarity with humanity as a whole again discloses the same void. The secret of the Christian hope is this, that it reveals an eternal purpose for the individual which is at the same time a purpose for humanity. In fact, the individual goal and the universal goal for all mankind are so inextricably one that the individual can attain his meaning and his goal only as a member of humanity in its consummation.

All human, philosophical or religious teleology suffers from this either/or: either that it allows the individual to be dissolved in the general and universal, and thus imperils the meaning of the most precious thing which he has—his personal being—or that it promises to the individual a fullness of meaning which separates him from the totality of mankind. But the coming Kingdom of God revealed in Jesus Christ has the peculiarity that what brings the individual as a person to the fulfilment of his being is precisely what overcomes the isolation of the individual from others and links him with the whole of humanity, namely, divine love. Human teleologies are either abstractly universal or concretely particular. The former suffer from their bloodless impersonality, the latter from their eudaemonism and egocentricity. This is so because man, when he conceives ends, either must grasp the ideal in its abstractness or desire in its concreteness. The Christian hope, however, is both universal and personal because it is not rooted in the will or the being of the "I" but in the will of that "Thou" which calls both man as an individual and humanity as a whole unto Himself, and thus frees men both from the egoism of desire and from the abstractness of mere ideals. But this revealed end, which is neither abstract, universal nor a matter of individual desire, can certainly not be conceived as an idea of humanity: for reason is necessarily generalizing and abstract and the individual is of necessity irrational. The two factors cannot be combined by man; there is no possibility of such a combination conceivable by man. Nor in history has it anywhere emerged as such (6). It is present only through God's self-revelation in Jesus Christ and nowhere else.

But what about the truth and certitude of this hope? To wish to prove the truth of the revelation which is the foundation of the hope would mean that it had not been understood. Faith cannot and is not intended to be proved. For proof implies falling back upon the universal and timeless, and just that eliminates the very idea of revelation and faith. Revelation certifies itself—in faith; it has its own certitude peculiar to revelation. Faith has the right to be incapable of proof because it rests upon a truth which both precludes and forbids man the possibility of self-justification before the forum of reason. Such also is the type of certainty characteristic of the hope which is our theme.

This faith in which hope is rooted, this hope which is implicit in faith, is, however, at the same time a matter of experience. Not experience of the senses, of perception, but experience of true personal encounter. To require proof in the sphere of personal encounter means to overlook the essence of personal being, to attempt to make of the person an object. The hope which springs from faith is so much a part of the life of faith that one must say: the future, for which it hopes, is the present in which the believer lives. To understand this more precisely, a twofold investigation is needed: one concerning the relationship of faith and history, and one concerning the understanding of time.

Chapter Four

FAITH AND HISTORY

NOT all religions have an interest in history (1). On the contrary, in the majority of religions history is not at all the focus of attention. The mystical religions of the East are indifferent to history because for them the world of becoming—hence history—is of no ultimate significance. History—that which is in process of development—is the sphere of the transient, it is non-being in contrast to the eternal, which, as the sphere of the timeless, is that which alone truly is. Hence, because true being, that is to say the timeless and eternal, is the real object of religious interest, the world of the historical falls outside it.

Equally indifferent to history are the polytheistic religions of nature. Nature, in the fascinating mystery of its life, is the sphere in which the divine is manifested. But nature and its processes are characterized by eternal recurrence. Its symbol is the circle which ever turns back upon itself, the cycles of day and night, summer and winter, birth and death. Man too, as a member of the world of nature, is an integral part of this cyclical process—only of course in so far as he is understood collectively (see pp. 15 f.). For behind the dying generations are ever springing to birth the new generations of the living. Man, understood as a species, becoming and passing away, forms no exception in the cosmos of the ever recurrent but fits into the rule. There is no reason therefore to interpret his story in any other terms than those of a happening within the life of nature—the sphere of the ever recurrent.

The idea of the history of nature is a new datum and only conceivable on the soil of the Western Hemisphere, where the spell of the conception of eternal recurrence was broken by the intrusion of a fundamentally historical type of thought; that is, on the soil of Christian Europe (2). It took several centuries, however, for this historical mode of thought, which was concerned almost exclusively with the history of humanity, to be transplanted to and become at home in the realm of nature. The proof of this lies in the fact that even the Greeks, who did more than any other people for the investigation of nature, were far removed from conceiving a history of nature even as a possibility.

There are but few religions where the myth of eternal recurrence, the cyclical type of thought, appears to have been overcome and which therefore disclose a fundamental interest in history. They are religions of vital theism, presupposing faith in a Lord of the world, who as Lord is distinct from the world and from nature, which He has created and to which He assigns a goal. The world has a beginning and an end. The circle, ever returning upon itself, is transformed into a straight line and the thought of world history is born. In accordance with this idea of world history, happenings in time, and especially human existence, are no longer merely an appearance in space but a movement towards an end; human history is therefore no longer appraised as a purely transient phenomenon of no ultimate value, but in virtue of the fact that it is movement orientated towards an end, as a thing of immediate and unqualified concern. No longer is it possible to assert that there is nothing new under the sun; rather, history is the field in which what is new and of unique occurrence happens. History as a movement towards an end has assumed a direction and a meaning, an absolute divine meaning which makes a total claim upon man. In the life of man there takes place a decision for or against this meaning; human life is laden with the responsibility of decision. Simultaneously with the idea of history emerges that of man's responsible personality. Because God is personal, personal being is distinctive; man is raised above the life of nature—not as in Greek philosophy by his faculty of reason, but by the fact of his responsible personal being, by the significance which belongs to decision in God. Thus history as world history and history as the field for personal decision come into view and imply each other. Because God as Lord and Creator of the world gives to it a direction and a meaning and because He allows man to co-operate in this meaning through surrender to His will, therefore history, both that of the individual and that of humanity as a whole, is charged with divine and decisive significance (3).

This new and revolutionary vision of things appeared at about the same time in two neighbouring localities—Persia and Israel (4). In both cases the intrusion of a historical into a non-historical consciousness was connected with certain historical events and personalities. Both the religion of Israel and that of Persia are "founded" religions and, unlike nature-religions and mysticism, not "simply there" and "have not always been there". Both these religions are historical as well in the circumstances of their origin as in their world view. They spring to birth through quite specific revelatory events. Both their content and their mode of origin are stamped with the same personal-historical character. This of course is not a matter of chance: God is recognizable as the personal Lord only through revelation in persons. The historical character of the manner of revelation conditions the historical character of the content of revelation.

Only one of these two religions—the Israelite religion of revelation—succeeded in retaining its character as historical. The religion of Zarathustra sank back into the cyclic-mythical type of heathen religion above which it had so clearly risen and remained without historical influence and consequences (5). But the religion of Israel persisted in the form of two world religions—very different from each other—which in their creative influence on the course of history far surpassed its immediate successor, Judaism: namely, in Islam and in Christianity. All three have as their distinguishing features, so far as content is concerned, faith in God the Creator and Lord and, so far as origin is concerned, a revelatory historical event.

But in Christianity alone has this historical and personal

element been carried through to its logical conclusion. The religion of Israel is based upon a multiplicity of prophetic revelations and revelatory events. It is difficult to say just where the origin of this religion lies, whether in the mythically-coloured figure of Moses, and in the still less historically realizable figure of Abraham, or in the first clearly historical figures of the writing prophets. Corresponding to this ambiguity in its historical origins is the fact that the conception of a divinely appointed end of history is still obscure throughout the Old Testament and, as it were, only dimly perceptible behind the mists of a purely nationalistic Messianism and prophetic visions of the future in which the earthly and the heavenly, the temporal and the eternal mingle confusedly (6).

It is quite otherwise with the faith of the New Testament. Here the many, as forerunners, recede behind the One. But this one decisive event of revelation—the Person of Jesus Christ—stands exposed to the full light of history. He began His public ministry in the fifteenth year of the reign of Tiberius the Emperor when Pontius Pilate was governor of Judea and Herod tetrarch of Galilee (7), and—what the oldest creed singles out and stresses in the Gospel tradition—"was crucified under Pontius Pilate". He is plainly fitted into the chronological scheme of world history. Even if many individual features of the Jesus tradition are legendary, if others have been distorted through the faith of the Church, through "Church theology", in the interests of evangelization—it remains firmly established that Jesus of Nazareth the man, whom the Christian community reveres as its Lord, is a historical personality whose portrait is no product of a myth-creating imagination but corresponds to the objective facts of history as granted by unbelieving historians. Jesus is, as the evangelists record of Him, a unique actuality of history, not interchangeable with other historical personalities. This uniqueness of historical occurrence belongs to the very basis of the Christian faith. It is implied in the fundamental apostolic confession: "The Word became flesh" (8).

But the uniqueness which the New Testament specifically stresses has wide implications which go far beyond this general historical sense. It is especially the fact of His death upon the Cross to which the consciousness of uniqueness for faith refers. The death upon the Cross is understood as the decisive event of atonement. Atonement and redemption, effected through the death of Jesus, is an event which lies outside the dimensions of the historical. Hence it is something which the historian as such cannot grasp and which it lies in the power of faith alone to apprehend. Here we are confronted by an action of God, an act of divine self-disclosure and self-communication; that is, by something which cannot be established as a historical occurrence. Whereas the uniqueness which the historian can appreciate in the person and story of Jesus is a relative uniqueness, what faith apprehends as God's act and word in atonement and redemption is something absolutely unique, something which by its very essence has either happened once for all (9), for all times and for every man, or has not happened at all. For the atonement of which the New Testament speaks is an act of God which, if it is really atonement, is unrepeatable. Now the faith of the Christian community and the faith of each individual Christian consists in the appropriation of this event which has happened once for all on the Cross of Jesus.

Thus here—and here alone—the situation is that an event which is relatively unique in the sense of secular history is apprehended by faith as an event which by its very essence is absolutely or unconditionally unique. The historical event on Calvary, fundamentally appreciable by everyone as such, is the visible shell of the invisible kernel—the absolutely unique—which can only be apprehended by faith (10). It is just this which is meant by the words of St. John's Gospel in which the fundamental significance for faith of the life of Jesus is summed up: "The Word (of God) was made flesh." That which lies outside and beyond all history as its ultimate source and goal has become historical, the eternal has become temporal.

In so far as the category of uniqueness as opposed to the eternal recurrence of natural processes is the stamp of the historical as such (11), the Christian faith, in virtue of its relation to what is unique in a twofold sense—the historically and relatively unique and that which is absolutely unique for faith—may be regarded as the unreservedly historical faith. There is no second example in the history of religion where faith is so unconditionally linked to the absolutely unique as is the Christian faith when thus seen as faith in what has happened in Jesus Christ. It is a symbolically significant expression of this truth that the time of world history should be reckoned backwards and forwards from this event—the birth of Jesus Christ—as its central point, that the years should be counted "*ante* and *post christum natum*". This implies, of course, that the interpretation of history opened up by the Christian faith has passed over into world chronology (12).

But the historical nature of the Christian faith contains two further important aspects through which again the historical is endowed with ultimate significance. The first of these aspects is that of personality, the second that of humanity as a whole. The Christian faith is unconditionally personal, and it is also unconditionally related to the totality of mankind. It is unconditionally personal in several senses. Principally and fundamentally it is so in the sense that it is centred in a person, and indeed in a historical person, understood as absolute. In Jesus Christ Christian faith recognizes the divine Person—the mystery of the personal in God Himself. The Word in which God reveals Himself is now no longer merely a prophetic word but a historical person. The prophets of Israel authenticate themselves by their affirmation: "Thus saith the Lord." They point beyond themselves to the One who gave them this word. But Jesus, unlike the prophets, makes no reference beyond Himself to the Giver of His message and mission, to Him who spoke or gave the word. He utters in His own name the divinely authoritative "I am", just as in the Old Testament God speaks the "I am". Whereas the prophet in his own person is but the unimportant messenger and bearer of the divine message, in the New Testament Jesus Christ as Person is identical with the content of the message. The latter has been embodied in a personal life: the Word became flesh. Since this is the essential peculiarity of the Christian faith, having no analogy in any other religion (13), Christian dogma formulates it as such in the doctrine of the Trinity, which expresses the unity of the Revealed (the Father), the Revealer (the Son), and the event of revelation (the Spirit). The trinitarian Christian creed alone makes this claim to personal revelation, and this fact constitutes the stumbling block both for Jew and Moslem, just as the implied claim to exclusiveness is the stumbling block for Hindus and Buddhists.

But the Gospel of Jesus Christ is personal in yet another sense. We are not merely told about a man named Jesus that He is in His very person the Revealer of the divine mystery and the author of divine atonement, but it is stated that this revelation, this redemption or atonement, was effected personally as a personal struggle of the man Jesus with the insidiousness of temptation and the powers of darkness. Jesus did not simply passively suffer the Cross; He took it upon Himself and became obedient unto death, even the death of the Cross. *Therefore* God has given Him a name that is above every other name (14). It is not just a question—as might appear from the later historical development of dogma—of a metaphysical event resulting from the physical incarnation of the God-Man, but of a personal historical deed, a voluntary suffering and self-surrender.

To this objective historical factor there corresponds on the personal human side, in the matter of personal appropriation, a faith which again is not faith in a doctrine but a faith which might better be indicated by the formula—trustful obedience (15). Belief is not just the acceptance of a dogma, but something "existential", an event in the sphere of personal life, which Paul describes by the words "to die with Christ" and "to be crucified with Him"; it involves the surrender of one's own person and its claims, its self-will, in favour of the living God who confronts it in Christ. Faith is the utmost conceivable personal deed, a self-surrender to the self-offering Redeemer. Faith in Jesus Christ implies a total transformation of one's personal existence.

This personalism is bound up with a radical universalism. It is not possible in this matter to understand the personal in the sense of the merely individual and private. Rather the real significance of the work of Christ affects humanity as a whole. For before the coming of Christ we are as sinners linked together in a single lump of sinful humanity, and similarly in Him we are linked together by faith in one totality of redeemed humanity. That is the meaning of the antithesis between Adam and the Christ, the first and the second man (16). Just as sin is on the one hand the most utterly personal guilt, on the other, an indivisible mass of sinful humanity, so the redemption wrought by Christ is a matter of the most utterly personal decision and at the same time a corporate redemption of humanity as a whole. In contrast to all mysticism, the Christian faith is concerned with world history, with the history of mankind as a whole (17). To be a Christian means without qualification to think in terms of corporate humanity. To mark off an area of personal interior religion as opposed to the sphere of public social questions is thus excluded in the nature of the case. For to believe in Jesus Christ means to hope for a universal redemption and consummation of humanity and all that is human. The goal disclosed in Jesus Christ is no private bliss of souls in the beyond, but the coming Kingdom of God implying the fulfilment of all human history as well as the fulfilment of each individual human life in its personal destiny. Personality and sociality, the individual and society, man and humanity, are to be viewed as a single unqualified whole. The reality of history in its aspect of decision and responsibility on the one hand, and on the other, in its aspect of world history as a unity and totality—both factors are understood by the Christian in an absolute and radical sense.

We have seen that the Christian faith is in several respects, and in each of them, historical in its essence without reservation. A further question is whether and in what sense it is concerned with the *writing of history* and in what relation the science of history stands to faith. We suggest this, in itself, far-reaching question because just in most recent times certain fanciful assertions have been made by theologians which would tend to obscure the correct insight into the relation of faith and history.

It has often been asserted by Christians that the thought of world history is of Christian origin. This statement, though somewhat exaggerated, is not *sine fundamento in re*, and that for two reasons. To begin with, it is quite simply a matter of fact that before the beginning of the Christian era there was no writing of world history, but only of national history. Secondly—and this is much more important—this fact is not accidental. The idea of humanity and human history as a unity is by no means self-explanatory. It arose as a matter of historical fact through the Christian faith. God has created the whole world and rules it by His providential guidance; he who through faith sees the world and its history in God's vision sees it as a unity, as *one* Kingdom, despite the multiplicity of its kingdoms. God has created man, and in Him, the divinely created, all men have a common origin. To the one Father God corresponds the unifying conception of the family of peoples. Just as the one origin in creation, so the one redemption and fulfilment as the goal of history gathers the destinies of nations into a comprehensive unity. In this sense it may well be said that the conception of world history is Christian in origin and subsists through the Christian faith.

On the other hand, it cannot be denied that with the ever closer interrelations of the peoples—a process which has been going steadily forward since the time of Alexander the Great and the extension of the Roman world empire, a purely pragmatical unity of history has been becoming a practical necessity. The modern historian can no longer think except in world historical terms, because actual events, even to the tiniest needs of the citizen's household budget, are globally conditioned. The idea of world history therefore, even without the Christian faith, would have become an urgent practical exigency and retains its meaning and its necessity even where the writing of history has lost all conscious connexion with Christianity.

And not only is the recognition of the unity of the historical process but also that of its specific character derived from the Christian faith. For only through Christianity did it happen that man learned to understand history as something radically distinct from the processes of nature (18). This statement too is an exaggeration, but one in which there is truth. The Christian faith causes human existence to be understood in an otherwise unknown dimension, where decision and personal encounter are characteristic; and it is precisely this feature which distinguishes history from nature. The interest of faith in history—unconditional, as we saw, from the Christian point of view—has its repercussions on the writing of history and sharpens that sense for the specifically historical, which is the distinguishing mark of the good historian. It is certainly not insignificant that nowhere is so intensive an investigation of history to be noted as in Christian Europe.

But even here we must not try to assert too much. There were excellent historians and an acute understanding of the historical long before the entrance of Christianity into the world (Herodotus, Thucydides) and historical science exists quite independently of any Christian point of view. The curiosity of erudition and enthusiasm for scientific research are completely independent of the power of the Christian faith-impulse.

And yet the question must seriously be asked: What would become of history if Christian faith vanished from humanity and a materialistic type of thought became predominant? The present-day Marxist interpretations of history can only give us a faint idea of that, because even they are still richly fed from Christian sources. Likewise, modern Positivism has enabled us to some extent to realize how easily the sense of the specifically historical element fades and how quickly it happens that people begin to study history as a natural science as soon as it becomes possible to interpret humanity only as a phenomenon on the level of nature (19). From this point of view the truth emerges that Christian faith, with its category of the absolutely unique and the absolutely decisive, keeps alive the sense of the specifically historical. It reminds us that history is to be understood not as something objectively given but as a reflex of the way in which man interprets his being—and that means fundamentally his faith or lack of faith.

Historical knowledge and the interest of faith in history are two very different things. The one is concerned with the relatively unique, the other with the absolutely unique. But they coincide at one point, namely, the event of which faith affirms: *ho logos sarx egeneto*. Jesus Christ is the Word of God: on the other hand, the Word of God is a historical person, a historical event. Hence just here, kerygma and paradosis, preaching and historical report are one. The logos as history and the logos as divine revelation are fused. The Gospel can mean both things: the story of Jesus and the Word of Christ and of salvation. The *logos tou staurou* is both passion narrative and preaching of the Cross.

How is that possible? How can the relative win absolute significance? It cannot win it, it has it; just because, and at the point where, it is at one and the same time relative, human, temporal, earthly and divinely absolute; the presence of God, eternity in time, heaven on earth. This is the theme of the New Testament, what the church has tried to formulate in the doctrines of Incarnation and Satisfaction, the historical which is also the end of history, or the eschatological. As Jesus is the end and the fulfilment of the law, so is He also the end and fulfilment of history. Because at one point of history—of that history which the historian describes or recounts—unconditioned salvation, the absolute will of God is revealed; because therefore at one point the relatively unique and the absolutely unique are identical, Jesus *is* the Christ, *is* salvation. Hence the historical and history in the sense of salvation, of the eschaton, belong indissolubly together. What this means for history must be discussed in Chapter Nine (20). But first of all we must turn to the consequences which this has for the understanding of time—and of eternity.

Chapter Five

THE CHRISTIAN UNDERSTANDING OF TIME AND ETERNITY

BEHIND the problem of history stands the much more fundamental question of the meaning of time. Never yet in the history of human thought has the problem of time stood out so clearly as at the present day. Since Bergson's sensational work *Time and Freewill* (1), the stirring effect of which went far beyond specialist philosophical circles, the puzzle as to the meaning of time has not ceased to command discussion. As a result of George Simmel's *The Problem of Historical Time* (2), but above all through the pioneering work of Heidegger's *Being and Time* (3), it began to compel attention as one of the main philosophical concerns of our day. Einstein revolutionized the basis of physics by a new understanding of time. Theology turned to this problem relatively late (4) and only in most recent times has it shown itself to be a key to the understanding of the New Testament message as a whole (5).

We cannot avoid the question: What contribution has the New Testament and Christian faith to make to the understanding of time, a problem so far the exclusive concern of philosophy? Is there such a thing as a specifically Christian understanding of time and, if so, how is it related to the original views which contemporary philosophy has worked out on this theme? We can hardly accept as sound the opinion of Cullmann (6), who has done so much to elucidate the New Testament idea of time, when he says that in order to grasp the New Testament or primitive Christian view of time we must think as unphilosophically as possible. Certainly the Christian understanding of time is different from that of the philosophers; but we understand its otherness rightly only when we do not ignore the work of contemporary philosophy but remain, on the contrary, attuned to it and in reaction to it. Otherwise it might happen only too easily—as the example of Cullmann shows—that in thinking to be faithful to the New Testament view of time we speak not only as unphilosophically as possible, but even at times simply falsely. And the aim of modern philosophy since Bergson has been precisely to overcome the traditional notion of time which has its roots in Plato.

The linear conception of time which Cullmann rightly stresses is in fact not, as he supposes, a special feature of the New Testament but is what everyone means when he says time. We term it, in distinction to any sort of philosophical interpretation of time, *the primal experience of the time-factor.* Everyone knows that time passes away. Everyone knows that the moment which was just now and is now gone never more returns. What men of all times and countries have been conscious of as the painful experience of time is the unceasing flow of the time stream, transience, the irreversibility and inexorability of this movement from the "not yet" to the "now" and onwards to the "no longer". Precisely this feature, the character of the one-way street, this time-form which is different from space by the fact of its linearity and irreversibility, is "the deepest source of the world's sorrow" (7), Karl Heim rightly says. The flow of time is inseparably bound up with transience, mortality, the not lingering, the not being able to return to what has once been, and just that constitutes the linearity of time. Space is open to us in every dimension; we can move, whether in thought, whether in reality, from any one point to any other, and we can as often as we wish repeat this movement. The time stream does not permit us this freedom; it carries us powerfully along with itself from the "not yet" to the "no longer"; there is no turning back and no abiding. This is everyone's experience of time; this naïve straight-line conception is assuredly not a peculiarity of the New Testament (8) but is the time experience of " everyman".

Time as experienced is, however, different from time as thought, time as it appears to reflection and exact knowledge, and indeed because in reflection this linear aspect becomes still more thoroughgoing. In spite of the fact that time flies, there is for living experience such a thing as a present, a "now". But reflection makes of the experienced present a mere *punctum mathematicum*, the passing moment incapable of extension, where the "not yet" becomes the "no longer". Measured time is of this kind. Although "for the happy man no hour strikes", the thinker and the mathematician can accord to the present not even the slightest extension. This fact was already noted by the first man who pondered on the nature of time—Augustine (9): the present is without extension. The ideas which he felt to be implied in this discovery—viz. that time is "nothing", since we have "not yet" (the future), have "no longer" (the past), and the present is a point without extension—need not yet occupy our attention.

Bergson starts from this consideration that for the thinker, and especially for the measured time of the physicist, time is but a point and sets in contrast to this *philosopher's time*, *time as experienced* (10), the time which everyone is aware of, where the present, although fleeting, is yet not simply without extension. That is the time of every man who on the one hand feels transience, the sweeping onwards of the time stream, to express his bitterest sorrow, but who on the other hand lives out the present, however fleeting it may be. Every man has indeed the linear, but not the radically linear, experience of time. In spite of all conscious reflection, there is such a thing as *durée réelle* (Bergson). Lived time is not a radically linear experience where point is added to point, each only touching the other; in time as lived there is a certain intermingling of elements, a mixture of the past and the present.

Thus, for example, the life of the organism shows an intermingling of past and present. The seed which *was* is present in the tree which *is*, the tree is in some way identical with the seed, the plant with the shoot. The organism represents a suspension, although only partial and fragmentary, of the time stream; it grows old, it has *durée réelle*. The same applies still more to human existence. I am what I am not only as what I am at this precise moment but also as a result of what I was—just like the living organism; but in distinction to it, I am also always my past in virtue of my memory. Memory is the presence of the past—it too brings about an overcoming of the time stream, although but partial and fragmentary, a partial suspension of pure linearity and transience. Memory produces permanence in transience.

Here the work of Heidegger begins, his interpretation of human existence as "being in time". He too does not attempt to formulate a philosophy of time but simply to bring into conscious reflection what every man experiences as time. He certainly experiences time as transience; but he also experiences it as a certain unity of past and future in the present. I am never without my past and I am never without my future. Even to-day I am he who I once was, I am my own history; it belongs to me; without it, without the knowledge of my past and the persistence of my past in me, I am not a man; the presence and the responsibility for my past gives to my being its human character. Even so is it in regard to the future. Only as one who anticipates his future in expectation and aim can I be human; for only in reference to my future do I experience my freedom. Just as I am my past I am also my future. What I plan, am anxious about, fear or hope, belongs to my present. The fact that my past belongs to me I experience particularly in the sense of guilt; the more man feels responsibility for his past, i.e. bears his guilt, the more is he a human being. The more a man penetrates into his future, in planning or expectation, in fear or hope, the more does he experience his specifically human existence.

Thus there is in fact *durée réelle* in the onward-sweeping stream of time. But that this is only a very relative, fragmentary and all too piecemeal phenomenon is clear from the fact that I—everyman—know that my being is a being "orientated towards death" (Heidegger). Here are no philosophical theories of time but in fact what everyman experiences as his temporality and knows in experience. He does not *think* these things *about* time, he is *implicated in* time which has this character; it is his destiny, his reality, an extraordinary hovering between persistence and annihilation, between a holding of the present and a constant losing of the present.

We must distinguish between this universal awareness of time and the way in which man in reflection reacts to it, the way in which his consciousness of time colours his total world-view. The experience of time is common to all; differences arise in regard to the *interpretation of this experience*. First of all, we must speak of the mythological view of time. The man of the myth-religions, i.e. man who understands his being from the point of view of nature, sees his life as part and parcel of nature, and thus regards it as something integral to the ever-revolving course of natural processes. What he experiences as linear time he interprets as merely a part of the unending revolutions of nature—the process which ever turns upon itself and has neither beginning nor ending. The conception of time as non-linear, as circular, is therefore distinct from the *experience* of time—everyman's experience: it is rather a specific *interpretation* of time, an interpretation which makes the time experience part of an eternal process. The individual man is indeed mortal and transient. But the forces manifested in the revolving course of nature's life, like the latter itself, are eternal, unchanging, abiding, immortal. Through his integration in the order of nature mortal man somehow shares in the eternity of nature.

To be distinguished from this mythological interpretation is the philosophical one which in India and Greece slowly struggles free from the former. The philosopher deals with the problem of time and transience. He does so either by means of an ontology proceeding from the object or by means of a system of ideas springing from the subject. Briefly, the sequence of ideas characteristic of ontology is the following: the transient, hence the temporal, is not that which truly is since it constantly passes into non-being. Time, linear time, the time stream, represents an unceasing movement towards non-being. That which truly is, is the timeless: that which has no share in this movement from the "not yet" to the "no longer".

The second form in which philosophy seeks to overcome temporality is that which arises from reflection on the truth. The truth which I think is timeless. The true has no relation to the temporal. What is true, is true from all eternity, unaffected by time. So also are the ideas by which I think the truth timeless. Not only that. The subject too, the "I", the thinking consciousness, which thinks the truth, shares in timeless eternity through that very process. Hence the true "I" is the timeless eternal "I", identical with the truth, while the mortal "I", imprisoned within the time stream, is not the true self. I am therefore composed of two elements, the eternal spiritual "I", identical with eternal truth, and the temporal, transient "I".

This theory, whether in its objective ontological or in its subjective form as an interpretation of knowledge, has been reproduced again and again in various forms since its first appearance in the Vedanta and the philosophy of Parmenides and Plato, and forms—especially as expressed in late Neoplatonism—an integral part of the Western history of ideas. It is *this* philosophy of timelessness which Cullmann has in mind when he sets in contrast to each other New Testament and philosophical thought. But this type of thought should not be confused with the cyclical thinking proper to mythology, although the latter—even in Plato—is constantly reflected in it. Fundamentally the philosophy of timelessness and mythological thinking in terms of cycles are radically distinct.

Into this world where the alternative is that between the cyclical thought of mythology and the idea of timelessness the Christian faith intervenes. It declares that the span of world-time runs from the beginning of creation to the completion of redemption. For it, world-time is a straight line which runs from a beginning to an end that is not identical with the beginning. But the decisive thing is not this linearity —which it has in common with Judaism. The decisive thing is rather that in the midst of time eternity has revealed itself, that He who is above and beyond all time—Christ, the same yesterday, to-day, and for ever—has entered into time, has become clothed with temporality (11), in an event which differs from all other events by the fact that it is unconditionally once-for-all. The Christian faith is founded upon the uniqueness of this event which is incomparable with all other events (12). On that basis, and no other, everything is to be understood, both time and eternity and the relation of time and eternity. Temporality, existence in time, takes on a new character through its relationship to this event, Jesus Christ, the *eph hapax* of history, the once-for-all quality of His Cross and Resurrection, and it is thus newly fashioned, as we shall soon see, in a paradoxical manner that is unintelligible to thinking guided by reason alone. We must consider in detail the aspects of this new orientation. All three dimensions of temporality, of being in time, are reorientated by faith:

1. *My Past.*—The man who understands himself anew through faith in Christ takes full responsibility for his past. He does not see it lying behind him like the skin which the snake has shed; he knows himself to be identical with it. He is in fact not only in full solidarity with his individual past but also with the past of humanity. He knows himself to be identical with Adam, created by God and fallen from God. He realizes his oneness with humanity, divinely created and estranged from its divine origin. He knows that in his present he is corrupted by the sin and guilt of humanity. He knows, however, that this guilt is effaced and forgiven through the Cross of Christ and that he is no longer alienated from God by sin. The barrier, sin, has been overcome by the Cross of Christ, the broken relationship with God is restored. Further, he recognizes in Jesus Christ that which precedes his past, his existence in God's election before all world-time (13). As one who is elected from all eternity in Jesus Christ, he is exalted into the eternity of God and raised beyond the stream of time. His being has its deepest root in the eternity of God preceding all time and all creation; "Thine eyes saw all my days when as yet none of them was" (14), they saw me as the one destined to eternal life in Jesus Christ.

But the believer enjoys all this through his exclusive relationship to what has happened in history, the uniqueness of Jesus Christ, the Crucified and the Risen. He has it, not as a result of any gnostic vision but as the fruit of penitence, by the fact that he is himself gathered into the death of Jesus Christ, shares now in what happened then, and because his self-security, his self-praise are destroyed by that historical event, because the divine Word of Grace takes the place of human self-confidence. So remarkably and variously interwoven are his past and present in this event which gives him an utterly new orientation towards his past.

2. *My Future.*—Equally fundamental is the change brought about in regard to the dimension of the future. Of course my being does not cease to be a being unto death. The seriousness of this view is not diminished but, on the contrary—we deal with the point in more detail in Chapter Eleven—increased by the thought that death is not simply fate, it is rather the ordinance of God as a punishment for sin. Being unto death is being unto the judgment of death. But this negative aspect is not the final and decisive thing: that is rather the turning towards the positive through the gift of Christ, towards the fact that in Christ my being unto death has become a being unto life eternal. He who through the awareness of sin is buried with Christ in His death is also through the awareness of forgiveness risen with Him (15). The Crucified is no other than the Risen One and communion with Him is communion with His risen life. Thus death is not the terminus, the last stop, it is only a point of transition to eternity. Anxiety and sorrow, which determine the character of temporality from the standpoint of the future, have become the triumphant certainty of eternal life and of participation in the Kingdom of God. The fear of death has been replaced by hope, by secure, confident and firmly based hope, secure and firm through the certainty that God is for me and not against me, the certainty that nothing, not even death, can separate me from the love of God which is in Jesus Christ (16). To move into the future means now to wait for the future coming of the Lord Jesus Christ.

3. *My Present.*—If even in the natural human experience

of time, the temporality of everyman, the present is the decisive thing, because it alone has full reality—the past is no longer, the future is not yet, only the present belongs to me—that is still more true of the new life, of life in Christ. The *durée réelle*, which the experience of time distinguishes from the *punctum mathematicum* of conscious thought, is of course, as we saw, a very precarious reality, a hovering between being and non-being, an almost illusory stay and pause in the ever-sweeping movement of the time stream. It is burdened with the load of the guilty past and overshadowed by the anxious expectation of the future and by fear of death. But as a result of the fact that this burden of guilt, this carefulness and fear of death, are removed by faith in Christ, the present now becomes a living reality. Hence it is clear that *durée réelle*, the real present, is God's own mode of being. For God alone transcends the time stream; He alone embraces the span of past and future, He alone is unchanging from all eternity. The present of God does not crumble away like the temporal present, it alone does not hover between being and non-being. We share in this plenitude of the divine present by the gift of the Holy Ghost, through whom Christ is present with us. The life of the Christian, in its difference from that of everyman, is life in the Holy Ghost, life in the radiant present of God. It is—if only in a borrowed and provisional form—in very truth eternal life. The life of the believer is in fact eschatological, a manner of life according to ultimate reality. The witness of the New Testament is unequivocal that the Holy Ghost is the pledge and first-fruits, the anticipation or first instalment of the eternal life which is to come.

Only provisionally, we said: for we still live in this body of death (17), still being unto death is a bitter reality. But this natural reality, this temporality of everyman, is, as it were, covered by another reality, that of life in Christ, just as a second shot in a film passes over a first and is unrolled. It remains valid that inasmuch as we are Christians "we have eternal life" (18), that "we live, although we die" (19). But this eternal life is still enwrapped in the temporal experience common to everyman; hence it is true to say with regard to it: "Ye are dead and your life is hidden with Christ in God" (20).

One final and extremely important thing must be said. The decisive manifestation of Christian living as life in the Holy Ghost is the reality of *agapé*, of self-giving love. That is the very life of God Himself. God *is* love (21). And what Christ operates through faith is just this, that the love of God is shed abroad in our hearts, that man through faith is gathered into the love of God as the reality of his new life. Thus love is greater (22) than faith and hope because it is God Himself. "Whosoever abideth in love, abideth in God and God in Him" (23). Love is the sensitivity of the "I" for the "Thou". This means essentially: for the divine "Thou" which has disclosed itself to me in the Christian revelation. In so far as this happens, the co-relative thing also happens necessarily—that my "I" is sensitive to the human "thou". Union with God in Christ expresses itself and works itself out inevitably in communion with my fellow-man. This very reality is what we mean by the present. It is the merit of Eberhard Grisebachs in his work which bears the title *The Present* to have insisted tirelessly upon this sequence of ideas, that only the man who loves enjoys the full reality of the present, because he alone is present with his fellow-man, and the latter with him. Everyman cannot truly love and has no real present because his present, as we have just said, is loaded with the burden of the past and shadowed by anxiety and care about the future. He can never therefore be truly present with his neighbour since he is a prisoner of himself and is ever preoccupied with himself. He never enjoys true fellowship with his neighbour, for he is separated from him by the weight of his own past and anxiety about his future. But because Christ removes from me the load of the past and my anxiety about the future I can be fully present with my neighbour and he with me.

Love is thus the necessary fruit and also the infallible criterion of faith (24). In love the reality of the Holy Ghost is manifested in me, Christ Himself, God Himself, is present with me. In love alone does man attain the fullness of his true life; for he is made for love just as he was made through love. Love is thus the most distinctive gift of the Spirit (25); it is shed abroad in our hearts through the Holy Ghost (26) so soon as it has become true that we no longer seek our lives in ourselves but receive them as the gift of God through faith in Jesus Christ.

4. Such, according to the witness of the New Testament, and it is confirmed by the experience of true believers in all ages, appears to be the transformation of life wrought in man through faith in that which has happened once for all in time. But this actual change in temporal existence is accompanied by a new understanding of time, and indeed such an understanding as is fundamentally different from all others and utterly unintelligible, completely paradoxical, to all those to whom the experience of faith is alien (p. 48). This new understanding of time is implicit in the life of the believer wherein time and eternity are fused. To formulate it as such is a matter for reflection and theology, not for faith itself. We have now to expound this new interpretation which is the secret of the believer but which concerns time as world-time.

(*a*) Time has a beginning, it was created simultaneously with the world. God Himself is not in time, He stands above time in the same sense and in the same way as He stands above the world. Augustine was the first to formulate this insight of faith. He anticipates too the view of the modern physicist (27): there is time only where there is a measurement of time, only where there are clocks, physical bodies by whose changes time can be measured. Time no more than the physical world is the product of the fall. God's relation to time is the same as His relation to the physical world. Thus it is false to assert in the Biblical view that time is uncreated, existing before all creation (28). Before all creation there existed nothing but the eternal God who is Lord of time and the Giver of time. That time has a beginning is a statement which modern physics does not at all contradict but is, on the contrary, inclined to assent to (cf. Appendix, pp. 57 f.).

(*b*) Just as time has a beginning so also will it have an end. It will be dissolved, in the fullness of time, in eternity. The representation of eternity as an endlessly long stretch of time which has been put forth recently in all seriousness in the name of New Testament exegesis is absurd (29). For in that case the difference between God's mode of existence and that of His creatures would be merely quantitative, and the qualitative difference between time and eternity would be expressly denied (30). If that were so God would not really be Lord of time and it would not be true that a thousand years in His sight are but as yesterday (31), that for Him the future is just as much present as the past. The well-justified reaction against the Platonic idea that eternity is timelessness must not lead us into the opposite error of supposing that the eternal is to be thought of as distinguished from the temporal merely by the endlessness of its time elements. What the real Biblical view of eternity is must now be discussed.

(*c*) Only through the clear delimitation of time as having a beginning and an end does time really become a straight line and is the cyclical conception proper to myth religion dissolved. Only so does time become historical time. The formula "the end of time equals the beginning of time" (32) must be recognized as the quintessence of cyclical myth-thinking. The first Adam and the second Adam are clearly kept apart in the witness of faith (33); otherwise, with the completion of redemption, the fall would be again possible and everything could begin again in an endless circle.

(*d*) But beginning and end are held together by God's eternal plan, and God manifests His Lordship over time just by the fact that from the beginning He aims at the end. For this reason there is history not only of humanity but of the cosmos. All is moving towards an ultimate goal. Everything has its place within this world-history. The goal and the meaning of this world-history towards which all is orientated is eternal life in the communion of God and creature. This insight into the essential character of time is possible only through the revelation of God in Jesus Christ. Jesus Christ, in whom my life gains new foundations, is the Word that was in the beginning, in whom and through whom and unto whom all things were created (34).

After what we have said about the Christian understanding of time the Christian thought of eternity can be quickly summed up (35). To speak of eternity means to speak of God. God alone has eternity, God who is the Lord of time, the Lord of the world. Eternity is not therefore, as in Indian and Greek ontology or in the Platonic system of ideas, that which is timeless or the negation of time. The Biblical thought of eternity is strictly parallel to the Biblical thought of omnipotence: God's Lordship over time. The Biblical language may easily mislead us. The eternity of God is expressed Biblically in two different ways, each of which in itself cancels out the other, viz. eternity = unending time and eternity = negation of time. If eternity were merely unending time God would not be Lord of time and He would share in the transience which belongs to the essence of the time series, to linear time. God, however, is precisely the abiding, as the One who is, for whom the distinctions of time, time-distances, have no significance in that for Him a thousand years are but as yesterday, He who sees the end of time in the beginning, who foreknows and fore-ordains the future. The expressions of negation alternate with those of unending time, so that we cannot accept either the one or the other as adequate in themselves. But the third term, to which both sets of expressions point, is inaccessible to our thought. We can grasp it only indirectly in the notion of Lordship over time.

This implies that God's relation to time is not purely negative. He is indeed transcendent over time, but He has created time just as He has created the world. Hence He wills that time, like the world, shall be filled with His glory. He wills therefore that the end of time shall be the consummation of time, time that is filled with eternity (36). We know this just because God has taken time into Himself, because in His Son He has entered into time. Only because this has happened have we knowledge of God, of His plan in creation and redemption, of the final goal for the sake of which the world was made. By the fact that God has revealed Himself in time,

He has imprinted upon it its historical character; He has given it direction and meaning, the possibility and the necessity of decision. Time, because it is historical, is something other than the merely neutral time stream; it is charged with the tension of decision, of faith, and of penitence.

The Lordship of God over time is only an indirect expression of His eternity. A more direct expression is only possible through analogy: God is life, He is the living God. God is the absolutely living One to whom is proper nothing of the transience, the existence in death, which cleaves to all temporality. God's being is changelessness and immortality. Our life in the present—that of everyman—consists in an uncertain hovering between being and non-being; our present constantly crumbles away in that every moment; hardly does it arise, when it is gone. Hence our temporal existence—the mere form of time linearity—is penetrated with sorrow. Our moments are hedged in between the "not yet" and the "no longer". No doubt experienced time is *durée réelle* as contrasted with time as thought. It is so because it embraces past and future in a unity. But the power to do this is limited; hence time drops away from us and the moment will not tarry. But God embraces past and future in an unqualified sense, time does not flow away from Him, He controls it; He has therefore absolute *durée réelle*, real undivided, unconquered, indissoluble fullness of life in the present. The divine moment thus holds together past and future in an indivisible unity.

But we may find a yet more positive expression for the divine eternity.* We recognized that the present which is given to us in faith is love. This love is the love of God, the being of God, if I may say so, the substance of God. The substance of God—we have seen in our *Doctrine of God* (37)—is pure actuality, *actus purus*. The theologian Biedermann, who was a pupil of Hegel, has attempted the most abstract definition of the divine being: the One who is in Himself and for Himself. This definition is correct; only it defines—as is inevitable in a purely speculative theology—the hidden God, the *Deus absolutus*. But, if such abstractions are at all intel-

* See translator's note at end of chapter.

ligible and permissible, the God of revelation would have to be defined as the One who is in Himself for us, as love grounded in His own being, rather than first awakened by the beloved object; hence self-giving love, *agapé*. God's being in so far as it is revealed to us, is being for us, accessibility to the "thou". God is for His creation, for us (38); this is how he is revealed to us in Jesus Christ.

But as He reveals Himself so is He in Himself. He is in Himself self-offering, He is in Himself love. And this divine self-giving is before all worlds. He is the love with which the Father has loved the Son before the foundation of the world (39). God is in Himself not only the One who is in Himself for Himself, but at the same time the self-existent Being who exists for us; and this is the ground of creation. Therefore God's eternal present is not the silence of sheer self-existence, but the conversation between Father and Son which has no beginning and no ending, self-communication which does not arise only through the creation of a world but which is before the foundation of the world. God's self-existent being is not solitary but the dialogue of love in eternity. The eternal life in love which He bestows upon us is the essence of His own being. The present which we hold in Christ is really God's making His very self operative within us; God's love is shed abroad in our hearts by the Holy Ghost (40). Therefore the believer shares in eternal life even though this eternal life is still in the body of this death; hence it is the plenitude of presence only in a provisional manner. But this love is the *eschaton*: that which remains when all else will have vanished (41).

We are conscious of the fact that in making these statements about the eternity of God we have reached the limit of what can be expressed in human language. We could not have said these things if they had not been expressly declared to us in Holy Scripture. But we must say them when the question of what eternity means is raised. In this we are recognizing what it is more important to recognize than anything else: the nature of the true present, of the true properties of our humanity. Only from this point of view is understandable what the Bible tells us about the future and eternity as our own future, and how this future through faith becomes our present.

Appendix: The Biblical conception of time and the Kantian antinomies of time

It is well known that Kant dismissed time as a mere sensible form of the thing-in-itself by pointing to the fact that we must make statements about time which stand in contradiction to each other. The following two contradictory statements are a necessity of thought: firstly, time has no beginning and no ending. For every beginning would be in itself the end of preceding time and every end would be the beginning of a succeeding time. Secondly, time has a beginning and has an end. Otherwise an eternity would be enclosed in the present moment; but an eternity cannot be delimited. "It is a superficial notion to say that time without beginning or ending is not a self-contradictory statement and that only the idea of time as having a beginning and ending is a contradiction in terms" (42). Kant overcomes this antinomy by saying that time is only a sensible form and not a final reality, not a thing-in-itself.

From the point of view of Biblical faith, we have no reason to repudiate the Kantian doctrine of antinomy, quite on the contrary: it confirms within the limits of human thought what we know by faith about time and eternity. The Kantian idea of sensible form and appearances corresponds to the Biblical conception of the creaturely status of time. Theologically, the idea of God is co-relative with the Kantian thing-in-itself, and with Kant we state that the sensible form of time has no application to Him, since it has validity only for the apparent or (as we would prefer to say) for the created. Thus far our agreement. Nevertheless we, from the point of view of faith, proceed to make statements about time which Kant would have to reject. We say: time has a beginning and an ending, it cannot be without beginning or ending, because like the world and with the world it is created. The thought of creation has as little place in rational thought as the thought of revelation. But we do not say that through thinking we recognize the fact of creation and thus of the commencement of time. Rather we state specifically: so we believe and so we teach on the basis of revelation. But Kant confines himself to what is attainable by rational thought.

Now it is very remarkable that modern physics appears to be approaching the Christian position not on the ground of rational speculation but as compelled by observation and experiment (it should be remembered that Einstein's theory of relativity took its point of departure from the mutually contradictory observations of Fizeau and Michelson and was repeatedly verified by measurements). Both from the recognition of the precisely calculable energy rays of the elements as from astronomical knowledge of expanding space, and the law of entropy, we are compelled to adopt the hypothesis of a world beginning in time. Exactly here as in the unproved supposition that a three-dimensional idea of space is alone valid, the error of Kant might be seen solely in the fact that he concerned himself too exclusively with what is unthinkable and took too little account of the possibility of correcting thought by experiment. Just as space as thought does not coincide with space as actually measured—as is known, Guass was cautious enough to check by measurement the soundness or otherwise of *a priori* Euclidean geometry—so real time is something other than time for thought. At this point the philosophers of our time, Bergson and Heidegger, took up their work and worked out the difference between real and conceptual time. How closely in so doing they approached the Christian interpretation of time we saw at the beginning of this chapter.

Translator's note to page 55

Gegenwart and *Gegenwärtigkeit*. The author's thought, here and on the following page, rests upon a fine linguistic and philosophical distinction between these two words, both of which refer to "the present" or "presence". The former suggests the present as a mere *form* of time, the latter the present as lived, as filled with *content* and meaning, or, more specifically here, the being present to someone in personal encounter. Brunner here means that by faith and love the present becomes charged with eternity for *us*.

Chapter Six

THE ECCLESIA AS THE PRESENT REALITY OF THE FUTURE AND THE TRANSFORMATION OF THE IDEA OF REVOLUTION

IT is clear from the foregoing considerations and from the witness of the New Testament that in faith the future is already present. The ecclesia, the community of Jesus Christ, wherever it is a genuine fellowship of faith, knows itself to be living a genuine Messianic eschatological existence through the presence of the Holy Ghost. Jesus, in His preaching of the Kingdom of God, proclaimed the new æon which was to come not merely as something realizable in the future but as something present in Him and already come in Him (1), though this proclamation was clothed in the form of a mystery; for before His death on the Cross the self-announcement of the Messiah could only have been misunderstood. But He was not yet the Messiah in revealed majesty, only in the form of the suffering Servant of God.

The primitive Christian community, however, which since the resurrection recognized in the crucified the Messiah and the Christ, and experienced His living risen presence, knew itself henceforth to be a Messianic community, a communal-personal life, the bearer of the new life of eternity and of the powers of the divine world (2). At the same time it knew that this newness of life was still hidden within it, wrapped in the mantle of the old life, hence only a first-fruits, provisional and incomplete and waiting for the consummation. Such is the paradox of the primitive Christian, the truly Christian life; it is characteristically both a "now already" and a "not yet".

This paradox appears in the fact that exegetes hold contradictory views about the relationship of present and future in the primitive community. Some speak of a "realized eschatology" and see in the event of Pentecost the Parousia proclaimed by Christ (Dodd) (3), while others relate the primitive community to the framework of contemporary Judaism and its purely futuristic apocalyptic (A. Schweitzer) (4); others, again, see the decisive fact in what happened once for all in Christ but none the less regard the expectation of what is to be as the culminating moment of the Christian faith (Cullmann, Ed. Schweizer, Kummel, etc.) (5), and others yet again view this orientation towards the future as a purely mythological expression of what is really meant—the new character of the present (Bultmann) (6).

After what has been said about time and eternity, there can be for us no doubt that the primitive Christian existence, the mode of being of the ecclesia, is paradoxical in the sense that in it the life of the world to come is a present reality, but a hidden reality, waiting for future disclosure and apocalypsis; though it is to be granted that, in the New Testament, emphasis on the "now already" and the "not yet" varies in the different writings. But it is common to the whole Christian witness that both the "now already" and the "not yet" applies; that is to say, the fellowship of faith lives both in rejoicing over the newness of its experience and in longing and sure hope of that which is yet to come (7).

The Christian ethos arises from this dualism of possession and anticipation. It is an ethos which flows from the received newness of life, from the reality of *agapé*, and which is therefore determined not by imperatives and commands, but rather by recollection (8). Its norm is constituted by the admonition to actualize what has already been done in Christ; it is an ethos which is distinguished from all ethical systems by the fact that it is not subjected to a law but consists in a bringing forth through the guidance and inspiration of the Spirit what is according to the will of God. If the Spirit reign in you, then you are no longer under the law (9)—that is the Magna Charta of Christian freedom. On the other hand, again, it is necessary to assist the leading of the Holy Spirit by admonition, by imperatives, and even by law, since all too easily the guidance of the Holy Spirit develops into a false ecstasy and the too confident reliance on His leading into a false quietism.

But even with this limitation the element of newness discloses itself as a principle of revolutionary life. The early Christian and, we repeat, all genuine Christian faith is revolutionary existence. Above it stands as motto the apocalyptic word, "Behold, I make all things new" (10). In spite of the hardening process of institutional and bourgeois life Christianity has proved itself to be the greatest revolutionary force in world history. The fact that it has not been so considered by the generally recognized revolutionary leaders, but rather appraised as a reactionary force and that the factor of hope integral to the Christian faith has been branded as opium, paralysing the will to remake the world, is certainly due in part to this hardening process, but above all to the fact that here two opposite ideas of revolution are involved—to discriminate between which and to examine the basis of which is one of our most urgent tasks.

The true Christian revolution is essentially a consequence and an accompaniment of the fundamental revolution which God alone can accomplish. The "Behold, I make all things new" is not the voice of a human leader, but the voice of Him who sat upon the throne and who declares the new life to be the end of all history, a new heaven and a new earth. God alone can truly revolutionize, He who is the Creator and Redeemer. Men cannot do so because everything that they do stems from the old and therefore brings with it the curse of the old, of sin and unrighteousness. When man himself takes in hand the new shaping of human affairs he must finally admit that nothing has essentially altered, since the old leaven of malice is still there, spoiling the seemingly new day. The "I make all things new" can only be said by Him who can create out of nothing—and just that is reserved to the Creator of the world.

But the situation is not that this new creation leaves no room for the co-operation of man. Since God became man, since in Jesus Christ the beyond entered this world and the eternal became temporal, man has been called to co-operate with God (11) in the task of renovation. But this process of renewal has quite other laws and quite another mode of working than the programmes of revolutionaries. The first and fundamental difference is this—that the change begins with man himself. "If anyone is in Christ he is a new creature" (12). That is the experience of the first Christians and of genuine Christianity in all ages. The revolution begins at the innermost personal centre. For in the last resort it is the personal subject which must be the decisive guiding force in the process. Before man can really create something new, he must himself be renewed. That such personal renewal can be effected through faith by the Spirit of God is the witness of the New Testament and of Christian experience. This renewal begins at the point where man's own doing never suffices: in relationship with God. "Thy sins are forgiven thee" (13). Man seeking himself in his own strength becomes the forgiven sinner, whose sin was that he relied upon his own freedom and self-assurance for what God alone can effect. The revolution begins from within, in the heart, and consists in the fact that the independent man becomes the one who is utterly dependent on God; and this is an act in which—what is incredible to the unbeliever—the slave becomes free, the sinner a child of God. The true revolution consists in this innermost transformation, which is wrought through the Cross of Jesus Christ and which means birth from above (14) by the Holy Ghost.

The revolutionary character of the Christian faith means: only the regenerate man can create truly new conditions. The revolutionary recognized by the world, the typical instance of which is the Marxist of our days, says on the contrary: the transformation of conditions, the abolition of capitalism and its replacement by the classless society of communism, brings into being the new communistic man. In a certain sense that is true; totalitarian communism creates, in fact, the new communistic man through communistic education controlled and dictated by the state. But then it becomes manifest that the prognosis which we made from the standpoint of Christian faith is verified: this new man is only a variant of the old, and the conditions which he creates are only variants of the former ones. Slavery instead of the hoped-for freedom, and instead of justice the new injustice of state pillage; instead of humanity, complete inhumanity. Revolution shows itself to be the worst form of reaction—a lapse into the most primitive tribal organization, into organized sub-humanity.

The Christian faith revolutionizes the idea of revolution in that it perceives the only real revolution to be one which works from within outwards, and all others as mere camouflaged reaction. The contrast goes still deeper: the Christian faith sees true revolution to consist in the fact that man surrenders his claim to freedom and receives his true freedom from dependence upon God. Only by men who recognize their freedom to lie in obedience and trust towards God can a new society, an order of justice and humanity, be built up. So-called revolutions which begin as an impulse towards freedom end always in a monstrous mass slavery and collectivism which robs man of his true human values.

But why is it that, in spite of the fact that for 1,500 years it has had the greatest chances, Christianity has not succeeded in establishing the kingdom of justice, humanity, and peace and shaping the life of the nations of the West? We have already mentioned what must be at least a part of the answer to this question: the hardening process by which Christianity has become institutional and bourgeois. What is now called Christianity and is known as such, as a result of the last 1,800 years of history, is not the life of the ecclesia which is shown us in the New Testament but a compound of the old Adam—corrupt sinful humanity—and a Christian façade, if we may say so, a Christian envelope to a core of Adamic humanity. The hardening process which so soon robbed Christianity of its revolutionary impulse and inspiration can be variously interpreted (15). We mention only one aspect: the development of the church from the ecclesia or the assimilation of the church to the state and its forms of organization. The institutionalization of the church in the Roman Papacy represents a transformation of the church from within; the state nexus of Protestantism is a continuation of what began with Constantine and Theodosius: the dependence of the church on the state.

This process has a deeper reason in the fact that Christianity ceased in its early days to trust in the power of the Spirit and sought security in office, sacrament, and formal creed. In proportion as it did so its revolutionary power and impulse was broken. It ceased to be a brotherhood and became a corporation. It ceased to be a new life and became a philosophy and theology. It made its peace with the unrighteous world; it became a mere cult society in the world and ceased to work as a revolutionary ferment within the world.

That is part of the answer to the failure of Christianity. The other part of the answer lies in the fact that the ultimate revolution transcends what man can hope to accomplish by his own action as the co-worker with God. The "Behold, I make all things new", does not mean what can or will be done by the community of Christ; that is, by the fellowship of those who are inwardly regenerated. It means rather what God will do at the end of time, at the end of history, by the resurrection of the dead. The fact that the new life in man through faith, although a reality, is only provisional because and so long as we remain in the body of this death marks the limit of the possible in the Christian revolution.

The Christian revolution, we said, begins in the inner life, where no man can change himself, and is effected by the power of the Holy Ghost. It makes of the self-seeker one who serves others in sincerity of heart. It makes of the unjust, a just man; of one who seeks happiness, a man who aims at truth and justice; of one who seeks power, a man who serves the highest power. That is the essential revolution. But this renewal remains hidden, a mystery. And yet: the change does not only happen in secret. The early Christian ecclesia stood forth openly as a new phenomenon and aroused the attention of the heathen. "See how they love one another"—even the heathen had to bear witness to the fact. The ecclesia is in itself an essentially new factor in world history—a visible adumbration of the Kingdom of God.

But the new inspiration does not remain confined within the framework of the ecclesia. Wherever a part of the genuine ecclesia exists, something of its life streams forth into the world and becomes the new leaven which leaveneth the whole lump. The new inward life becomes a new social life: new marriage, new family life, new manners, a new conception of justice, new relations between masters and servants, a new estimation of childhood, of woman, of the weak. But it is an essential law of the working of this revolution from within outwards that it needs time and proceeds as a gradual evolution rather than by fits and starts, that it lays more emphasis on the motive than on the outward visible effect, that it regards with mistrust, rather than aims at, the outward change which does not of itself follow from the inner transformation.

All this makes it an object of suspicion to the revolutionary. The latter aims at immediate changes, and when conditions are ripe easily produces them. It is not difficult for the determined revolutionary to make revolutions, i.e. to change conditions, to abolish the old order and to put in its place something new. Whoever thinks in terms of externals first is sure of success, if only he works with a clear system and has the power of suggestion, of representing plausibly to men that this reforming programme will fulfil their wishes and remove their distress. From the point of view of such a one the Christian faith, with its hope in what God will accomplish, with its reference to what will come to mankind from the beyond, must appear a temporizing manœuvre, an idle and false consolation of suffering humanity by other-worldly hopes, and so, as a most stubborn reactionary power. "Opium for the people" was Marx's description of religion (and he had in mind the Christian religion).

But Lenin was the first to realize that deadly enmity existed between the Christian faith and his communistic revolution. For revolution as he understood it could tolerate no scruples derived from bourgeois morality concerning love of one's neighbour. The resolution to produce by force the total transformation of the outward order did not permit him to shrink from any consequences of Machiavellian thinking in terms of ends. Hence he set up as means to the end the totalitarian state, with its methods of terror and the immediate purpose of the dictatorship of the proletariat. He realized that totalitarianism spells the denial and contempt of God; perhaps he did not realize that its collectivism spells the denial and contempt of man. But he saw that the two things were mutually exclusive. Hence he passed from the Marxist contemptuous toleration of religion to a determined fight for its annihilation. But the mistake of his calculation was as follows: the peoples, the proletarian masses of Europe, who were at first attracted by the success of his revolution, began to fear the methods which this revolution employed in the interests of quick results. In proportion as they came to realize that the totalitarian state could not be, as Lenin had naïvely supposed, a mere temporary measure, but that, as the clear-sighted Stalin was the first to see, it must be established definitively with a view to unlimited duration, they began to recognize in this revolution the worst type of reaction and to dread it as such.

Revolutionary Marxism was the only form of the idea of progress which at the collapse of the bourgeois evolutionary theory of progress still retained a certain plausibility, because it was able to impute that collapse to the capitalist bourgeoisie. Evolution has become incredible, long live the revolution! But now that the revolution has been unmasked as a terrible illusion what hope remains? Is perhaps the Christian revolution in a position to fulfil the hopes of the peoples? Can it promise a paradise on earth now that we have been forced to realize that evolutionary development is heading for catastrophe and that revolution does not bring forth the kingdom of justice, freedom, and humanity, but on the contrary destroys all humanity and freedom?

Chapter Seven

THE CHRISTIAN HOPE OF PROGRESS AND THE UTOPIAN MILLENNIUM

IN the experience of newness of life through the Christian faith and in the reality of the ecclesia is grounded the hope of interior spiritual world transformation. For, if it is true that when a man is in Christ he is a new creature, then there exists essentially for every man the hope of becoming other than he is, the hope that the godless can be sanctified through Christ, transformed through the power of the Holy Ghost. If the ecclesia is in fact something new under the sun, then the hope exists that this still tiny body can become a great people, embracing finally all the nations of the earth. Even though modern exegesis stresses the fact that Jesus' so-called parables of growth—those of the mustard seed and the leaven—refer not to growth but simply to the contrast between the small, insignificant beginnings and the greatness of the ultimate goal, yet it is undeniable that the letters of the apostles are full of the thought of growth. In the Church there is to be growth in every part (1); the Church as a whole must grow up into the fullness of the stature of Christ (2). Hence in the Acts of the Apostles and apostolic letters we are told with joy and gratitude of the extensive spread of the Church in distant lands. Both this extensive and intensive growth belongs as well to the actual experience as to the theology of the faith and its fellowship. As already in the story of Pentecost it is noted with grateful astonishment that on that day about three thousand souls were added to the Church (3), so the continuous theme of the Acts of the Apostles is its account of how the Christian seed grows, how the Word of God proves itself to be a power not of this world since it constantly spreads in spite of all resistance on the part of men. The Christian faith implies the duty and the will to an evangelistic activity which recognizes essentially no boundaries. Hence missionary effort has gone forward unceasingly throughout the world and the thought that no man should be excluded from hearing the Christian message has inspired the missionaries of the Gospel to undertake the boldest deeds and to shrink from no obstacles. The command to evangelize was voiced plainly enough: All peoples and every creature (4).

Wherever this expanding Gospel goes, it brings to birth new life by the service of man as co-worker with God, the Kingdom of God is set up; for wherever Christ is Lord over man's heart, there the Kingdom of God is—although as yet in its concealed and provisional form, there the transcendent breaks into this world.

This event, of course, in its essence, is something quite hidden according to the word of the apostle: "Your life is hid with Christ in God" (5). But it is inevitable that it should be manifested in fruits of the Spirit (6). Where Christ reigns in the heart, a change takes place, not only in the hidden depths but also in outward conduct. A new relationship to the fellow-creature comes about, new marriage and family life ; there is not only a new disposition behind all activity in the world, but also a new activity. There, from the centre of innermost personal renewal, there comes to pass that slow and secret revolution which really alters conditions because first of all men themselves have been changed, there arise new manners, new law, a new shaping of life, new art, new literature, new culture. There, even in the outward husk of human life, the state, there comes to be much that is new.

Those *Mayflower* Pilgrim Fathers who left their old home in order to build up in the new world a new type of communal life, according to the ordinances of God, were no dreamers. Just as little was William Penn a dreamer, who, equipped with a royal charter, set out for the land which was called after him, Pennsylvania, in order there to attempt his sacred experiment of constructing a state according to the laws of God. Wherever the powers of God break through into the earthly historical world, there takes place something similar to the gushing forth of water in the desert. A new undreamed of life begins; something of what is meant by the coming of the Kingdom of God is realized, even though only in a provisional and imperfect fashion. Despite all its horrors the history of Europe and of the West is a testimony to that fact. The seed of the Kingdom has in truth not been unfruitful. It has come forth and borne fruit some a hundredfold, some sixtyfold, and some thirtyfold—even though alongside it and at the same time quite a different seed has sprung up and borne fruit (7).

And yet this is not what is meant in the New Testament by the coming of the Kingdom of God. When Jesus proclaims the Kingdom of God and its advent He means the ultimate, the perfect, the wholly other, the end of history, which sets a bound to this whole historical world, this whole earthly life. We shall not yet speak of this. But that foretaste which also comes from the beyond, the Kingdom of God in its concealed and imperfect form, is none the less a reality, and the hope of such inward transformation is justified even though the greater Christian hope refers not to this but to the end of history. Indeed, this faith and this looking forward to an inward transformation as an earthly adumbration of the Kingdom of Heaven appears in fact to have its New Testament basis in the conception of the millennium.

Of course we must be clear that what is meant in chapter 20 of the Book of Revelation, the only place where the millennium is spoken of, is something wholly other than this reflection of the transcendent within history. For that apocalyptic millennium is introduced by a resurrection of the dead which, as the first resurrection, is expressly distinguished from the second, the ultimate one, and in which only a small section of humanity, those who had not worshipped the beast, are resurrected. These thousand years, so we read in the Apocalypse, are a time of peace and good because during this time the powers of evil are fettered. But after the thousand years the latter break forth from their captivity, a new reign of terror begins on the earth, until shortly afterwards the ultimate, the consummation of the kingdom, will come.

This plainly fantastic theory is the only one which in the New Testament expresses the idea of the millennium. Later on, it received manifold interpretations and transformations of which we can recall briefly only the most important. The first of these transmutations is that which has been defined as the early church chiliastic eschatology. It does not distinguish between a provisional and a final state, hence does not deal with an interim millennium, but is concerned with nothing other than the New Testament promise of the Kingdom of God, which it understands as a factor realizable within history. The Kingdom of God comes upon the earth and transforms earthly historical life into a state of perfection, yet without transforming the temporal and historical foundations of existence—in this we see a contrast to the teaching of Jesus and the apostles. Thus in this conception we have the consummate fully revealed eternal life contained in the framework of earthly temporality. If, forgetting the original meaning of the word chiliastic, we wish to call this idea of an *earthly* consummation chiliasm, then we must say that this chiliasm recurred in many sects of the Middle Ages and of the Reformation and post-Reformation periods and is also dominant in certain forms of modern religious socialism. "Kingdom of God upon earth". And that not thought of in provisional terms as in the case of the Biblical millennium but as something ultimate, like the Kingdom of God proclaimed by Jesus.

A second transformation is that of Augustine. He interprets the millennium as referring to the history of the church (8). For him therefore the millennium is not the object of hope but the experience of actual churchly life. This conception has, in common with that of the Apocalypse, merely the temporary duration of a thousand years. The church, both Roman Catholic and Protestant, has assimilated this view in so far as it has expressly identified the thought of an intervening kingdom with church history. The millennium idea is again dimly reflected in certain church theologians who, like Spencer, cherish a hope of better times.

A new turn was given to the theory by the Christian utopists, who, without expressly referring to the millennium, sketched out the ideal picture of a Christian world-state and hoped more or less for its realization in the future. With Thomas More we call Utopias these fanciful dreams of future good. The Renaissance Catholic Thomas More was followed by the Lutheran Martin Bucer in his writing *De regimine Christi*; later by the orthodox Lutheran Valentin Andreae, the author of *Christianopolis*, and the Dominican Campanella with his *Sun-state*. From this time onwards the Christian thought of progress merges in that of rationalism. The most recent imposing form of secular utopianism is to be seen in Karl Marx's teaching about the classless society to be introduced by communism—an ideal which he describes quite in the fashion of the wishful pictures of the utopists, in fact almost in the terms of the early Christian chiliasts (9). The difference between the rationalist and the Christian faith in progress lies essentially in the following points:

1. The rationalist faith in progress is founded on the *faculté de se perfectionner* of human reason. This, as we have said, is hope based on self-security. The Christian faith in progress is, however, hope based on the certainty of God. Just as Jesus is the pure gift of divine grace, so also is the church and its reflections in the world, and the new life is the gift of the Holy Ghost to Christians.

2. Whereas the rational faith in progress is a victim of the illusion that the mere development of reason in the formal sense must automatically guarantee an increase in material well-being, the Christian hope is built on the faith that the Holy Ghost controls the heart of personal life and so brings about a moral and spiritual change therein.

3. In the Christian context, the growth is not simply as in rationalism, a matter of addition and increase; rather the growth of the new comes about only by an ever-repeated destruction of the old, a radical change in the direction of living. Here applies the dictum of Chr. Blumhardt: "Die, so

that Christ may live." The hope is therefore from this point of view, too, the opposite of hope based on self-certainty.

4. But after these distinctions have been made the common factor must also be stressed: the Christian faith in progress, too, is in fact a hope which does not leave out of account the factor man, whom it regards as an instrument and co-worker with the grace of God, and which thus entrusts the amelioration of the world to human activity also in so far as this latter wills to be and is nothing other than an instrument of the action of God. So the apostles were able to say: "Your labour is not in vain in the Lord" (10). Thus here too man is not a *quantité négligeable* any more than in the rationalist hope of progress, though he can only be the tool of God, not the real *auctor* of the betterment.

In this sense all who in the history of Christianity have rendered some great service have expected results from their action and from that of other believers. All who have gone to distant lands and have undergone the greatest privations have done so in the confidence of thereby contributing to the spread of the Kingdom of God. All who, impelled by the love of Christ, have made an effort at some one point to improve matters, whether it be in the church itself, in education, in the shaping of law, in care for the weak of all kinds—they have done it in the certainty that thus some leavening of secular life by the leaven of the Gospel would take place. Without this faith in progress, the action of the Christian would necessarily be paralysed and his joyful deeds be emptied of all inspiration. This faith in the possibility of a better future through the effectual action of the Holy Ghost belongs to the very foundations of the Christian faith.

But it must give us cause for reflection when we note that the Reformers rejected Christian utopianism as so much Judaism—e.g. the idea that before the resurrection of the dead the pious would set up a world kingdom (11), or the Jewish dreams that before the judgment day a golden age would dawn in which the pious would exercise a world dominion (12). This conception of a terrestrial Utopia within history, of a kingdom of justice and peace built upon a

Christian basis, they condemned as *judaica opinio*, obviously because in it the Old Testament promise of the Messianic kingdom is understood as an earthly possibility within history (13). Here rightly there is no allusion to the millennium of the Apocalypse. That extremely fantastic conception of a partial resurrection while earthly history still continues is silently passed over as was customary since Augustine.

But why should the possibility of a Christian world empire, of a universal order of righteousness and peace, brought about by the powers of the Holy Ghost and of faith, be dismissed as illusion and fantasy? Must we set limits to the creative power of the Holy Ghost? Should we not rather trust that, just as God made real the miracle of the Christian revelation and of the ecclesia within history, so also He might complete His work extensively? Was it really only a sound and sober distrust of enthusiasm or was it perhaps a doctrinaire but sinful pessimism when the reformers finally dismissed the thought of a kingdom of justice and peace to be eventually realized within history?

We are here confronted by a decisive question which is of the greatest relevance for present-day Christianity. Certainly the belief in progress based on reason is exploded, and we know why it was such a short-lived dream. So much the more the Christian hope of a millennium to be established by God Himself gains in significance. Why should it not be possible for God to bring about within the historical world, i.e. under the conditions of the normal historical life known to us, a kingdom of peace and justice and thus to make Himself fully manifest? Can anyone undertake to prove that this is not possible?

The Reformers obviously were of the opinion that they could furnish this proof; otherwise they would not have dared to brand these ideas as *judaica somnia* and to decide formally to reject them. How, then, should this proof be made?

1. Historically. History shows that all those experiments which were attempted with such sincere faith and penitence, that of the *Mayflower* Pilgrim Fathers, that of William Penn,

that of the Hussites, and many less well known, ended in great disillusionment. To be sure, the first generation of Pilgrim Fathers and Quakers created in fact a communal life that perhaps, through its brotherly order, stood out as new in contrast to the states of western history (14); but with the second generation the outlines of the new structure became blurred, it was no longer so characteristic as at first, no longer so different from what had been left behind, until with each new generation the difference between the old and the new became slighter and finally utterly disappeared. And in this it was a question not of a great state or a world empire but, on the contrary, of small communities in which there were present specially favourable Christian presuppositions for the building of a Christian communal life. In this connexion it is significant that in the story of the Pilgrim Fathers—in itself so gladdening and refreshing to read—with the second generation, the creation of a police force became necessary. That was a tacit admission that spiritual and moral inspiration was not sufficient to secure the establishment of peace and justice, and that even in this Christian community the usual sanctions of force must be applied. The history of all Christian communistic experiments shows the same thing (15). They began with voluntary equality and the renunciation of privilege; they then proceeded to develop a legalistic structure until the latter became intolerable. Up to the present there is no contrary example proving the possibility of establishing permanently and on a big scale a community inspired by Christian brotherly love, an order of peace and justice. Nevertheless this argument from history is not conclusive. It might be one day. . . .

2. Therefore the fundamental theological proof must be added to these examples drawn from history. It is assumed that we are dealing with a fellowship of sincere Christians each of whom is resolved to submit himself wholly to the law of Christ. Must it not be granted that even these who seriously wish to live the Christian life are still sinners? Certainly they have been born again and are persons in whom a new life has arisen from within—but still they are such as need

daily repentance and forgiveness because they, too, still live in the body, because there still clings to them the being of the old Adam, which is constantly at strife with the new man.

Secondly: how stands it with the new generation? Who can guarantee that the children of true Christians will themselves be Christian? The very fact that faith is a free gift of divine grace precludes the idea that one generation can be a guarantee for its successor. Of course Christian education can do much, but it is not able to ensure that the children of Christian parents will become Christians.

Thirdly: all those sacred experiments have begun on the favourable assumption that all the participants are men who seriously wish to be Christians. But where has it been promised us that the hour will come when all men are Christians, and not nominal but true Christians, so that a Christian order would correspond to the will of all? In the articles of the *Augustana* and in the *Helvetica posterior* there is an appendix which throws a flood of light on the idea of the Christian world state : *ubique oppressis impiis* (Aug.) or *oppressis suis hostibus impiis* (Helvet.). This means therefore that the exponents of the utopian idea do not suppose that all men will have become Christians but that the Christians will be in a majority, which will allow them to rule over those of other persuasions, or of none, to bring them by force under Christian control; i.e. to set up a kind of Christian dictatorship. But this means that the kingdom of justice and peace is weighted by a very dubious mortgage.

Of course, the champions of the Christian utopia could give another and more democratic turn to their theory, as follows: it suffices for the establishment of a Christian order of peace and justice if the Christians are only a powerful inspired minority group who by their unity and determination would be able to carry others along with them. But the experience we have of such Christian governments in the course of history can hardly set aside the doubt that still more in a Christian *world* government Christianity would go by the board. The essence of the Christian ecclesia is precisely the freedom and spirituality of its structure contrasting with all legalism. The Christian *agapé* cannot be embodied in a civil polity without becoming thereby something entirely different. All in all, we must subscribe to the sober judgment of the reformers.

But at the same time we must not give up the hope that by a strengthening of the truly Christian elements, both in the cultural and in the social political life of humanity, much could be bettered.

The Kingdom of God cannot be established in this earthly historical world because it is incompatible with two factors which are inherent in the latter: with the power of sin still operative even in the regenerate, and with the power of death. From the hidden depths of human nature and its fear in the face of death and from the tragic rent in human history caused by death, in spite of all counter-action by the Holy Spirit, negative powers emerge which prevent the historical earthly forms of human life from receiving a decisive change for the good. Just for this reason the Christian hope is fixed on an event which will work not merely within the framework of human life but will transform its fundamental structure: it is fixed on the life of the world to come.

But we have yet to decipher the meaning of a second Biblical-apocalyptic symbol which represents the polar opposite of the millennium: the idea of the Antichrist. The Christian hope of progress is limited not only by the fact of sin and death, but also by the fact that, just as there is a growth of the good, of the seed sown by God Himself, so also there is a growth of tares sown by the power of evil (16).

Chapter Eight

THE NEGATIVE PROMISE: ANTICHRIST

IF we may take the apocalyptic idea of the millennium as a symbol of a Christian hope of progress derived from faith in God's action in history, the New Testament offers us in the symbol of Antichrist, of the Satanic power of evil increasingly and effectually at work until the day of the resurrection, the antithesis of the former conception. Of course the New Testament and history both bear witness to the fact that there is a current and provisional advent of the Kingdom of God. We experience it above all in the ecclesia, in the brotherhood based upon communion with Christ; but we experience it also in the reflections of the Christian spirit in the social and cultural life of the world, whose structure does not spring from the Christian faith but which, mostly without anyone being aware of the fact, assimilates the action of Christ and mirrors something of His Spirit. The greater, deeper, more far-reaching are the effects of the Word and Spirit of Christ in the hearts of men—and who would set a bound to them?—so much the greater are these influences of the Christian fellowship on the world outside.

But if we find this hope of progress pictured in the parables of the mustard seed and the leaven there stands beside them the parable of the wheat and tares, and everywhere in the New Testament we meet the thought that the historical world stands under the influence of forces inimical to Christ and God, that Antichrist opposes Christ, and Satan, God. The Revelation declares that after the thousand years has run its course, during which time these hostile powers were held in check, a new outburst of them will follow which will surpass everything previously experienced in the way of terror. We find a similar thought in the so-called apocalypse of the Gospels, where Jesus says that the last days before the coming of the end and before His appearance in glory will be so terrible that they would be unbearable if God in His mercy did not shorten them (1). This means that just as there is a progress in good there is also a progress in evil; on both sides there is growth and accumulation.

It is just this fact that rationalistic optimism constantly overlooks. It is of course not to be denied that from century to century there is an ever-increasing inheritance of knowledge, of the technical means of controlling nature, of means of communication, and organization, and therewith a constant increase in human freedom and power. But not only does the heart, the inward centre of man, the disposition, remain untouched by this progress, rather it is that the growing power constitutes a twofold temptation to man: the temptation of an effective misuse of power and that of intoxication by power, of the mad sense of independence, of self-deification. The relatively most innocent aspect of this state of affairs is that pictured in tragi-comic fashion by Goethe in his *Apprentice to Magic*: the man who has learnt the art of invention and of acquiring knowledge has not at the same time learnt how to employ it usefully in his own service. He is threatened with destruction by the very fact of his own progress. He is destroyed by his own machines and through sheer progress loses control of them.

The second consequence is intrinsically more dangerous. Since all progress leaves unaffected the fundamental egoistic tendencies of human nature, and the bitter strife among men in spite of the unifying power of communications goes on apace, the effect of progress must be to render this strife so much the more murderous by the accumulation of the means of destruction. The first big consequence of world-unity created by technics is to be seen in the world-wars, and inventions of all kinds have a tendency to contribute in the first instance to the making of war. Thus progress drives humanity automatically to suicide. But progress can have a still more deleterious effect. Since man sees the scope of his power and freedom growing from century to century and from decade to decade, while his moral powers do not increase in the same proportion but have rather declined, this success goes to his head in such a way that he thinks himself his own god and holds the idea of religion as dependence on God to be a superstition unworthy of enlightened humanity. The culmination of outward progress coincides with the emancipation of man from belief in God, and therewith from all moral law. The climax in the development of means of power synchronizes with a complete unfettering of the egoistic will, of the instinctive forces, and the will to power.

Nor is that all. The self-deified man has learnt not only constantly to augment his technical means of power but also to develop complete mastery in acquiring domination over men's minds. He not only organizes men outwardly into a completely controllable collectivist state but he organizes also the conversion of men to the required collectivist-technocratic-totalitarian mode of thought and surrender of judgment(2). Hence the contrast between this impious human state control and the Christian faith and fellowship becomes ever more pointed and complete. It becomes clear that here lies its real enemy, seriously to be feared or respected; for universalistic liberalism, which intrinsically must equally well be its enemy, has shown itself to be too weak in will, too little systematized and too liable to be disintegrated by individualism, to be seriously counted. Thus the man of progress becomes Antichrist and the struggle against Christ develops into a life and death struggle.

But the force of Antichrist cannot be explained merely by an increase in the scope of freedom, i.e. indirectly. When Christ becomes powerful, then the devil and the forces of Antichrist step forth out of their hiding place into the light. Whether we express this state of affairs in personal-mythological terms, or psychologically, matters not at all. The success of Christianity does not allow the devil to sleep; he must assert his rights; when the presence of the holy makes itself powerfully felt, it awakens the counter-action of the unholy. The first-fruits of the Kingdom of God in the historical world does not remain long without experiencing a counter-thrust from the depths of the abyss. This is a fact of history just as it is the teaching of the New Testament. The fact simply is as the Lord says: after God has sown His seed the enemy comes by night and sows *his* seed. And then both grow together until the harvest of judgment day, so closely interwoven that man cannot discriminate between them.

Even so, we have not said all. The form of Antichrist can assume a still more sinister guise. We meet this both in the personal life of devotion of the individual Christian and in the history of the church at large. The Christian faith itself, the new life created by the Holy Ghost, is not immune from the danger of distortion by dæmonic forces. The audacity of faith can quite imperceptibly change into customary sinful human folly, the superb confidence of faith into human arrogance; humility can be a camouflage of vanity; and self-sacrificing love, a subtle snobbishness. So the ecclesia, the sphere of divinely created freedom in the spirit, can become a duplicate of the collectivist state, a pseudo-Christianity which arrogates the claims of Christ and finds acceptance, a church which administrates in business-like fashion the grace of Christ and guarantees it by church office.

History confirms the word of Scripture that the devil can assume the shape of an angel of light (3): the confirmation would no doubt be stronger than we imagine if only our spiritual vision were sharp enough to distinguish between the true and the false light. So the two symbols, that of the millennium and that of Antichrist, stand over against each other in mutual limitation. Neither an optimistic nor a pessimistic view of history is permitted us. No limits are placed on the potential unfolding of the Kingdom of God within history other than those of historical existence itself. But we must recognize the fact that within history underground negative forces are operative which pretend to follow the Christian way in order that they may exercise themselves more effectively the more the cause of God gains ground. It is ingratitude and a sign of faltering faith in God not to reckon with the progress of the work of Christ in history; but it is childish folly and disobedience to Scripture to be unwilling to recognize the counter-action of evil and the limits of the progress of the Kingdom of Christ.

Then, is the ideal never to be realized? That it will ultimately become a reality is the plain witness of the Gospel. But in order that this may happen things must not only happen *within* history but historical existence itself, "the body of this death", must itself be done away. It is precisely this that is meant by the message of resurrection and eternal life—and with this message the Gospel is identical.

Chapter Nine

THE FUTURE ADVENT OF JESUS CHRIST AS THE MEANING OF HISTORY

HAS my life, has the life of humanity, has the life of the world, any meaning? That is the question which more than any other preoccupies the modern man. The question has not always been clearly formulated. The man of the myth-religions evades it by understanding himself and human history as a part of nature, to which, by the idea of eternal recurrence symbolized in the circle, he both accords and denies meaning. The element which in these cycles is isolated and grasped is in itself meaningless; but the persistence and the ceaseless repetition of what revolves is, as eternal, something meaningful. With man's differentiation of himself from nature this solution of the problem of meaning becomes impossible. The individual man who has become aware of his freedom can no longer be content with the collectivist interpretation of his being such as is given in the idea of his integration into nature's eternal cycle. By the distinction between nature and spirit he is lifted out of the circle and understands himself in his spirituality to be eternal and free from time. He discovers the idea of the immortality of the soul. At the same time he gives up the search for meaning in history, which he relegates to meaningless recurrence. As a result of the undisputed predominance of the Christian faith for 1,500 years, Western man has come to take it for granted that what gives his life eternal meaning is the same thing as what gives meaning to humanity and the world as a whole. Both the life of the individual and the life of humanity, history, the world, and the cosmos, have a meaning —an eternal meaning which sums it all up.

This belief in meaning which made intelligible both the

individual and the whole has been dissolved by the rationalistic faith in progress, by hope based on self-security. But this attribution of meaning, as we have already seen (p. 11), was only possible by a sort of forgetfulness. For what sort of meaning could the progress of humanity give to *my* life, the life of the individual man? The individual had, as it were, in order to attribute meaning to history, to resign meaning for himself in favour of a meaning for humanity as a whole. For no doubt a vaguely conceived humanity in the remote future might well share in the goal of progress, but not he, the individual man, of to-day. Humanity must, as it were, form a pyramid where each generation would climb higher than its predecessors until the last, climbing over all the others, reached the top.

This faith was a product of liberal bourgeois enlightenment, for whose comfortable existence it sufficed. For the mass of men, especially for the proletariat, whose present conditions were so unfavourable, this meaning, focused on an endlessly distant future, could not suffice. So from the proletarian mind arose the utopian idea of an earthly paradise realizable in the immediate future. In the Marxist ideology of the classless society proletarian man found something which was able to inspire in him and his children a vital hope and lend his existence meaning, since dialectical materialism placed the goal of humanity in a foreseeable future. But for the non-Marxist bourgeoisie the collapse of the belief in progress left only existentialist nihilism. Man, no longer able to find a meaning in his life, hits upon the mad thought of giving it and his world the meaning which it has not (1). But, however imposing this existentialist philosophy may seem in its madness, it knows at bottom that it is mad. For how should man, the image of nothingness, be in a position to give his life the meaning which it has not? Existentialist heroism therefore amounts ever again to a nihilistic despair of meaning.

The same thing happens to the Marxist proletariat. In proportion as it sees the classless society replaced temporarily by the totalitarian bureaucratic state system it comes to realize the utopian character of its Marxist hope and enthusiasm gives way to an ill-concealed cynical resignation. Thus Sartre's nihilism and Marxist disillusionment merge with each other.

Naïve souls have wanted to see in the utopia of the Jewish Marx a link with Old Testament prophetic Messianism, and indeed to derive the latter from the former. That is both factually and historically quite wrong. The Jewish Marx preserved nothing of the inheritance of his pious forefathers and knew still less; he scarcely read the Old Testament prophets. He is absolutely a child of the atheistic bourgeois enlightenment. But also, in fact, his eschatology is nothing other than the rational bourgeois thought of progress in a new synthesis. It too is hope based on self-confidence, and atheism is not a fortuitous element but an integral part of his whole system (2), which is built up on the thought of absolute, not relative, freedom, as a result of which all religion as spelling dependence on God is to be utterly denied. Prophetic Messianism is the fundamental opposite of all this. It is hope based on the certainty of God and on trust in God, and complete dependence on God is the life-breath of it.

At one point there exists a certain parallelism between the Old Testament and the philosophy of progress, whether in its bourgeois or Marxist forms: the pious man of the Old Testament does not seek a fulfilment of meaning for the individual mortal—the latter sinks unresistingly into the shadowy realm of Sheol: he seeks only the fulfilment of the divine will in the Messianic kingdom. By contrast the Christian Gospel is characterized by the fact that the promise of the future advent of Christ implies a fulfilment of meaning both for the individual and for the history of humanity as a whole, even for the cosmos. And in a second point the future hope of the Gospel is distinguished from that of ancient Israel: the future, regardless of the fact that its coming is awaited, is already a present experience. The life of the ecclesia, life in the *agapé* of God, is an already experienced Messianic present and therefore meaningful in the highest degree. The life of the individual believer, like the life of the church from which it is never to be separated, has a content of meaning already (even though only as first-fruits) by the experience of what will ultimately be revealed as the meaning of all history: of the *agapé* of the divine reality disclosing itself as present for the "thou". For this reason the Christian lives in the joy of a present fulfilment of meaning as much as he longingly awaits it in the midst of the sorrows of this present life. In fact it may be said that the *problem* of meaning hardly arises for him, because his life is filled with the active realization of what gives it its basic meaning. Whoever lives in the power of love asks no question about meaning because he possesses truth and puts it into effect.

The New Testament has this in common with the Old Testament hope of the kingdom: that not the happiness of the individual nor even that of the community stands in the foreground, but the realization of the will of God, the ultimate glorification of the Lord of creation by His creatures, the *doxa theou*—the glory of God in the face of Jesus Christ (3), reflected in the hearts of the faithful and in the perfect self-giving of God to His creation which takes place on Calvary and is completed in the Resurrection. The question of meaning is solved by the life *in* Christ which yearns for fulfilment through the life *with* Christ (4). If the individual believer has the meaning of his life in fellowship with God through Christ and the consequent realization of his true humanity, he hopes also for its consummation in the life of the world to come, wherein the meaning of history as a whole will be fulfilled.

World history, as we are able to grasp it through the reports of historians, does not contain its meaning within itself. Only by means of illegitimate refashioning to efface all meaninglessness was the Hegelian philosophy of history able to represent history as an unfolding of intrinsic meaning. For the meaningless is one half of history. This error is not, however, greater than that of the cynical and blasé interpreters who have only a superior smile for the attempt to find a meaning in history. But it would only be a false pseudo-Christian gnosis if we supposed that through faith we are in a position to surpass the work of Hegel and from a yet higher point of vantage to explain the meaning of history. What we know through faith is but this twofold truth: firstly, we know that history has not its meaning in itself, but rather that meaning comes to it from beyond itself through Jesus Christ, the Coming One, the Redeemer, and the Bringer of the Kingdom of God. Secondly, in Him who not only is to come but has already come we recognize both things—the meaning and the fathomless meaninglessness of history. The meaning of history would seem to be the formation of the divine image in man, of the true humanity rooted in true fellowship with God, the *agapé* of the Kingdom of God. But this meaning is embodied in actual world history only *sub contraria specie*, concealed, muddled, falsified, by self-deification and world-deification and by the consequent egoism and egocentricity of man. This mixture of meaning and non-meaning in history looks at us from the face of Him who wears a crown of thorns, over whom the representative of Cæsar speaks the "Ecce Homo" (5). But the slain and crucified Christ is none other than the Risen and Glorified One who in His second coming will complete His work. Through Him world history will receive its ultimate meaning, which through creation it contained in itself but which it lost through sin.

Thus we know that wherever we find some trace of the humanization of man in the historical process we see a revelation of its meaning, but never do we discover it apart from the filth and ruins of inhumanity: in the story of that strikingly human Nefertiti of ancient Egypt, of whom we also know, however, that she sacrificed hundreds of thousands of human lives for the building of her royal tombs; in the story of that most sincere of seekers after truth and humanity, Socrates, who was condemned by his Athenian fellow-citizens to drink the hemlock-cup, in that same Athens which built the temple of the Acropolis and was exalted by the tragedies of Æschylus. It is as though man in history were seeking *humanitas* and true humanism without ever being able to find them. They are sought in religion, apart from religion, and in opposition to religion; they are sought in the state, and in opposition to the state, they are sought in culture and outside culture; but either the truly human escapes man through the violence of its non-personal excesses or man misses humanity through the narrowness of his too human personal striving after self-realization. Man—humanity—is unable to find himself. And the one and only time when he was fulfilled—true man incorporating true humanity—he was destroyed by the world-state of Rome as well as by the Jewish religion because man refused to recognize in His person that kingdom which was not of this world (6). Thus is He the unrecognized meaning, the incognito King of humanity, whose manifestation is awaited by the community of believers in His second coming in glory, in the event which will bring about the end of the world.

But the New Testament goes still further. Just as the revelation of the meaning of my personal life will shed light on the hidden meaning of humanity, so the latter will reveal the meaning of cosmic history. The Bible shows the history of man to be embedded in the history of the cosmos but, unlike heathen mythology, does not merge it in the circular course of the cosmos. The cosmos is orientated towards man, as man is foreshadowed in nature. The history of humanity begins with the history of nature as so much natural history of man. On the other hand, the history of the cosmos culminates in man. As the earth is the unforeseeable exception in the planetary world, as the world of organic life is the unforeseeable exception among the unimaginable dead masses of the universe, so man is the unforeseeable exception in the organic life of this earth (7). The opinion so often heard today, that this teleology pointing to man might well have been possible in the geocentric world-picture of antiquity but has now become impossible as a result of the enormous extension of our world-view initiated by Copernicus, does not take into account what Kant calls the second Copernican revolution: viz. the recognition that it is man himself who has been responsible for this enormous widening of the picture, that, as the knowing subject, he has gained in significance just as much as he has shrunk when considered as the known object. Man ousted from his centrality in the universe by an objective view of things is the being who, by this same power of insight and recognition, again places himself at the centre. The vastly extended universe is *his* universe, which *he* measures, whose dimensions *he* calculates, whose expansion *he* establishes. This Einstein-picture of the universe exists as an idea in the mind of *man*.

If it is true that God is the creator of the world and that He has revealed His being to us in Jesus Christ, then man, the only creature made in His image, is, because of that fact, the centre of the universe and the goal of world history. But this applies not to man as he now is, rather to man whose true being is likewise revealed to us in Christ; hence man whose true being is not yet realized. For it hath not yet appeared what we shall be. But when He shall appear, the Risen and Glorified Lord (8), then we shall be like Him. To us, as we now are, applies the word of Nietzsche's Zarathustra: "Man is something that must be overcome." Not as we are in actuality but as we are in Christ—that is the goal towards which the world is moving because it has been created for His sake, and in Him, the Son of God, has its meaning (9).

Such is the cosmic teleology of the New Testament through which the creation story of the Old Testament first unfolds its hidden meaning. For the word by which the world was created is none other than that which is the Son unto whom are all things. That which is revealed in Jesus Christ and, although only secretly, the advent of the Kingdom of God, the eternal life revealed in Him, the love and the fellowship of God breaking forth in Him, is not only the meaning of my life and your life—the life of the individual man—not only the meaning of the history of humanity, but the meaning and goal of cosmic history.

This *telos*, this ultimate reality, is already present—in faith. The Son of God is present to us in faith; as yet only in faith, not in sight (10). We experience His presence as that which gives us true life in the present—as His love which is shed abroad in our hearts by the Holy Ghost (11). For the man who lives in the love of God, the question of meaning is already solved; it is solved by the actual realization of meaning in the activity of love which flows from the joyful certainty of sharing in the consummation of all things—at present in joyful anticipation and hope, but then not merely by faith but by the blessed vision of eternal life in the fullness of its undimmed presence.

The answer which Christian faith gives to the question of meaning is peculiar in two ways. Firstly, because this meaning is a present experience and at the same time a hope of that which is to come. Secondly, because it is the most utterly personal thing and at the same time the most universal of all things. It is the most utterly personal, the sole truly personal thing, because it is love. It is personal hope because I know that nothing can separate *me* from the love of God (12), that therefore I through love am bound for eternity. But it is also the most universal, because this love is not only my personal end but also the end of humanity and of the world. This love is, however, not merely my personal hope and the hope of the whole world; it is through faith my present experience and my true life now, life in Christ.

Chapter Ten

THE SIGNIFICANCE OF THE CHRISTIAN HOPE OF ETERNITY FOR LIFE IN THE PRESENT

TWO things may be understood by this. Firstly, the significance which must be attached to this hope in the total structure of the Christian creed. The hope of eternal life is not just a part of the faith, the final section, called eschatology; it is rather the point at issue in the faith as a whole, without which therefore it would not simply be minus something, but without which it would utterly cease to exist, exactly as the apostle says of the resurrection of Jesus: "If Christ be not risen then is your faith vain and ye are yet in your sins" (1). This might also refer to the significance of this hope for the present life, because, as we saw, it is precisely this hope which makes man enjoy fullness of life in the present. Hence it is characteristic of this Christian hope that it belongs both to the present and the future, that it is both experience and expectation. But no more of this.

We mean significance for the present life in the sense: what sort of difference does it make for his present life whether man has this hope or not? Is a human life which knows nothing of this hope really poorer, and in what sense, for what reason, is it so? And we must make the question still more precise. For it is not the same whether we inquire about the condition of the man who never knew anything of this hope or about that of a man who has lost it. It is the latter case which we have in mind: for we are thinking of the post-Christian Western man. Through the Christian faith of those who went before him there were opened up to such a one dimensions of existence which were closed to the pre-Christian man. Hence we put the question thus: what does man really lose when he loses the Christian hope of eternal life? Since, as we have suggested, the consequences of the loss are incalculable, it can only be a question of indicating some of the most important of these, at least those which seem to us among the most important.

Firstly: *Panic fear of the end.* No one who loves and knows the literature and art of times in which the *exspectatio vitæ æternæ* belonged to the solid foundations of life (2) can resist the impression that there prevailed in those times a certain peace and reflectiveness which has increasingly faded in modern times. It is usual to make responsible for this change the rise of technology, which has so much quickened the pace of life. But the real order of cause and effect is the reverse: man has developed technics because he has already lost peace, and he has lost his peace because all that formerly he could calmly await from eternity he would like—now that he has lost faith in eternal life—to crowd as far as possible into the limited span of earthly life. The believer may wait in hope; he who has no hope must hurry. The gate threatens to close—then all is over. For ever.

This anxious impatience to scramble for as much as possible and pack it into life affects not only the scramble for material goods, for fortune, and for pleasure, but applies equally to the attempt to establish an order of justice and humanity. Here lies the true source of utopianism and the will to revolution which it kindles. And from that point of view, on the other hand, religion with its eternal hope must appear as opium, as a fatal paralysis of revolutionary energy. But that this panic fear of the end, the greater it is, makes so much the more difficult the solution of social problems should be clear to anyone who knows how stupidly men behave in a panic, how panic endlessly magnifies the objective danger and reduces to *nil* the real possibilities of rescue.

Secondly: *The tendency to nihilism.* The loss of the Christian hope of eternal life does not necessarily and certainly not immediately mean the plunge into nihilism. The history of thought in Europe shows us rather how many intermediate stages had to be passed through before finally this terminus was reached. But we see clearly in a historical survey what ought to have been obvious from the start: all intermediate solutions, from rationalistic belief in immortality to the deification of the idea of humanity in the positivism of Comte, have no historical permanence; they resemble easily disintegrating elements which in disintegration possess great luminous power, while this very luminosity is an unmistakable sign of their disintegration.

Humanity in emancipating itself from the Christian faith and its hope of eternal life, as we have seen, acquired a substitute for the Biblical thought of the Kingdom of God in the various forms of belief in progress, and these for a time possessed convincing power sufficient to conceal from it its loss. But the hour must come, and is now undeniably come, when this substitute-hope is finally breaking up. And now the final consequences in nihilism stand fully exposed with terrifying brutality and clearness.

Perhaps there will arise even yet an after-glow of the idealistic surrogates of an Hegelian or Schleiermachian philosophy of the history of human development. Why this hope can have no substance we will show more precisely later. In any case, in present-day Europe the alternative to the Christian hope is that of more or less open or concealed nihilism, as Nietzsche clearly foresaw and proclaimed (3). Nietzsche himself of course thought to find salvation from his nihilism in heathenism and the teaching of eternal recurrence(4). At bottom, however, he knew well enough himself that this way of escape was illusory; nor has anyone followed him therein.

But we must clarify further the idea of nihilism, just in regard to the nexus between present fullness of life and hope (now lost): the loss of the hope of eternal life stands in a reciprocal though hidden relation with the *loss of personality*. We consider only one aspect of this: how the loss of the hope of eternity depersonalizes man.

The Christian idea of the human person is integrally connected with this eternal hope. That has been shown in detail elsewhere (5). The question is what kind of valuation of man still remains possible when this connexion is dissolved;

i.e. when man is no longer understood as destined for eternal life. If we disregard the idealism of Kant and its derivatives, which hardly possess vitality to-day, there remains as a serious philosophical alternative only existentialism, whether in the form expounded by Heidegger or Jaspers—we can hardly admit Sartre's outlook as a serious philosophical possibility. For Heidegger, man is to be understood in his true sense when he sees and accepts in full awareness the fact that his being is a being unto death, when therefore he affirms freely his irreversible doom to die.

But what kind of true being is this? Is it qualified humanity or personality distinguishing itself from the mass of the human species? We must answer that this personal existence has no foundations; that one cannot be seriously deceived about its emptiness. This personal dignity—and that is what is meant by the idea of true being—consists in fact in nothing other than the merciless clearness with which it is recognized that there is no such thing as personal dignity. This insight—as Thielicke has convincingly shown (6)—simply cannot be understood otherwise than as coming from the Christian faith, from the New Testament understanding of man, but which at the very moment when it is taken over denies its origin. This philosophy of being unto death is a stepping over the threshold from Christian faith to nihilism The next step, according to Heidegger, must then be the philosophy of Sartre, where the full bankruptcy of personal existence is concealed, for dim eyesight, only by the completely groundless appeal: "Emancipate yourself entirely." The declaration of bankruptcy is unmistakable for him who has eyes to see; the plunge into a purely cynical valuation of man is unavoidable, it has already taken place as is expressed openly in the literary work of Sartre (7). This adds up objectively to just what the apostle Paul puts forward as the only alternative to belief in the resurrection: "Let us eat and drink, for to-morrow we die" (8).

Thirdly, there remains only one further possibility: *the concealment of death*, the attempt to deceive oneself about it, by seeking to take from it its terrors and giving it as far as possible a smiling face. This trick is so transparent that no one can think of it seriously except as a pure lyrical fancy, a piece of more or less conscious æsthetic self-deception. Hence this way of dealing with death is essentially innocuous. On the other hand, the repercussions on social and political life, outside the sphere of reflection and intellectual debate, are the terrible reverse of the innocuous.

Fourthly: *the absolute valuation of natural vitality*, the brutal justification and operation of the *will to power*. The removal of all the metaphysical foundations of personality which positivism effects is the direct preparation for totalitarianism. The nobler positivists—a Comte, a Mill, a Spencer—still lived unconsciously on a Christian or idealistic inheritance. But the age of the totalitarian state has brought to the light of day the inevitable goal of positivism. When the transcendent ground of responsible personality is withdrawn there is no longer any limit to the expression of vitalistic crass earthliness, the will to power must make itself absolute and unleash itself in boundless ferocity. That is the step which Lenin took beyond Marx, and Stalin beyond Lenin: the radical destruction of utopian illusions, the establishment of the supposedly temporary totalitarian dictatorship as a condition of permanency, the cynical smile at the surviving traces of bourgeois idealism among the old guard of the communists (9).

Such are the effects of the loss of faith in eternal life. Nihilism is no pre-Christian, no extra-Christian, possibility, it is something essentially post-Christian. For only from the Christian faith comes the courage for merciless self-recognition, only from it springs the clarity with which man becomes aware of his nothingness, whereas heathendom is able to hide from itself that vision by the myth of the circle of eternal recurrence or to argue it away by the philosophy of timelessness and its implied conception of immortality.

The philosophical teaching about immortality rests on a dualistic teaching about man which divides him into a better and a worse part, bisecting him into an upper mental and a lower sensual half. This attempt succeeds so long as man is in a position to relegate the evil in himself to this lower nature, the "not I myself". The moment when this self-apology no longer succeeds, when man sees himself as responsible for evil: that is, in the moment when he recognizes himself as a sinner, the idea of immortality cannot further be sustained. In that moment the alternative emerges clearly: either nothingness is ultimate or eternal life as the gift of God. Since only through the Christian faith is this self-recognition as sinner possible, therefore only in a world where the Christian revelation has once taken place, can nihilism develop itself to its full and terrible extent, i.e. it is a post-Christian possibility (10).

Only in the Christian faith are the two factors seen as a unity—death and sin. And therefore in it alone is the force which conquers sin also the force which conquers death: the redemptive action of Jesus Christ.

What in this chapter we have seen from the negative side: how the loss of faith in eternal life finally destroys the human person, we shall recognize in the next chapter from the positive angle: how Christ, who restores the person by overcoming sin, bestows upon it in the same act the gift of eternal life. At the same time we shall see that neither the question of death nor that of sin affects merely the individual, but that both can only be rightly understood when they are placed in the larger context of the history of mankind as a whole.

Chapter Eleven

THE MYSTERY OF DEATH

ALL attempts to give meaning to life from within the context of earthly historical existence come to grief on the fact of death. For what ultimate worth can be assigned to interpretations derived from the spheres of culture, humanism, or society, when the creators and guardians of eternal values are in the end mercilessly dismissed and plunged into an abyss of nothingness? If life is really a being unto death, what could an attempt at interpretation be other than a masquerade or pretence, like the performance of an actor who plays his part in all seriousness yet with the underlying realization that it will last only for a few hours? Are not the cynical jokes which the gravedigger cracks in the last act of *Hamlet* more just to the awful reality of death than the pathos of the funeral orations which seem to follow the unwritten law of making the audience forget that death brings an inexorable conclusion to all these fine speeches? If there is no hope beyond death then we can use the very word "hope" only with reservation, knowing full well that it is not really hope.

What is death? Much that is true may be said about it without even touching the mystery which shrouds it. In any event death is a phenomenon of delimitation, one aspect of which lies within our ken, the other beyond it. We know to some extent from what is partially disclosed to us the meaning of dying. In particular, the doctor or the biologist has such knowledge. He knows what phenomena mark the onset of death, what are its concomitants, and what follows so far as we can see. He establishes the fact that at a certain moment the circulation of the blood ceases, the secret quantity called life gives no further sign of itself and that a series of processes set in, the term of which is the disintegration of the functional unity of the living organism: the latter decomposes. From the moment called death man ceases to yield any of those tokens of himself which we associate with life, especially those in which man reveals himself as a person, as spirit and as subject.

Not all organisms die like that of man. There are certain elementary modes of life, one-celled, which do not die but which by the ever-repeated sub-division of cells in ceaseless growth possess a sort of earthly immortality. All present-day living organisms, plants and animals, man included, are the products of such splitting of cells and have therefore in themselves an infinitesimal particle of living substance which was alive millions of years ago. Nevertheless it is true of man that he dies like all the other higher animals. Comparative physiology teaches us that human death is no exception but, on the contrary, the rule, the confirmation of the general law of nature that all that lives must sooner or later die. Hence we are tempted rather hastily to draw the conclusion that the death of man is a purely natural phenomenon with nothing surprising or mysterious about it.

But the truth is that man does not die like other higher animals, any more than he lives like them. Human existence is an exception in the world of living beings; for man is the only living being who is a person. Hence his death is something other than the death of animals. The singular feature of man lies precisely in the fact that his life—and his alone—is a being unto death. He alone lives in the anticipation of death, is aware of its coming. This sure knowledge of the imminence of death lies like a shadow over his whole life. Man alone goes to meet death in full awareness. He alone knows what he loses in death. The more man is aware of the specific nature of his being, the more is his dying distinguished from that of the animals.

The more man is man, the more he realizes the subjective nature of his being, realizes that his personal life distinguishes him radically from all other living creatures. So much the more does his death become an impenetrable mystery. What he has often seen, what is thus truly nothing new, nothing mysterious to him, is just not his own dying. He knows absolutely nothing of these two things: what the death of a person is and what the "I die" implies. The death of an organism, the dissolution into its dead component parts, of that which is bound together into a bundle of life—*that* he can observe and comprehend—although even that is an exaggeration; for as little as man knows what life is, so little knows he what it is to die. But he can at least grasp some meaning in the death of the organism: the decomposition into its component parts of that which functioned as a unity. But what the death of the "I" must be, that no man can fathom by reason. For how something should disintegrate which is not composed of parts we can have no idea. Still more the fact that "I", this man in his uniqueness, his inconvertibility, his irreplaceability, is to die is as mysterious to me as it is absolutely certain. In this matter experience offers me not the smallest point of comparison. I shall know what it means only when I undergo it.

And thus the death of man is surrounded by surmise, expectation, uncertainty, the effect of which is to make his death radically different from that of any other living creature. The sure knowledge that he will come to die is accompanied by the ignorance of what then happens to the person and by the anxious hope that he will not die. Even the most hard-boiled materialist, who his life long has loudly voiced the conviction that death is the end, realizes when the hour of death comes that his theory is only a hypothesis which may or may not be correct. He too then notices that as a person he is something other than an animal with a specially large and differentiated brain. He then sees that his materialistic theory does not cover his personality and that his alleged explanation of death amounts to ignorance. The more man is man, the more he becomes aware of the mystery of death.

But, furthermore, man revolts against death, and this revolt is something other than the repelling instinct of the animal, the final manifestation of his instinct for self-preservation. It is not merely the naïve instinct for self-preservation, characteristic of the human animal, which thus revolts against death; it is something arising from depths of the spirit, a feeling that man himself cannot understand, which says: it ought not so to be, it cannot so be. Indeed, even the man who his life long has asserted that death is something quite natural and who has faced it with the calmness of the stoic, he too is no exception in this matter; he too finds himself revolting against death as something which ought not to be. No doubt man in his conscious mind can silence this rebellion against death; but by this time we should know that man is not only what he is consciously and what he can consciously control. We should learn much that would surprise us about rebellion against death precisely from the dream-life of those who deny such rebelliousness.

We have been speaking so far of the death of everyman. But we must go on to discuss the various interpretations of death which distinguish men from each other. First there is the prevalent modern idea that man is finished when he dies. There are still many who suppose that this conception is the necessary consequence of our scientific knowledge of neurology, neuropathology, physiology, etc. What in fact we have established through research is an extensive parallelism between mental and material processes, the dependence of mental processes upon the structure of the brain and its functioning. But all that we know of this is far from proving the materialistic argument or even giving it convincing support (1). Materialism is not knowledge but a metaphysical theory, and of all metaphysical systems the worst founded and the most frequently disproved by conclusive reasoning. The very fact that an interaction as well as a parallelism exists between mental and physical processes should make us cautious, especially the argument, never refuted since Dubois Reymond's famous "*Ignoramus ignorabimus*", that a man can never know how something objective becomes something subjective. The problem of the relation of soul and body is impenetrable, the materialistic interpretation has nothing more to do with knowledge than any other and, like many others, it does not hold water when confronted by the actual experience of dying (2).

Widely spread among all peoples and at all times is the idea of a survival of the soul after death, i.e. the view that death means the separation of soul from body. This view appears in many varied forms (3), from primitive animism to the philosophical doctrine of immortality. It assumes the form of the Indian teaching of Karma about the reincarnation of the soul in another life in a state corresponding to its ethical worth. Again it appears in the idea, first found in ancient Egypt, of an other-worldly judgment, in which some souls will be assigned to a joyful and radiant world, others to a dark, joyless, and tormented existence in the beyond. In such conceptions we catch a glimpse of man's understanding of himself as a responsible person. For the history of Western thought, the Platonic teaching of the immortality of the soul became of special significance. It penetrated so deeply into the thought of Western man because, although with certain modifications, it was assimilated by Christian theology and church teaching, was even declared by the Lateran Council of 1512 to be a dogma, to contradict which was a heresy, and likewise from Calvin onwards it was assumed in post-Reformation Protestantism to be a part of Christian doctrine. Only recently, as a result of a deepened understanding of the New Testament, have strong doubts arisen as to its compatibility with the Christian conception of the relation between God and man, and its essentially pre-Christian origin has been ever more emphasized (4).

We consider this doctrine here only from the one point of view, that of understanding death. If the soul is immortal in the sense and for the reason which Plato and his successors teach, then the problem of death is solved because death has no power over the deeper side of man as person. We then know that we are so constructed that nothing can happen to our essential being in death. Death can affect the immortal soul as little as the waves of the tossing sea the lighthouse; it defies them by virtue of its solid construction. It remains unshaken and unimpaired. Likewise the soul. This means, however, that man and time do not belong essentially together; the true man, the noble part of man, is timeless, only his baser and lower part, his corporeality and sensuality, are a prey to death. The body is mortal, the soul immortal. The mortal husk conceals this eternal essence which in death is freed from its outer shell.

That this dualistic conception of man does not correspond to the Christian outlook can be shown from various angles. The contrast stands out most clearly in the two following points. The effect of this Platonic dualism is not merely to make death innocuous but also to rob evil of its sting.

Just as death affects only the lower part of man, so also does evil. The latter consists only in the sensual and impulsive. I myself am not truly responsible for evil, only my baser part, which is as it were fastened on to my better higher and true being. Evil is thus no act of the spirit, no rebellious revolt of the ego against the Creator, but merely a sensual or impulsive nature which has not yet been tamed by mind. In brief, evil is the absence of mind, not sin. Evil is not revolt, contradiction, but merely lack of education. It has no relation to God and His Will, it is a merely immanent thing, a misunderstanding which at present exists between my lower chaotic life of impulse and the formative power of my mind. My higher spiritual life, on the other hand, is akin to God, a spark of the divine fire, logos emanating from the divine logos, consubstantial with God. The second aspect of the contrast to the Christian view is as follows. Man in his spiritual and higher being is divine, not creaturely. God is not His creator, God is the all of which the human spirit is but a part. Man is a participator in the divine in the most direct and literal sense. Hence, since this mode of robbing evil of its sting runs necessarily parallel with the rendering innocuous of death through the teaching about immortality, this solution of the problem of death stands in irreconcilable opposition to Christian thought. One believes either in the immortality of the soul—and it is only necessary to believe so long as one has not mastered the proof—immortality being essentially demonstrable—or one believes in the God of revelation.

But the man who stands before God in faith knows that he must die. What the philosopher says about being unto death is fully accepted by faith (or, rather the philosopher has derived it from nowhere else but the Bible) (5). Just as little as a bisection of man is possible from the point of view of evil, is such a bisection possible in regard to death. Not my body dies; *I* die. I can relegate dying to my inferior being just as little as I can relegate my evil. For I myself am a sinner *totus ego*.

Hence, since I cannot find escape in a bisection of personality, I must take my death seriously. But these two statements are related not only through parallelism; it is not merely a question of a "just as"—rather the second follows logically from the first.

Because I know myself before God to be a sinner, therefore I discover something new about the character of my death: that it is the wages of sin (6). For what is sin? It is the revolt of the human "I" against its creator, the rebellion of the dependent one who deems that he must and can win his freedom. By this revolt the original character of created being as a being in God is destroyed, or in terms of the parable: man is driven out of paradise, the cherub with the flaming sword guards its entrance, there is no returning thither. Sin cleaves to him, it is reckoned to him as guilt. The guilt of sin separates him from God and robs man of the life which lay ready for him in God. For God Himself is life; whosoever is separated from Him is cut off from the sources of life. For this reason, death is not something which does not take place until the end of life. Rather, death is the signature of this so-called life. It is just this that is meant by a being unto death. The bodily physical death is only the final and full revelation of the sinful character which inheres in this sinful life—of the fact that it is a prey to death, that it is orientated to the goal of destruction and bears in itself the marks of its own nothingness, because it has lost its ground in the One who is the source of all life and is Himself life.

Death is therefore for the Christian understanding an ordinance of God, but it is not an original element of the divine order in creation; on the contrary, it has arisen from disorder. It is the reaction of the divine anger to human rebellion. The Old Testament Psalmist already interprets it thus: "In Thy wrath are we consumed and in Thine anger we suddenly pass away" (7). But only through Christ does this insight become clear, decisive and fundamental. Only then it is said: death is an enemy (8) just as it is the wages of sin. Of course, these are mythical expressions; but what is meant is more plainly recognizable in this mythical form than in abstract language cleansed of myth. Nevertheless, let us attempt to express it apart from myth: that man must die, God teaches him to recognize as something utterly contrary to "nature", as unnatural as sin itself. And these two factors —the being a sinner and the having to die—are necessarily linked because separation from God implies separation from life, manifested ultimately in physical dying.

Is then the thought—so we men of the scientific era must ask—that death is the consequence of sin at all tenable for modern man, since we know that millions of years of dying creatures precede the existence of man, that the history of mankind represents the latest event, the last page in the thick book of earthly history? In actual fact, creation just as little as the fall of man, can be included in the chronology of ascertainable world-facts, hence neither can we include therein that death which is the wages of sin. In the dimension of ascertainable world-facts there is to be found neither God nor creation nor sin. These ideas belong to another dimension—that, namely, which concerns man as person.

In God's presence are we persons, as sinners we encounter Him and recognize death to be the wages of sin. But this recognition, springing from our confrontation by God, cannot be embedded in any scheme of world history. This experience of encounter with God produces a history which cannot be recorded in any chronicle. And yet it does not stand somewhere above or outside of history. It gathers its pregnant significance from an event which has taken place at the heart of earthly history, but whose meaning cannot be grasped by the historian as such, can be apprehended only by the believer. This event is the Christ—that which happened once-for-all, the unconditional, the unique.

We have seen earlier how this uniqueness stamps history itself as the sphere of the unique. We see now how it confers uniqueness upon the character of *my* life. Through Christ I come to appreciate that the being unto death is ultimately serious, that there is no possibility of escape from the orientation towards death, neither through the cyclical conception of heathen mythology, nor through the philosophy of timelessness with its teaching on immortality. For both of these types of thought imply that sin is not taken seriously. Both invite me to delegate my responsibility to some factor other than I myself—something impersonal and natural. That escape is forbidden to me when I see myself confronted by Christ. Hence through Christ alone is the meaning of my death exposed to me.

And that from a point of view about which we have not been able to say anything so far. In the presence of Him, the second Adam, we recognize ourselves as the Adam who was created by God and has fallen away from God. We recognize our personal guilt as sinners, as existing in solidarity with the sin of mankind. The light of Christ illuminates the unity of human history as a history of fallen creation. My sin is no private affair but something universal which I have in common with mankind as a whole. I recognize the true nature of myself only when I see myself not merely in my private experiences but as integrated into the history of mankind. I am always both myself and humanity as a whole. Thus this body of death is not only this my individual body but at the same time the body of humanity in its bondage to death, in the multiple manifestations of its mortal sickness and hate, of which the history of humanity wherever it is truly reported is full. In my confrontation by God I am not allowed to avert my gaze, in wrath, from this history, to feel myself superior to it, for it is also my history. The same Christ who has died for my sins has died for the sins of all. In so far as I know the second fact I know the first. I know therefore that my death is not merely my private affair, my individual destiny, but an integral part of thc common human death—not because the individual is subject to the law of the species, as a natural biological fact, but as part of the meta-history of *humanitas*, which falls outside all biological categories.

The biological fact of death, the extinction of life, is only a shell or container—and at the same time symptom and effect—of something rooted deep in the spiritual history of man and humanity, just as my own bodily life is only the bearer and husk of my life as a person. The cause of death which the doctor establishes is not the real cause of my death. I do not die of this or that illness, just as little as I, this person, called "I myself", live on albumen, carbohydrates, vitamins, etc. The responsible person "I" lives by the creative Word of God. So also I die to God when, because, and how, He wills. "In Thy wrath are we consumed." What the doctor establishes is only the shell of death. Its essence is hidden in the mystery of God.

That this is the interpretation of death as seen in the radiance of Christ becomes clear when it is realized that not only death but also life is relevant to the act of dying. The deep implications of death are revealed in the fact that with dying begins the resurrection of the dead. "For ye are dead and your life is hid with Christ in God" (9). As the death of Adam spells my spiritual death, so the death of Christ gives me eternal life; not merely me, but all who belong to the new humanity and the new world of the resurrection.

Before we pass on to consider this new theme, let us cast a glance once again at the doctrine of the immortality of the soul. It cannot be explained by weakness of faith on the part of the church that it took over a point of view which stemmed from such a different source—that of Greek philosophy, and was so utterly foreign to its own essential teaching. Somewhere in the Christian faith there must have been some opening through which this foreign doctrine could penetrate. Assuredly, from the Biblical standpoint, it is God alone who possesses immortality (10). The opinion that we men are immortal because our soul is of an indestructible, because divine, essence is, once for all, irreconcilable with the Biblical view of God and man.

No doubt it is part of the Biblical teaching about the divine image in man that we are created and destined for eternal life. Of course we have marred this orientation by sin and, so far as we are concerned, are irredeemably a prey to death. The being unto death has now become the law of our empirical existence. Thus there is here no possibility of a Platonic-Socratic *anamnesis* as a result of which we might find our way back to this eternal destiny. There is in us no eternal unimpaired, indestructible essence to which in face of evil and death we might have recourse. All that is the Platonic idealistic Vedantic outlook, not the Christian one. This way is barred to us by the judgment "Thou art *totus* a sinner", therefore "thou art *totus* in bondage to death." For us as we are in ourselves, that is final. But in Christ we have the message that for God that is not final. What we have marred has not been destroyed by Him. Rather the Word which was in the beginning, which created us, comes again to us in Jesus Christ—not as a human possibility of *anamnesis* but as a divine possibility of a *restitutio imaginis*. It is bestowed on us again specifically as the Word of our original destiny (11): the orientation which we have lost is restored, the threads broken by us, which bind us to eternity, are again bound up; and in the light shed by the Logos which created us we recognize that for God we have not ceased to be destined to eternal life, that our sin cannot ultimately destroy that orientation, but rather, if only indirectly, bears witness to it. The *misère de l'homme* is the *misère d'un roi* even though it be *d'un roi dépossédé* (Pascal). On this rests the contradictory character of our humanity: orientation towards eternity in the empirical existence of a being unto death.

As we have just said, we cannot discover this eternal destiny in ourselves by the method of *anamnesis* (12). We can only become aware of it when it is revealed to us by the Word of God. It is founded only upon and has its subsistence only in the Word of God. But in this divine Word, as the ground of our personal existence, this orientation towards eternity is rooted. "Whenever God speaks or with whomsoever He speaks, whether in wrath or in grace, the one addressed is immortal. The Person of God who there speaks and His Word show us that we are creatures with whom God wishes to speak for all eternity and in immortal fashion" (13). In this formula of Luther is expressed a genuinely Biblical Christo-centric faith in immortality. Not in the way we are made but in God's creative summons have we our eternal life, which has not ceased to bear witness to itself, even in our sinful mortal mode of existence. Our eternal life is rooted in the "thou" of God who addresses us, not in the "I" which we speak to ourselves (14). But the philosophical belief in immortality is like an echo, both reproducing and falsifying the primal Word of this divine Creator. It is false because it does not take into account the real loss of this original destiny through sin; but even as this false teaching it would never have arisen were there not some surviving memory of our true origin. In spite of sin, man does not cease to be a person and to know that he is such; but as a sinner he cannot help falsely interpreting his personal existence. So we may never say that the doctrine of immortality is completely wrong, but what is true in it can only be appreciated in the light of Christ, at the point where it is also unmistakably told us what is false in it. "With whomsoever God speaks, whether in anger or in grace"—it is just this last point which the doctrine of immortality is unaware of. Yet a trace of it appears in the already mentioned mythical conceptions of a judgment beyond the grave. But the manner in which this judgment is decreed is again tainted with the same radical error which clings to the philosophical doctrine of immortality, with the self-justification of the good man who sustains the judgment of God, with the self-security of the sinful man who is in bondage to death, with the evasion of the truth about human nature. Therefore the recall to eternal life is necessarily a summons to judgment, a summons which leads straight into the heart of death.

Chapter Twelve

DEATH AS THE TRANSITION TO ETERNAL LIFE

CHRISTIAN faith is faith in the saving and life-giving significance of the death of Jesus Christ, the apostle tells us, and he sees in it the message of the foolishness of the Cross, the epitome of the entire Gospel (1). Man who has become a sinner owes God his life. He has forfeited life. It is wrong to regard the New Testament pronouncements which express this in terms of punishment or of the sacrificial cult as due to an echo or influence of heathen primitive mythical conceptions. The case is exactly the opposite: in all sacrificial rites of atonement and in all juridical conceptions of atonement we see a foreshadowing of this secret connexion between sin and death. The disappearance of the thought of atonement from modern jurisprudence is one of the most palpable symptoms of the secularization of our thought, and also one of the most harmful factors making for the disintegration of society.

If it is true that man owes to God his death, each man his own death, then it is evident that man himself cannot pay off the debt; for death hastens to anticipate him without his initiative and suicide is forbidden him by the law of God. Furthermore, it is not primarily a question of physical-biological death, but of the death of the human person. It is a question of a dying in which the falsely autonomous man surrenders his false freedom and the divinity which he has arrogated. We ourselves are not able to perform this sacrifice, we are not able even to recognize its necessity, we have only some vague surmise about it. This surmise becomes clear recognition only when we are confronted by the Crucified, only in the moment when we appreciate that His death took place for us (2). *Quanti ponderis sit peccatum*—nothing less than the vicarious passion and death of the Servant of God is necessary for our realization of this gravity. On the Cross, before our very eyes, the weight of our sins is weighed; the balance necessary for that process is the life and death of the Son of God. Only in Him can we measure what our condition is. By that event once only, once for all, the cataract of our self-deception is pierced and we are given a clear-eyed awareness of ourselves (3).

It may be debated whether this recognition might not have been achieved in some other way; it suffices to know that in actual fact it has never become a reality in any other way. It is a recognition which requires a courageous insight into the truth such as is inherent in no man. No man dares to see himself as he really is; every man, even the most sincere, shirks and eludes this self-exposure (4). The Cross of Jesus exposes us inexorably, but in such a way that we are able to bear this exposure because at the same time the unconditioned grace and love of God are promised us. Only against that background are we capable of the audacity of self-recognition. Only because we become aware of the fact of forgiveness do we dare to take the last step towards self-awareness, do we dare to recognize the death of Christ as having taken place in our stead as a vicarious death (5). Only when it is seen as a revelation of the unqualified love of God can the death of Christ be understood by us as an exposure of our inmost selves.

But through this recognition is effected that dying which is concerned with our false personality and autonomy, our falsely won freedom and self-deification. Here first our false pride receives its death blow, here alone do we bend under the judgment of God, which discovers to us the nexus between sin and death and causes us to realize that death is the wages of sin. This is what Paul means by his word about dying with Christ (6), this is the meaning of being baptized into His death (7). By this our self-identification with the Crucified is achieved our voluntary assumption of His death, and in this death of the old man the new man is born. This death is the beginning of our resurrection to eternal life.

This realization of the significance of the death of Christ is only possible because Jesus Christ is proclaimed to us as the Risen Lord. Faith in the resurrection of Jesus is not simply a form of expressing our faith in the saving significance of His death (Bultmann) (8); rather it is that His death can have saving value because He, the Crucified, is also the Risen One. The miracle of the resurrection is the presupposition for the fact that we can believe in the atoning significance of His death. Only in this sequence of thought is it right to say that to believe in the saving power of the Cross and in the resurrection of Jesus Christ is one and the same thing; for only so is preserved the nexus between sin and death, on which all depends. Only so does dying with Christ imply the beginning of a resurrection to eternal life.

Faith in Jesus Christ is faith in His resurrection and implicit faith in one's own resurrection. But this *faith* is already the beginning of a *new and risen life* because faith in the death of Jesus as marking the judgment on my life implies an actual dying, even though not a dying in the biological sense. To believe means objectively to die—i.e. to die as that false ego which is identical with sin; and likewise to believe means objectively to rise again as the new man—Christ in me. Let him who will call this Christ-mysticism (9); only let him consider that this mysticism, this immediacy, is also in the highest sense mediacy, because it is faith in something that has happened once for all in history (10).

The decisive issue is that through this faith in Jesus Christ there springs to birth a new life which remains hidden in the shell of the being unto death, just as metaphysical death is indeed a reality though it is concealed in the framework of biological death. The new life, however, is none other than the reality of the world of the resurrection, the reality of the risen life, of the eternal life of God. It is life in the Holy Ghost. But the Holy Ghost is God. Life in the Holy Ghost is not something merely believed in, but a reality experienced in faith. The Holy Ghost is the effectual newly-creating power of God, power which is recognizable in its effects, power (11) which manifests itself as new life flowing from the unseen, just as previously death was manifest in the midst of life as the hidden worm gnawing at the root of life.

Faith, or rather life in the Holy Ghost through faith, means a real participation in the coming world of the resurrection. It is only a beginning of the life of the world to come, *aparché*, first-fruits, and *arrabon*, a pledge, a first instalment, an adumbration. But none the less a real participation just as the first instalment is a real payment. The mere incipiency of this new life is the same thing as the hiddenness of the new under the forms of the old. Therefore it is said. "Whosoever believeth on me, though he were dead, yet shall he live" (12). The believer really lives a new life—"if a man is in Christ he is a new creature"—but this new life is not visible outwardly, it is rather hidden beneath the husk of the old deathly existence—the being unto death. The Christian is the man in whom the being unto death has been changed into a being unto life; the most evident mark of this change is *agapé*, which confers on the believer, in the midst of the stream of transiency, plenitude of life in the present.

But the strange and characteristic fact is that this new life assumes the form of a dying: "I die daily," says Paul (13). The living deed wherein the new life is accomplished is at the same time and ever again a *mortificatio*. "*Si deus vivificat facit illud occidendo*" (Luther). This inversion, whereby that which was called life stands revealed as death, and at the same time what is now seen to be the new life accomplishes itself in dying, constitutes the paradoxical structure of this changed existence. But physical death, imminent for everyman whether he believes or not, has lost for the believer its former significance. It has lost its sting (14), for it is no longer the end but only a transitional stage, a door on the other side of which the plenitude of eternal life awaits us. Therefore to die is "gain to me" (15). Through the hidden working of faith at the heart of the personality there has taken place a reversing of the switches. Life is no longer a journey into death, but into eternal life, and death has now only the significance of a transitional stage on this journey.

How does the resurrection, which so far we have expounded from the point of view of the personal life of the individual, affect the story of mankind as a whole? It is certain that to die with Christ marks the beginning of eternal life. The drama of the *recapitulatio*, the interruption of the line of Adam, the severing of the orientation of mankind towards death, begins at the centre, the hidden depths of the person. To that personal centre the truth applies that we have passed from death into life (16).

But just because this beginning takes place in that hidden sphere, faith points beyond itself to an event in which what is at present hidden shall become fully manifest. "For ye are dead and your life is hid with Christ in God. When Christ who is our life shall appear then shall ye also appear with Him in glory" (17). The hiddenness of that which is most personal waits for its ultimate manifestation in the story of mankind. What is now true only in the depths of interior personal life shall then be openly revealed. This "now" and "then" is essentially one thing, but in the order of dispensation constitutes the difference between the phase of faith and that of sight. The decisive battle has taken place, the fundamental victory has been won through the Cross and the Resurrection; this once-for-all event is the object to which faith is relevant. The most personal and interior is not therefore even an adequate expression of the hiddenness of this happening unless it be that the very fact of that relevance is to be described as the most interior element. This relevance has a threefold application in point of time; it is directed to what has happened once for all. It is directed to what is now effective in the sphere of the Spirit; it is directed to what will be as the ultimate manifestation of that which is now hidden. Thus it is faith, love, and hope. As hope it aspires from what is at present revealed towards that which is to come. Between this "now" and "then" lies the event of physical death, which has, however, lost its sting. That which was the main point in the perspective of natural sight—namely, the question what happens after death?—has become secondary in the perspective of faith; and the question should now be framed: how does death affect the final consummation of the Resurrection, the end whose beginning lies already before death in the present life of faith? This question cannot be answered until the close of Chapter Fifteen.

Chapter Thirteen

THE PROBLEM SET BY THE BIBLICAL REPRESENTATION OF THE END OF HISTORY

1. *Mythological elements in the New Testament message*

THE need that is now being felt for an existentialist exegesis with a view to de-mythologizing New Testament ideas brings to a new and acute stage (1) a problem which has agitated Christian theology for the past 1,800 years. To one who expects from the revelation of Jesus Christ the final word about the relation of time and eternity the problem is pressing, particularly in regard to the apocalyptic conceptions of the New Testament. In our preoccupation with the new form which it has to-day assumed we ought not to forget that the problem is fundamentally an old one, and that its old form, expressed most sharply in the demand for a necessary spiritualization of the Biblical kerygma, is to-day, for those outside theological circles, far more important than the new guise in which it now to an unjustifiable extent dominates theological discussion. For the new setting of the problem the exegete Bultmann is responsible; for the old, the philosopher Fritz Medicus with his book *Mythology in Religion* (2). It will be of value for the critical appreciation of the new setting of the problem if we include it in the context of the 1,800 years' history of de-mythologization.

For it has always been attempted by the elimination of mythical elements from Christian doctrine to give a more true and radical expression to "what was really meant" and lay concealed under mythical modes of expression. It was always the fact that the Bible spoke so "humanly" and "naïvely" (3) of the ultimate things which gave occasion to this demand—which, of course, formerly did not go under the repulsive title of "De-mythologization". It was always, as to-day, on the one hand, offence at the inadequate form of expression, on the other, the determination to express what was meant more purely or essentially, which characterized this intellectual movement, whether its point of departure was, as in former centuries since the time of Origen, Neo-platonic idealism or, as to-day, existentialist philosophy (4). But again and again the champions of the Biblical data have asked the question whether in reality this purified philosophical expression was still an expression of the same thing, or whether in fact, against the will and intention of the purifiers, the matter itself might not have changed through this chemical process of purification.

With regard to earlier attempts at de-mythologizing, we have gradually got the matter straight. It has become clear that the intended purification has in fact led to a change of substance. For, as far as the old form of de-mythologizing is concerned, what happened was that, unconsciously to most of its exponents, the God of the Christian Gospel, who acts in time, was replaced by the timeless Divine Being of idealistic philosophy. To-day the demand for de-mythologizing doubtless proceeds from quite a different point of view, with conscious repudiation of this idealistic interpretation; but the question must be raised immediately whether the interpretations produced to-day by quite other means—namely, those of the existentialist philosophy of Heidegger—do not in point of fact lead to a transformation of the essence of what is intended in the Christian kerygma.

First of all we must concede to all the exponents, old and new, of the hypothesis of de-mythologization that the Bible—the New Testament as well as the Old—uses forms of expression which are inadequate to the matter it is intended to convey. It speaks of God in anthropomorphic terms with a surprising carelessness; it speaks of the Transcendent and Ineffable with a massive tangibility of style. It is thus offensive to one accustomed to the abstract language of philosophy; its pronouncements, because of this very crudely mythical character of its style, are felt to be incredible and unacceptable. This impropriety and crudity are shown in two ways:

by the symbolism of personal being (anthropomorphism) and by the symbolism of God's intrusion into history (miracle). The symbolism of personal life comes out in expressions such as God the Father, the King, the Ruler, the Judge—thus in crass anthropomorphism. The symbolism of divine action appears in such conceptions as: God comes, God speaks, does, hears, creates, saves, etc.

It is obvious that the Bible, that Jesus Himself and the apostles, do not shrink from using these expressions in unrestricted vividness, because clearly everything depends for them on emphasizing the personal life of God in opposition to all abstractions. And likewise they use this massively tangible vividness of language for a second reason, because they wish at all costs to make clear the livingness of God, His activity, His self-revelation in history, in contrast to all timeless being. But in this respect it should not be overlooked that the error of confusing God with the world or with finitude is avoided by a third series of symbols—those which express equally crudely and massively God's transcendence of the world, His infinity, His incomprehensibility, His supreme power of disposal: God is beyond all that appertains to this world, He can be compared with nothing, therefore no image can represent Him, and His action in time is rooted in His thought and will, which are before all time.

When now, on the other hand, we investigate those ideas by which, in the interests of purification or spiritualization or de-mythologization, philosophy wishes to replace Biblical symbolism, we see that they all belong to the category of abstraction. Thus the opinion seems to be that abstraction is the criterion of spiritualization: the more abstract, so much the more spiritual. This of course is in accordance with the philosophical approach which, behind all concrete existence, seeks being itself; behind all mere appearances, their ground; behind all truths, the one truth. But it remains unnoticed how in thus interpreting Biblical statements by the aid of abstract categories the original meaning of such statements is often transformed. The "Lord of all being" is supplanted by "being" itself (5); the "Thou" who addresses man is replaced by an "it" which man himself conceives; instead of the God who acts, we find a changeless timeless being, a timeless truth. The Biblical world of the living God is transmuted into the Platonic world of ideas, into the ontology of timeless being, into the absolute of the *Advaita* doctrine, the absolute which has no interlocutor but is simply the eternal ground of all that is. Nor is this all. Rather it becomes clear that this abstract conceptualism is not just to be regarded as a non-symbolic adequate representation, but that in place of the "thou"-symbolism there enters a—of course refined and rarefied—"it"-symbolism, and in place of the symbolism of time we have the symbolism of place. No metaphysic, however abstract, escapes the necessity of speaking symbolically of the ultimate, of using inappropriate images derived from our human world to convey its meaning, however abstract and spiritualized this symbolism pretends to be. Our choice is not between a non-symbolic but adequate and a symbolic inadequate system of representation, but rather between two sets of symbols: the symbolism of personal life and action in time and that of things, of the impersonal, and the timeless. The specific character of myth lies in its association of personal symbolism with that of action in time.

When once we have grasped this situation our eagerness to de-mythologize will have notably cooled, and our efforts will be limited to bearing in mind the essentially symbolical character of Biblical speech and to our refusal to understand immediately and non-symbolically expressions which are intended symbolically. In this attempt the Bible constantly assists us, as we have already pointed out, partly by its choice of symbols and partly by its specific interpretation of them. Thus, for example, it is clear that no apostle thought of God as dwelling in heaven (Bultmann), since the Bible itself expressly denies this idea of localization and expresses plainly enough the omnipresence of God and His exaltation beyond all space, although it often seems as if this fact were not always realized. By this approach, which remains aware of the consciously symbolical character of Biblical speech about God and His action, and also of the impossibility of speaking other than symbolically about the divine, we should be able to understand more precisely what the Bible wishes to say to us. In this connexion it will become clear that there are differences in the extent to which this situation is borne in mind; there are doubtless more or less restrained pieces of symbolism, and it will always require careful consideration and a keeping in mind of the sense of Scripture as a whole to avoid an undue literalism or a false spiritualization.

After these general considerations we now turn to the special problem of the New Testament statements about the end of history. On the one hand we see the fundamentalist tendency to interpret the New Testament apocalyptic symbolism in a massively literal way and to regard the end of history as a cosmic drama of *dénouement* taking place within history. On the other, we have the demand of the partisans of de-mythologizing, who wish to relate New Testament eschatology in general to man's understanding of himself in the present and to appraise as mythological every statement about an event in the future.

The demand of the fundamentalists that we should understand every apocalyptic statement of the New Testament literally as referring to a future happening, and thus accept it as a Word of God binding for us, is impossible, if only because the greatest differences, indeed contradictions, exist between these apocalyptic schemes. Once we compare these fundamentalist apocalyptic guides with each other, it is palpable that they stand in mutual contradiction and treat the Bible with violent arbitrariness while at the same time asserting that they should be taken literally as the infallible Word of God. To mention only one point: how disingenuous is their interpretation of those passages which predict the coming of the Kingdom in glory, the event of the Parousia as something to be inaugurated within the present time, during the earthly life of Jesus. We have occasion to speak just in this connexion of this fundamentalist approach—although we have already essentially rejected it as missing the sense of Scripture—because in this eschatological debate non-fundamentalist theologians often refer to the Bible in a way which is distinguished but little from the fundamentalist use of Scripture. The decisive point which is to be made in regard to the fundamentalist conception of the end of history will be brought out in our fourth section (p. 131). We anticipate here the result: the Parousia, according to its very nature, cannot be interpreted as an historical event without ceasing to imply the end of history.

A simple acceptance of the New Testament apocalyptic eschatological schemes is no longer possible for us men of to-day. We no longer live in a world in which the stars can fall from Heaven. But still further than from such a naïve—and fundamentally dishonest—Biblicism are we removed from a theology of de-mythologizing which expects us to recognize an interpretation of New Testament faith which eliminates from it the whole dimension of the future. Before engaging in subtle discussions about the existentialist interpretation we should consider whether we are not trifling illegitimately with the whole idea of interpretation when we interpret the Gospel of Jesus and the apostles in such a way as to leave no hope at all of an eternal future. Can such an amputation of the dimension of the future from the Gospel be seriously considered as an interpretation at all?

The Gospel of Jesus Christ is the glad tidings not only of the forgiveness of sins but also of the conquest of death. To retain only the first and to interpret away the second as though it were merely an alternative form of the first can never be properly termed interpretation, but, precisely when it gives itself out to be such, only mutilation. The arguments which are alleged for this *quid pro quo* are in essentials the following:

(*a*) The pronouncements of the New Testament with regard to the end of history stem from Jewish apocalyptic, which is clearly full of mythology flowing from the Parsee religion, or on the other hand they have their source in the redemption myths of gnosticism.

(*b*) Such schemes of thought have no place in our modern picture of the world.

(*c*) By their essential connexion with the belief in an early advent of the Parousia and the end of the world they cease to be valid for us, just because this expectation has been unmasked as illusory by the actual course of history.

(*d*) Not in this mythical-apocalyptic form, but only as demythologized, has the New Testament message about the future an existential significance for modern man and for his understanding of himself.

To these assertions we make the following replies:

To (*a*): No doubt this affirmation is to a large extent correct. But we should not in consequence infer that our task is to eliminate as unessential to the real Gospel, and as so much worn-out myth, the relation of the latter to death or to life after death, to the future as bearing the goal of history, to the consummation of creation. It is rather so to understand in the light of the New Testament as a whole the truth intended to be conveyed by this apocalyptic symbolism that it stands forth as independent of the latter.

To (*b*): It is first of all a question of discovering whether a hope of the future so understood really conflicts with the modern picture of the world.

To (*c*): It is questionable whether the expectation of an imminent end has such vital significance for the New Testament message as has constantly been asserted since the time of Albert Schweitzer and the school of the thoroughgoing eschatologists.

To (*d*): This question has already been answered by the discussion in the earlier section of our study, especially in Chapters Nine and Ten, and to the effect that precisely the eschatological message, correctly understood as implying that the future and the eternal is both a present reality and a fuller reality to be awaited, is that which fills the existence of modern man with a new and decisive significance.

2. *The changed picture of the world and its implications for the Christian Hope*

Christian theology is wrong to suppose that it can ignore

the changes which modern knowledge has brought about in our view of the world, or in thinking that it can set aside as so much outworn apologetic the serious consideration of the problems which have thus been raised. This attitude is quite as unjustified as is the arrogance of those scientists who suppose that progress in knowledge has superseded Christian faith. We have a right to expect more self-criticism and courtesy on both sides, but this requirement is expected above all from the exponents of a faith where self-criticism has always been considered the decisive criterion of right belief. In actual fact we find it to-day more frequently among the representatives of science than among those of theology.

The most important change in the world-picture from our point of view is that which concerns our ideas of the time-span. It is undeniable, nor is it a trifling matter, that the men of the Bible who proclaim to us the message of salvation in Christ had quite a different image of the time-span from ourselves in the age of the Palamore telescope and of physics laboratories in which the time covered by the disintegration of elements can be measured. This change in the picture of time is partly a consequence of the revolutionary change in the conception of space which began with Copernicus and, through Newton, has led to Einstein and modern astrophysics (6). The net result of this change in our conception of the time-span, effected by exact observation and experiment, is a millionfold widening of the horizons of cosmic time. By means of the telescope we can now observe phenomena which took place hundreds of millions of years ago and the light-knowledge of which reaches us only now through the telescope. By measuring the time taken in the disintegration of elements it is possible to establish with some precision that so many thousands of millions of years must have passed since, as a result of the radiation of energy, that disintegration began. We can—within precisely definable limits—predict the beginning of the next ice age, which as a result of the radiation of energy from the sun must start in so many millions of years.

The apostles reckoned with a time-picture whose dimensions, accepting the date of the beginning of the world 4,000 years previously, could to some extent be surveyed, and within which therefore the thought of an imminent end of the world was not by any means strange. Within such a limited cosmos the life-span of the individual life was no negligible quantity; the age of humanity itself was identical with the age of the cosmos. The creation of Adam was separated by only six days from that of the creation of the world. In the framework of a universe thus adapted as it were to the measure of man the idea did not seem at all fantastic that an event in the history of humanity would bring to an end the cosmos itself.

We have only to set side by side the two time-pictures, the diminutive one of the Bible and the magnitudinous one evoked by modern science, in order to see plainly the reasonableness of the attempt to eliminate as inapplicable to us moderns all that part of the Biblical statement of faith which is conditioned by this view of the time-span, and, moreover, in the same interest to unburden that statement of all cosmological contents whatsoever. Such is the aim of the existentialist interpretation of the New Testament. Its argument that it is clearly absurd to endeavour to fit into our time-view, with its colossal dimensions, apocalyptic expectations which were appropriate only to that diminutive time-span is immediately obvious.

This process of de-cosmologization (7) could be performed most easily if we could free the faith altogether from its connexion with an event in time—as Albert Schweitzer in the final stage of the development of his thought tried to do; but the result even in Schweitzer's case is plain: the renunciation of Biblical faith in favour of an Indian philosophy of timelessness (8). Similarly, the school of Albert Schweitzer effects the emancipation of the faith from its involvement in time by resigning the idea of a *Heilsgeschichte* and exchanging the Christian kerygma for an existentialist philosophy (9).

If one is not prepared for this abandonment but wishes to hold fast to the idea of *Heilsgeschichte*, to the dependence of faith on the historical event of Jesus Christ, as the exponents of the existentialist interpretation still do, then that emancipation from the cosmological is attempted by drawing a distinction between history in the sense of chronology and meta-history. For it is evident that chronological history is tied to cosmology. But meta-history is something which has nothing to do with the process of world-history and which is not therefore, and cannot be, an object of scientific knowledge.

This solution, which seems like a stroke of genius, is, however, of no avail. For so long as faith is centred in Jesus Christ its object is a happening which belongs integrally to history too in the sense of chronology, and so to cosmology, even though it is perfectly true that the pronouncement of faith about this Jesus Christ is no object of secular knowledge but of faith alone. In fact the decisive point about the Christian faith, as we have seen on p. 35, is just that its centre of reference is an historical event which in both senses of the word is unique—in the relative sense proper to chronology and in the absolute sense proper to faith, and that just this duality is implied by the affirmation that the Word was made flesh. Nor is this all. By ascribing to the death of Jesus a saving significance (as do the existentialist interpreters) we have bound up with our statement of faith a cosmological-biological fact, namely, the physical death of Jesus, and thus have included death even in its biological sense in the scheme of the kerygma.

But this does not mean to say that we must make room for the ancient-Biblical world-view in the picture which modern science has sketched. That is indeed what fundamentalism tries to do by, on the one hand, taking over the modern neo-Copernican world-picture and at the same time seeking to connect with it Judaic apocalyptic whose conceptions stem from the ancient image of the universe—conceptions such as those of the stars falling from heaven (10) and Christians, on the return of the Lord, being raised to meet Him in the clouds of heaven (11). This leads indeed to a ridiculous and intellectually unsound confusion (12) as against which the demand for de-mythologization is fully justified. Likewise the distinction drawn by the de-mythologizers between history and meta-history is justified in so far as that for us moderns the changes in the cosmic world-picture must not be regarded, without further examination, as of decisive significance for the statements of faith about the future.

The history of man cannot simply be merged in the history of the cosmos, just as little as man regarded as *humanus* is no more than a species known to zoological science. It should rather be emphasized that man as *humanus* is something other than man as a living animal, although the *humanus* is rooted in the biological *homo sapiens*, and that likewise the history of mankind is something more than a piece or section of cosmic history, although that history is rooted in the history of the cosmos. Human history is governed by other laws than those of the history of nature, in spite of the fact that it is also subject to the latter. The most essential element characterizing the history of humanity is lacking in the history of nature: the element of freedom, both the freedom proper to the structure of man's created being and also the freedom of moral decision. Hence man has a different kind of past from that of purely natural creatures; he has a human past, he has a history in the human sense. Should it not be thence inferred that he has also a future in a different sense from the future of nature?

The event of the Christ is related to the *humanus*, not to the *homo sapiens* of zoology. That event determines our past as a human past in a manner which is simply unknown in the sphere of natural history. So also that event determines our future in a manner which is incommensurable to the plane of cosmic chronology. In the light of Jesus Christ we understand our history, our past, otherwise than we could understand it without that light. In the face of Jesus Christ we read a meaning in our history which is not and cannot be relevant within the sphere of nature. In the same way, we understand our future in the light of Christ otherwise than we could understand it without Him. We understand it as a matter of His future advent. How this spiritual future is related to the future prognosticated by natural science is a secondary question, but one which in its place must be honestly and realistically answered. Our main concern, however, is to leave the way free for an understanding of the eschatological future, which neither stands nor falls with the Biblical picture of time nor can be challenged by the modern scientific view of the time-span.

If we consider the question of an end of history from the standpoint of the history of humanity rather than from that of cosmic history or natural history, we perceive at once that it assumes another complexion. Viewed from within the history of man, the thought of a goal of history is not at all absurd, as it must be when considered from the angle of the history of nature. On the contrary, the history of man discloses radically apocalyptic traits. That is to say, that the history of man contains phenomena which quite unequivocally imply a transcendent goal beyond which history is unthinkable. It would be rewarding to investigate with some precision this apocalyptic element immanent in history. Here we can exemplify it only at one or two points, though these considerations must not be understood as proving from history the fundamental correctness of the New Testament proclamation of an imminent end of the time-series, but merely as showing, on the basis of historical insights, that nothing contradicts, rather much supports, the Biblical point of view.

1. The history of man right from its beginning and throughout all ages runs plainly in the direction of the creation of a unity of humanity in the sense of solidarity in a common destiny. That this does not imply the optimism of the belief in progress is clear from the fact that the first notable manifestation of this solidarity of man in a common destiny is the event of the world wars. The history of man begins with small unities based on the tribe which, as such, show a strong affinity with the gregariousness of herding animals. Gradually there arise from these small groups, peoples; from peoples, the federation of nations. But not until the revolution in the technique of transport and communications in recent times were the peoples joined together in such a way that what happens in one part of the world at once has repercussions in the others. This process of unification will

eventually arrive at its culmination, and no romantic attempts to retard it can succeed. Whether the final result will be a permanent state of war or, on the other hand, a monolithic world state or world federation no one can tell. But a serious weighing of world history must show that its ultimate term in one way or another is world unification.

2. The history of man runs consistently in the direction of an unceasing acceleration in the rhythm of experience. Events succeed each other at ever shorter intervals. What in earlier times required centuries for its accomplishment takes place to-day in the space of a few years. The swing of the pendulum becomes ever faster. This constantly proceeding acceleration in the pace of life must eventually reach a point when it can go no further. Perhaps we can include in this movement the equally plain steadily increasing luminosity of consciousness, leading to an ever more acutely rational and intellectual outlook. The prognosis of the psychiatrist might well be : an ever-widening split in the human consciousness.

3. In this connexion we must recall what was said in the chapters on Chiliasm and Antichrist. The process of formal rationalization, the ever-increasing scientific and technical mastery of man, has been in operation since the dawn of history. For a considerable time it has been interpreted in an optimistic sense, and in terms of belief in progress, until it was perceived that this formal rationalization did not produce at the same time a corresponding growth in spiritual enlightenment. Since this was not forthcoming, since on the contrary the increasing outward freedom and technical ability of man was not accompanied by a growing goodness or humanity, the antitheses in human history—as, for example, that between the individual aspiration towards freedom and collective regimentation, or between intellectual enlightenment and the irrationality of experience, but especially that between the Christian communion based on faith and the godless totalitarian state—inevitably grew in acuteness and proportions. But this increase of tension must one day reach an extensiveness when the fundamental structure

of man can no longer keep pace with it. Just as the acceleration of velocity in rotation leads at a given point to the disruption of the rotating body, so eventually these indefinitely increasing tensions will one day disrupt the total structure of humanity to a far greater degree than was the case in the two world wars.

4. Finally, the discovery of atomic energy has now brought it about that humanity, at least in theory, controls the scientific technical means to destroy itself as a whole—presumably without intending to—in the space of a few moments. Only a short stage separates us from the point when it would be possible for man to destroy not only himself but also the arena of history—the planet itself—by means of a chain of no longer controllable reactions. What until recently seemed to be only the apocalyptic fantasies of the Christian faith has to-day entered the sphere of the soberest scientific calculations: the sudden end of human history.

If therefore we ask the question whether the thought of an end of history, necessarily bound up with that of the Parousia, must be rejected as absurd in the light of the modern picture of the universe, we must answer: quite the contrary. What our insight into the history of humanity leads us to say on the theme of the end of history cannot be expressed otherwise than: *nihil obstat*. It might very well be that the end of history were the this-worldly aspect of the coming of the Lord. This thought has ceased to be absurd, i.e. to be such that a man educated in modern scientific knowledge would have to give it up.

3. *The significance of the expectation of the Parousia in the near future*

The school of Johannes Weiss and Albert Schweitzer, which liked to call itself the school of thoroughgoing eschatology, undoubtedly had the merit of drawing attention to the fact that Jesus and early Christianity expected the appearance of the Messiah in glory and the consequent end of this world in the very near future. We may interpret this fact how we will, but no one may doubt it who knows and takes seriously the texts of the New Testament. Since, however, this expected event did not take place, it is inferred that the whole primitive Christian eschatological-apocalyptic vision of salvation, which culminated in that end of history and was to have received its confirmation from it, was falsified and rendered invalid by the non-appearance of what was expected; i.e. by the course of events themselves. It is supposed that the Christology of the church developed in the course of the first centuries should be understood as a substitute for that vainly awaited event, and in the artificial elaboration of its whole structure bears the marks of the embarrassment in which it originated. Once that has been recognized, it is thought better to turn either to the Eastern philosophy of timelessness (Albert Schweitzer) or to an existentialist philosophy which refuses to recognize any revelational events (F. Burri) or to an idealistic philosophy of religion (M. Werner).

What now is to be thought of this whole theory? First of all, it is worthy of note that in the New Testament, as was inevitable, the non-appearance or the delay of the Parousia was clearly appreciated; that the apostle Paul, who in his first epistles hoped himself to experience the advent of the revelation of the end, later seriously faced the possibility that he would not experience it, but as a result by no means thought that he was mistaken in his faith, which was founded on Jesus Christ alone. This undeniable fact can only be explained if we suppose that the chronological element constituted by the nearness of the expected end had not at all the central significance assumed by the thoroughgoing eschatologists. Next it is to be observed that, alongside the prediction of an early end, two other equally trustworthy statements of Jesus have come down to us, the effect of which is at least to relativize the validity and far-reaching importance of that concerning His early future coming: "The day and the hour no one knoweth, not even the Son, but the Father alone" (13), and "before all these things come to pass the Gospel must first have been preached to all peoples" (14).

The reason for faith's relative independence of this chronological element lies in the fact that, differing in this from Judaic apocalyptic, for early Christianity the decisive event of salvation has already taken place (Cullmann) (15). It can be looked upon as a *Perfectum*. This event is that which has happened once for all in Christ the Crucified and Risen. With Him salvation has come; through faith in Him and the fellowship of faith rooted in Him, He Himself becomes a living Presence. He Himself, the Crucified, Risen Lord, is salvation. What is still a matter of expectation is this—that the now still hidden life of fellowship with the Christ, the salvation yet hidden under the veil of the flesh, shall emerge from its hiddenness, that the condition of faith shall become one of sight, the state of provisionalness and incompleteness in the possession of salvation shall become the *definitivum*, the consummation. Faith in the Christ as the salvation which God has bestowed, in the divine Presence mediated by His Person—although so far only under a veil of hiddenness—all that becomes the point of departure and the foundation for the later dogmatic development. The theory of the Christ-dogma as a substitute for the disappointed hope of the Parousia is utterly superfluous as an explanation of the former, and therefore purely arbitrary.

But how is to be explained the fact that Jesus expected an early end of history through His coming in glory, and inspired in His disciples this same hope? We confess that we have no explanation of the matter; we refuse to use as an explanation the, so to speak, optic illusion, the shortening perspective produced by the prophetic visions of the future. It is rather that, just like the thoroughgoing eschatologists, we are faced by something inexplicable; for it is a mystery to them also how Jesus, in taking over the Messiah-dogma of Judaism, which knows precisely nothing of such an imminent end, should nevertheless have cherished that expectation. It seems to us as little understandable as the fact, already mentioned, that this conception of an imminent end of the earthly æon was connected with those two other ideas, namely, that the day and hour no one knoweth but the

Father, and that the end can only come after the Gospel shall have been preached to all the nations upon earth.

All this is veiled in the mystery of the humanity of the Son of God, of the form of a slave assumed by the suffering Servant of God, who renounced His claim both to omniscience and to omnipotence.

The theory of realized eschatology is right in so far as it truly grasps where the centre of gravity of the primitive Christian faith lies; that is, in what has already happened in Jesus, in the Grace of the divine Presence already bestowed upon the ecclesia, in the Holy Ghost. But it is wrong in that it fails to bring out how deeply Messianic is the life of the believing church, in the sense that it awaits the fullness of revelation, the advent of the Lord in glory. In fact, in the early church the certainty and the potency of the hope in a future consummation was so strong that it crystallized in this expectation of an imminent end which precluded the idea of a future course of history spanning centuries or millenniums, and which therefore was necessarily deceived by the actual development of events. But who can exclude the possibility that the deferment of the end arose from a divine consideration of man's lack of preparedness? (16) And again we can discern in Christian history something like a law to the effect that, the more lively becomes the hope of an imminent end, the more intensely the church lives in the power of the Spirit of God, so that possession of the Spirit and expectation of a near end go together as in the primitive Christian community.

4. *The paradox of the end of history*

Quite apart from all questions of our time-picture and of a point in time there remains the chief problem: What is to be understood by an event which brings history to a close, which dissolves the course of earthly history by the dawn of eternity? We are here confronted by an insoluble dilemma, an antinomy. When we speak of the imminent end of history we obviously mean a happening which takes place in space and time, for it belongs to the essence of everything historical that it takes place in space and time, even though its full meaning cannot be grasped in space-time categories. It is precisely this confinement to the limits of space and time which constitutes the nature of events. But if we say end of history we imply something which bursts the framework of space and time and destroys the structure of the historical. Only so—only as what Karl Heim calls the super-polar—can it really be the ultimate saving synthesis which overcomes the tensions immanent in history as such. Only so can it imply the coming of eternal life, of the world of the Resurrection, the life of the world to come; only so can it terminate the onward sweep of transiency and death.

Yet it must be admitted that Christian theology has never done full justice to this paradox. Either, in terms of Judaic apocalyptic, it has understood this final event as a dramatic *dénouement* to history and has depicted it by means of images suggesting a cosmic catastrophe of enormous dimensions in order to impart to it the character of the truly historical; or, as a result of the true insight that this apocalyptic drama, just because it unfolds itself in the structural forms of the earthly-temporal-historical—however much the dimensions of the event are magnified—cannot mean the breaking forth of the eternal, Christian theology has altogether renounced the conception of an end of history and has sought to convey the idea of the ultimate in the static concepts of timeless eternal being. What the exponents of the one point of view hold against the others is always correct, and yet a formula which does justice to both aspects of the matter cannot be found. The apocalyptic dramatizers are reproached with obscuring by their apocalyptic mythology precisely the most important point, namely, the utter otherness of the life which is to come; they temporalize the eternal, they secularize the unworldly, they actualize that which transcends all facts; hence they conceal what should be the disclosure of the hidden by clothing it in the garb of a new apocalyptic servant-form. The Platonizing static philosophers who describe the vision of the changeless, perfect and eternal are accused—with equal justice—of surrendering what is precisely the most decisive Biblical point, namely, that the ultimate redemptive synthesis has the character of an event; they transmute the latter into a timeless scheme of ideas and leave the question unanswered whether one day this vision of the eternal and perfect shall be embodied in living reality (17).

Each of these interpretations has its positive and also its Biblical justification. It is not, as the Biblical fundamentalists are constantly trying to persuade themselves and others, that the apocalyptic and dramatic eschatology is the essentially Biblical and New Testament representation. Side by side with the Revelation stands the Gospel of John—to name only the two extremes. In spite of the powerful cleavage which exists between these two testimonies to the faith, again and again the thesis finds its supporters that, despite all differences in style and expression, the authors of the Apocalypse and of the Gospel of John are one and the same. In that case, the New Testament would be a dialectic to a degree not yet attained by any dialectical theology. Whether that be so or not, one fact stands firm, that in the New Testament itself the apocalyptic dramatization finds its correction, just as does the Platonizing static view. We do well not to try to cancel out this tension in the New Testament witness either by a too thoroughgoing de-mythologization on the one hand or, on the other, by a too unreserved theology of events.

Whoever takes seriously the terms eternal life, attraction of the changeless glory of the beatific vision, as opposed to the form of a servant and the hiddenness of faith, cannot but feel the inadequacy of apocalyptic dramatization as a symbol of the wholly other. And whoever takes seriously the words advent, Parousia, realization of the Kingdom of God, despite their inadequacy, will not be able to disallow the apocalyptic symbols and will never be able to content himself with a purely existentialist interpretation which is a theology without hope.

The church has attempted to extricate itself from this difficulty by, on the one hand, emphasizing death as the limit of earthly experience, by expressing its hope in the form of the expectation of heavenly life, and at the same time—though only in faint undertones—sounding the note of the *dies iræ, dies illa solvet sæclum in favilla*, though in the course of the centuries this faint undertone has become ever fainter. In the process there took place a substantial transformation of the New Testament hope of the end (18): it passed from being a universal hope relevant to all mankind to being a personal hope relevant to the individual life. No doubt in this way the life-history of the individual man finds its due fulfilment of meaning, its eternal consummation; but, on the other hand, the history of humanity remains without completion. This means, furthermore, that even the fulfilment of meaning for the individual is viewed as a purely private affair. Just what is the central feature in the New Testament kerygma—the union of person and fellowship, the historical roots of the person, and the personal character of history—is thus lost. Thus far Albert Schweitzer's verdict regarding the progressive de-eschatologization of Christianity is thoroughly justified (19). One need only think of Paul Gerhardt's lines, "Fullness of joy and blessed peace may I await in the heavenly garden", in order to measure this individualistic impoverishment of the New Testament hope of the Kingdom.

Yet it must not be forgotten that, side by side with this development in the historical church, there stands the very different type of apocalyptic hope entertained by the sects. This preserved, even though in the primitive forms of mythical apocalyptic, the universal element which related the New Testament hope to mankind as a whole, and this has kindled in it again and again its evangelical fervour and its revolutionary social-ethical dynamic. Thus the curious state of affairs is that the culturally higher type of Christianity represented the individualistic, and the culturally lower type the universal element in eschatology and the philosophy of history. From this survey, the obligation arising out of the New Testament itself becomes still more pressing: that we should try to find a formula for this ultimate hope which will combine the universal-historical element, the expectation of the

Kingdom of God, with the individual-personal element, the hope of eternal life.

Let us once more cast a glance at the interpretation of the eschatological proposed by the existentialist critics of the New Testament. Here we find that the concept of the eschatological is emptied of all that has reference to a future, that is, the object of hope. Eschatological means merely the ultimate seriousness of the decision for faith in the saving Word of Jesus Christ. This means that hope is completely dissolved in faith. "Eschatological existence is realized only in faith, not in sight, which implies that it is no earthly phenomenon" (20), thus, with express reference to the Pauline distinction between faith and sight (21), but in opposition to what Paul himself means, is this hopeless eschatology formulated. As if the vision to which Paul refers were an earthly phenomenon! As though a faith had any meaning for Paul which did not imply a fulfilment in vision transcending itself! In order to escape the impasse of an end of history, here not only is eliminated the apocalyptic dramatization, but all hope in the future and eternal generally, and that in the interests of an interpretation which is nothing but an amputation impotent to inspire and sustain life.

The dilemma which we have indicated has not its source in a changed picture of the world, it does not press upon faith from without. It springs rather from the paradoxical nature of the conception of an end of history itself. Neither the Platonized theology of the church nor the primitive mythology of the sects does justice to the eschatological statement of the New Testament. But the eschatological vacuum in theology was not realized so long as it was concealed—even within the orthodox church—by modern illusory forms of substitute-eschatology, such as the thought of progress. Not until the break-up of the latter and the stark emergence of nihilism have we been constrained, and perhaps rendered able, to trace our eschatological thought back to its New Testament basis, while remaining free from a non-Christian literalism. In so far as we make the witness to Jesus Christ, the Crucified and Risen One, the sole foundation of the eschatological affirmation shall we perhaps succeed in so speaking of the end of history as to bring out the personal meaning of individual life-history and also the universal sense of the history of mankind, indeed of the history of the cosmos as a whole.

Chapter Fourteen

THE PAROUSIA, THE COMING OF THE SON OF GOD IN GLORY

THE word Parousia, which in the New Testament frequently denotes the future coming of the Christ and of consummation, means simply in its literal sense: presence. But this plain word of everyday usage implies the overt realization of a present reality that is veiled, the disclosure of what in this life we saw *sub contraria specie*, in the form of a servant, i.e. "His glory the glory as of the only begotten of the Father, full of grace and truth" (1).

If we ask how far this thought of the "advent" and thus of the effectual presence of God in earthly life belongs to the essence of the Biblical message, the Bible as a whole gives a plain answer. From the very start of the saving story the central theme is that God comes, that salvation comes, that a movement from above manward is in process, the coming of that which is lacking and yet what alone can give life its full meaning, its wholeness, its harmony; that through this coming God imparts His effectual presence and dwells among us, that God is present with His people, I thy God, thou My people. That is not merely one among other themes of the Bible; it is the only one controlling all others. In particular, we hear already in the Old Testament the promise of the advent of the Messiah, in which the reign of God is to be effectually consummated. The Day of the Lord comes, and with it through judgment the splendour of His glory. "Behold, the days come, saith the Lord, when I will make a new covenant with the house of Israel and with the house of Judah . . . and I will be their God and they shall be my people" (2).

But still more is this so in the New Testament. The formula which because of its simplicity almost escapes our notice, "I am come", meets us frequently on the lips of Jesus. In His Person the advent of the Kingdom is now realized. The whole Messianic saving message of God's realized presence is contained in this word "come". For this reason the Baptist is concerned only with the one question: "Art Thou He *that should come* or do we look for another?" (i.e. the true Messiah) (3). He *has* come—that is the witness of the New Testament concerning Jesus Christ. Hence the difference between the Old and the New Testament is this, that in the Old the advent alone is the object of hope and expectation, whereas in the New, as that which has already happened, it is both the object of faith and also, as a realized experience of the divine, the meaning and the power of the present life of the Christian and the Christian fellowship. But this already realized coming and presence is of such a character that it is not yet completed but is only in its initial stages and therefore still awaiting its consummation. The coming of God to man which is the theme of the Old Testament is thus explicated in the New, in the three dimensions of time: He has come, He is present and He will come. In this unity of faith, hope, and love consists the existence of the church, of the Body of Christ. To remove one of these dimensions means to destroy the whole. Faith is nothing when it is not active in love. Faith and love are nothing when they cannot be fulfilled in that for which man hopes. In fact, one can simply describe the new condition of life thus: "Born again to a new and living hope" (4).

For that the Crucified is really the Son of God, that the Crucifixion is not a tragedy but victory, that the decisive event there took place by which God is present with us and we with Him—that is only true if its veil of hiddenness does not remain permanently. The Cross is only redemptive if it includes the certitude of resurrection. It is of the essence of faith that it is aware of itself as a provisional state which will eventually be superseded by the ultimacy of vision. Faith without hope is just as meaningless as faith without love. "If Christ be not risen then your faith is vain and ye are yet in your sins" (5). But the resurrection of Christ, who through faith has become our new life, implies our resurrection at His future coming.

In all three dimensions of time, it is the one Christ to whom the awakened heart is turned in faith, love and hope. In each of these acts, it is a question of Emmanuel, God-with-us, the personal God whose presence is realizable in the heart. Therefore hope can have no other object than that He who has *come*—in the form of a servant—*will come* again in glory. Here again it is a question not of something but of Him. It is a question of the future coming of the Lord in His glory, in the splendour of His unconcealed presence, in the true mode of His being, which is no longer subject to the law of *contraria species*. Hence the second classical expression for this event in the future is: apocalypse, unveiling, revelation in its fullness. In spite of our sonship of God granted us in faith, it is true of us also that we stand in a provisional condition. "Beloved, we are now children of God and *it doth not yet appear* what we shall be. But we know that *when He appears* we shall be like Him" (6). In both senses it is a question of the revelation of that which is now only a hidden realization of Presence.

Just as birth pangs imply birth, so faith implies ultimate disclosure—the disclosure of His and our true being, the emergence from hiddenness to light, unmistakable manifestation and unquestioned fullness of true life, where we no longer "see in a glass darkly, but face to face" (7). As the beginning of a discourse has no meaning if it is not brought to its completion, so faith has no meaning if it does not attain its goal in the fullness of revelation, in the apocalypsis which is called Parousia, in the Parousia which is called apocalypsis.

From all these considerations it is clear that this thought of the future coming is anything but a piece of mythology which can be dispensed with. Whatever the form of this event may be, the whole point lies in the fact that it will happen. To try to boggle at it means to try to boggle at the foundation of the faith; to smash the corner-stone by which all coheres and apart from which all falls to pieces. Faith in Jesus Christ without the expectation of His Parousia is a voucher that is never redeemed, a promise that is not seriously meant. A

Christian faith without expectation of the Parousia is like a ladder which leads nowhere but ends in the void. What Paul says of the resurrection applies exactly to the Parousia: "If Christ be not risen"—if there is to be no future consummation—"then your faith is vain and ye are yet in your sins."

But if we turn to the question *in what form* the event of the Parousia will take place, then we come upon pronouncements of the New Testament which are clearly mythical, in the sense that they are in fact unacceptable to us who have no longer the world-picture of the ancients and the apostles (Bultmann): "For the Lord Himself will descend from heaven at the voice of an archangel and at the blast of the trumpet of God and the dead will first be raised, then we the living will at the same time be caught up with them to meet the Lord in the clouds" (8). If we ask whether the apostle who thus writes meant his words to be taken literally, we can answer neither with a simple yes nor no. He can hardly have imagined God as blowing a trumpet. Nor may we presuppose too clear an awareness of the symbolism, of the impropriety of the expressions, either in the writer or in the contemporary readers of this letter. The modern reader demythologizes it, whether he will or no, whether he is conscious of his thought-processes or not, even though he be a fundamentalist. The only questionable point is the extent of the de-mythologization. We feel immediately that just here the world-picture of the Bible clashes with our own. At the same time everyone who has understood the central significance of the Parousia expectation realizes: here there is no other possibility of expressing the matter except the symbolic one, the consciously inadequate, exactly as when we call God Our Father, Our Lord, the Father in heaven, or as when we speak of the being of God as above, and of our own as below, and, again, exactly as when we say that God speaks, acts, comes.

It is of the essence of the ultimate event that its character as an event is unimaginable. For that reason it will be better to remain loyal to New Testament symbols, conscious both that they are symbols and that we need symbols. We shall constantly attempt in our theological reflection to express in abstract language what we say symbolically in prayer and worship—as for example we are doing in this book. But we shall be under no illusion that this language is not symbolical—for what is the concept of transcendence if not a symbol?—and, furthermore, we shall be aware of the danger of this movement from the naïvely symbolical to the reflective-symbolical, as we bear in mind what we have said above, and we shall not suppose that the measure of abstraction is a measure of approximation to the truth. That in this we are following New Testament lines, a Word of Jesus gives us a plain indication. On the one hand Jesus spoke very concretely about a coming of the Son of Man on the clouds of heaven (9). But another time He expresses the same idea in the language of abstract symbolism when He says it will be like "lightning which flashes from the east to the west" (10). That is to say—although again in terms of metaphor—that what is here in question is something not to be localized or concretely understood. The lightning flash is probably of all the possibilities of expression open to us the one symbol which expresses most effectively this transcendence of space and time. Lightning is, so to speak, a happening without temporal extension, its flash is nowhere and everywhere at the same time. Whosoever wishes to go farther in the path of demythologization must consider whether he does not end up in a philosophy of timelessness and a philosophy of the impersonal absolute; whether a change in the form of expression does not lead to a radical change in substance, in that the personally speaking divine "Thou" becomes an "it" conceived by the human mind and the acting God is transformed into timeless being. By these attempts to interpret the Word of Christ so that it is also a word of human self-understanding is not the theme of the whole Biblical declaration—the action and the coming of God, the Lord of the world—transformed into a monologue of man understanding himself out of the resources of his own being?

We know that our recognitions are piecemeal, that we see in a glass darkly—the man who speaks thus is no naïve believer in myths—and we say this quite specially with reference to our eschatological conceptions. But we know also that faith in the ultimate and all-fulfilling Coming of the Revealer and Redeemer is necessarily faith in the Crucified and Risen One, in Him who is made righteousness and life to us, even though we can only formulate this final revealing advent in terms of the stammering speech of apocalyptic symbolism. How should it be otherwise, since it will be the wholly other and only as the wholly other can it imply redemption and consummation? We are protected from arbitrary fantasies by the fact that this wholly other is related to what we already have in Christ, and to the newness of life which He has bestowed upon us, as the emergence of what has been generated in the hiddenness of birth to the bearing of it in hope and expectation. The ultimate is not the ultimate, is not the wholly other, in relation to the new life that has already come to birth. It is not the wholly other in relation to the Christ who through the Holy Ghost is already in us. He is, rather, "the same yesterday and to-day" (11). He is the One "who was and is and is to come" (12). But it is the wholly other in the sense that what is at present hidden will be the fully revealed, that what is yet concealed in the flesh will be ultimately consummated in the spiritual and glorified body. This dualism, on the one hand, the identity between the ultimate and what is already given us in Christ, and, on the other hand, the utter otherness of the mode of being of the ultimate as contrasted with what is now concealed, will become plain to us when we turn to the individual aspects of the Parousia.

Chapter Fifteen

THE RESURRECTION

IT is hardly questionable that the conception of a resurrection of the dead was the result of Persian influence upon Judaism, from whence it penetrated into the New Testament. No doubt there are hints of it in the Old Testament, but they all belong to the exilic and post-exilic strata of the Old Testament. We must accept the fact that the Old Testament, even the prophetic message, is not concerned about the fate of the individual after death, nor does it know anything about a consummation of the Kingdom of God beyond the limits of historical existence. In a later connexion we shall find the clue to this rather curious state of affairs. In the New Testament, however, the idea of the resurrection is already found as something known to everyone, even though not admitted by all circles of the Judaic religious community. Jesus Himself points to this by at once establishing the connexion with Old Testament thought: When the Almighty is there described as the God of Abraham, Isaac and Jacob, it is an indication of the fact that these patriarchs are represented as living in God or in the presence of God; "for God is not a God of the dead but of the Living" (1). But with Jesus too the accent lies, as in the Old Testament, not upon the resurrection of the individual, but upon the coming of the Kingdom, which now of course is no longer thought of as an event within history but as something breaking in from the transcendent.

The preaching of the apostles, however, has another point of departure and, at least at first, a different content. The point of departure is everywhere and quite plainly: the fact of the resurrection of Jesus. But this fact never stands in isolation as a *perfectum*. It is indissolubly bound up with the *factum præsens*: that this Jesus is present, that His presence is a living creative experience through faith and the Holy Ghost. Precisely as "church theology", as a testimony to the faith experience of the church, the words ascribed to Jesus, "See, I am with you always even unto the end of the world" (2), and "Where two or three are gathered together there am I in the midst of them" (3), gain special significance. The Pauline theology (and in this Schweitzer was correct) is Christ-mysticism, but this Christ-mysticism is also and primarily faith in Christ, faith in that which happened once for all on His cross. Likewise the farewell discourses of Jesus in the Fourth Gospel are the product of a Christ-mysticism rooted in faith in Christ.

But it is putting things the wrong way round to assert, as has been recently done, that the faith in the resurrection is "nothing other than faith in the Cross as a saving event" (4). The event of Good Friday left the disciples in a state of indescribable sadness and disillusionment. Had nothing further happened, faith in Christ would have collapsed, no ecclesia would have arisen, the knowledge of Jesus would not have reached us, the event of Jesus would have merged as an unimportant episode of Jewish sectarian history into the darkness of world history. That this did not in fact happen, that, rather, the tiny flock of Christ's disciples filled and conquered the world with their knowledge of Christ, took place solely and exclusively because Jesus Christ showed Himself to them as the Risen One, and, as the living present Saviour, founded in them a new life.

In what way this self-revelation of the Risen One happened is not so clear from the documents of the New Testament as the artificial consistency of an orthodox-fundamentalist Biblical teaching would like to suppose. In this matter there are a number of seriously deviating presentations in the New Testament itself. When Paul, not only the greatest missionary, but also the first and greatest theologian of primitive Christianity, presents himself to the church as a witness of the resurrection of Jesus alongside the first apostles, and not only claims equal authority and originality as a primal witness but was fully recognized as such by the primitive community, this means at any rate that the primitive church admitted a witness to the resurrection which could not be expressed in the words "that a dead man was raised again to physical life" (Bultmann) (5), and that the factuality of this event cannot be exhaustively indicated by such a crass mythical equation. On the other hand, when the appearances of the Risen One of which Paul speaks, and which in one breath he groups with his Damascus experience, are equated with mere visions, and thus written off as mere subjective experiences, the interpretation may be made if one can feel responsible for it; only it should then be borne in mind that the existence of the ecclesia and the whole history of Christianity and of the church is being founded upon a subjective illusion.

For our part we would prefer to interpret the manifold discrepancy of the Easter reports as an indication that the fact to which they bear witness is in the strict sense of the word eschatological; that is, the beginning of the advent of the eternal consummation, of the life of the world to come, which cannot be grasped in the categories proper to this space-time world (6). The resurrection of Jesus is as an event the utterly incomprehensible and transcendent, the beginning of the Parousia, of which the—one might say—obvious characteristic is its incomprehensibility, its non-co-ordinability (7), the utter impossibility of expressing it in the terms of our thought and ideas.

The resurrection is an incomprehensible event because it represents the inbreak of the eternal world of God into our temporal sphere. Thus it is something which no man can understand or describe, because it is the cancellation of space-time existence. But it is also quite plainly the self-testimony of Jesus Christ, of the Crucified, as the Living One. The New Testament reports emphasize in different measure and in different ways this twofold factor: The Risen Lord is recognizable as the same Jesus whom we knew in His earthly life and He is also quite other than He was in His earthly life. The story of Thomas, who places his finger in the wounds of the Risen Lord and thus assures himself of His identity (8), expresses in extreme fashion the first aspect, while the voice and the light from heaven which make of Paul the persecutor the apostle of Jesus, or the narrative of how the disciples on their journey to Emmaus do not at first recognize Jesus and only at the moment of the breaking of the bread become aware who this mysterious third Person is, at the moment when He vanishes as suddenly from their eyes as He had appeared—such and similar traits suggest the utter otherness of His being and mode of presence (9).

In any event, the common feature of all these resurrection reports is that He who died on the Cross has revealed Himself to believers as the Living Lord. Therefore with Easter day the new æon has dawned. But this new æon manifests itself not merely through the resurrection of Jesus but also just as much through the new life, the life in the Holy Ghost, life in the presence of the Risen Saviour (10), and in communion with Him a life which differentiates believers from unbelievers, from those in the world, and which makes them members of the Body of Christ, of the church. The very existence of the ecclesia, the life in the Holy Ghost and in His gifts, are so many signs and operations of the world of the resurrection breaking into the present. The eternity to come has become a present reality, the existence of the community of Christ is a Messianic or eschatological existence; it is life in the divine presence at the heart of temporality, the Kingdom of God in the midst of the world of sin and death.

The ecclesia of primitive Christianity is distinguished from the church and churches of later times by the power with which the new world of the resurrection is felt to be present, and also by the definiteness with which believers are conscious of this newness, of this Messianic character of their existence. The Reformed interpretation of the New Testament has not always caught this victorious note, because often it was deflected too much by the concern to equate the church of that time with the New Testament ecclesia. In particular, the Lutheran *simul justus et peccator* implied a clear shift of emphasis in the self-appraisal of the *novitas vitæ christianæ*. In the New Testament the emphasis lies not only on the fact that the newness of life is "only" for faith, nor even on the fact that it is *real* for faith, but absolutely on the fact of the newness of the life in the Holy Ghost as contrasted with the old life in the flesh. Therefore our interpretation must take as its point of departure the New Testament witness to faith, not this later adaptation to the popular church situation.

The self-testimony of the ecclesia leaves us in no doubt that the life of believers, the life of the ecclesia, is Resurrection life in its hiddenness; hence only a foretaste of the newness of life which the final revelation of the resurrection in the Parousia of Jesus Christ will bring. The newness of eternal life, the likeness to Christ, is as yet hidden and implicated in the body of this death; the light of Christ can as yet be only refracted through the medium of this old existence whose sign is the being unto death. But this does not alter the fact that it is already a manifestation of this transcendent world and that the coming of the ultimate must necessarily have about it the character of a bringing to birth. Christians do not live between the times but altogether in the new æon —even though at present only in the first stages of this coming world.

This is especially clear from the fact that the Risen Lord is called "the First-born of many brethren" (11). What He now is, that we are truly also; only we are so not yet visibly, only as yet in concealed fashion; that is, heirs of eternal life, participators of the resurrection. "But we know that we, when He has been made manifest, shall be like Him" (12). And yet it is true of this provisional mode of resurrection life that it consists in a process of constant transformation the goal of which is likeness to Him. For we *are* changed now from glory to glory in the same image (13)—into His image, the image of Christ—through the operation of the Holy Ghost. It is the life of the resurrection since it is the life of Christ. If the reality consists as yet only in faith, not in sight, it is yet an *experience* of faith, for "the law of the Spirit *has* freed me in Christ from the law of sin and death" (14). "We *have* passed from death to life since we love the brethren" (15).

So therefore the existence of the believer, i.e. life in Christ the Risen Lord, is itself resurrection. And yet only a waiting for the resurrection. "But if the Spirit of Him who raised up Jesus from the dead dwells in you, He who raised Jesus from the dead will also quicken your mortal bodies by His Spirit which dwelleth in you" (16). There is a parallelism between the old and the new; just as in what we call, in the natural sense, life, right at the heart of everyman's existence, gnawing at the root of life, sits death, so now already in us building up the new at the root of life is the life of Christ. The being unto death has already been changed into a being unto life, but it is as yet only a being-to, not a being-in. It bears outwardly still the *contraria species*; it still appears as a being unto death although it is no longer such in reality. Precisely the "I die daily" (17) is paradoxically the law of life of the new experience. The new, the *agapé*, the true present, lives just in this active dying. It is not accidental, but rather corresponds to the law of life, that the *agapé*, the love bestowed by Christ, is described in the New Testament Song of Songs almost exclusively in negative terms: it envies not, it does not boast, it is not puffed up, it seeks not its own. The self-assertive ego has now vanished, for now no longer "I", but Christ lives in me (18).

One of the plainest tokens of the new life is the certainty of the resurrection, the certainty that nothing can separate us from the love of God which is in Christ Jesus our Lord (19). "Whosoever believeth on me shall live though he were dead" (20). Of course each one will have to undergo the experience of physical death, but he will not die into nothingness but into Christ. Hence it is said "For me to die is gain" (21), for it means "to be with Christ." Hence the apostle can say outright, "I have a desire to depart" (22). Death has in fact lost its sting (23). For if it is true that the love which we have in Christ is the love of God, thus the presence and the life of God, then that fact implies that nothing can separate me from this love, from the knowledge that we have eternal life.

Two questions arise at this point: firstly, what does the resurrection considered as union with Christ imply with regard to the individual? Secondly, how is this individual resurrection related to the universal resurrection-event at the end of history, which will come to pass at the Parousia of the Lord? It is impossible to answer fully the first question in isolation from the second. The same thing applies to the second: there exists a mutual relationship between the two. But we cannot well begin other than with the personal individual aspect, since just as the being *in* Christ is only understandable from the standpoint of the faith of the individual, so also the being *with* Christ which is its completion.

The resurrection of the individual is in the New Testament plainly to be understood as a personal immortality. The Goethean "finding himself in the infinite, the individual will gladly vanish, to surrender oneself is joy", does not come into consideration. The New Testament faith knows of no other sort of eternal life except that of the individual person. This is what Jesus means when He says of Abraham, Isaac, and Jacob that they live, since God is a God of the living and not of the dead (24). In any case this could not be otherwise within the framework of personalistic Biblical thought which springs from the personal revelation of God. "I have named thee by thy name, thou art mine" (25). This "thou" is the Biblical category, not an abstract impersonal "it". "We shall be like *Him*," Him, Jesus, not an impersonal philosophical principle. The Spirit of Jesus Christ is creative of persons, not de-personalizing. The impersonal idea belongs to a philosophy of timelessness, to the philosophy of speculative thought, not to the Biblical world of revelation. "With whomsoever God speaks . . . He speaks eternally." Speech is the self-communication of the "I" to the "Thou". Where love is the ultimate meaning of revelation the person is ultimately valid.

Paul goes yet a step further. Just as in his interpretation of sin any division of the person into a lower and a higher part is excluded, since the person as a whole is made responsible and a shifting of responsibility for evil on to the lower half, on to something that is not I myself, is thus impossible, so also a division of the person in regard to death is precluded. Just for that reason the teaching of immortality in the Platonic sense is to be rejected. Paul expresses the opposite of it in a paradoxical idea, that of a pneumatic body (26), a spiritual corporeality. An actual experience, that of encounter with the Risen One, lies at the root of this conceptual paradox. Jesus is not awakened again to physical life (Bultmann) (27) according to the Resurrection narratives, but to a spiritual corporeality which on the one hand manifests itself in spatial limits, on the other, overcomes the limitations of space. This encounter with Jesus, who is both recognizable as the same and is free from the conditions of material corporeality, lies at the basis of his idea of the *soma pneumatikon*. This idea also expresses the wholeness of the person as an individuality created by God and named by Him. I, this particular individual, am called of God; I, this specific non-interchangeable man, am to rise again.

But the flesh will not rise again. The resurrection of the flesh stands of course in the creed but is excluded by what Paul says in 1 Cor. 15: 35–53. The resurrection has nothing to do with that drama of the graveyard pictured by medieval fantasy, and presented with extreme artistic realism, but all the more in opposition to the Bible, by Signorelli in the cathedral of Orvieto. Every man will rise again in his own likeness, his own unchangeable individuality, but not in his flesh. In any case we here stand at the limit of what can be expressed intelligibly. One can grasp the meaning of this paradoxical conception almost solely in negative terms. Two things must be excluded: the transient element, the flesh, is not to take part in the resurrection. But the individual person who is a special thought in the mind of God will not be excluded from eternity. Corporeality, even in its spiritual form, is the expression of the non-abstract, of the individual, and personal. What is in question is fellowship as opposed to union. In fact, Jesus goes so far as to speak of a sitting at the table (28) in the Kingdom of Heaven.

But how is this individual personal aspect of the resurrection related to the universal aspect affecting the history of mankind, to faith in the future coming of Christ and the universal resurrection which is bound up with it? In regard to this second question we are concerned not merely with the point in time but with the far more important question of the direction of salvation: does not what we have so far called the individual aspect imply a fundamental change in the direction of our hope, in the sense of a movement from here to there, the object of hope being not the coming of the Christ, but man's reaching heaven? Does not thus the individual hope of blessedness take the place of the coming Kingdom of God? And does not the resurrection of the individual become a private event in the history of the individual soul without any nexus with the Parousia, which concerns humanity as a whole and history as a whole? The remarkable thing is that the same Paul who in the first chapter of the Epistle to the Philippians speaks about departing and being with Christ, in the third chapter expresses equally plainly the expectation of the Parousia which will bring resurrection for him also (29).

We must connect with this what was said above (p. 109) about dying with Christ. This "with Christ" immediately lifts the individual personal event out of the sphere of the *purely* individual and gathers it into that of the history of mankind as a whole. My death as a dying in Christ, a sharing in His death, is not only mine, but that of man in general. For Christ is the second Adam, hence He in whom human history is recapitulated. I die not only my death but the death of man. My self-identification with Christ by faith makes the beginning of the new life in me a participation in the Kingdom, thus an event affecting mankind as a whole. As sin and death are a unity, so also the forgiveness of sins and eternal life are one. "Death is the wages of sin but the Grace-gift of God is eternal life in Christ Jesus our Lord" (30). What I experience as a believer is "the being translated into the Kingdom of the Son of love" (31).

But what appears from man's point of view as a grasping of the grace of Christ is from the angle of God, is in truth, a being grasped (32). The entering in, is in reality a being taken in, the movement which appears primarily as my movement thither is in truth His movement from thence to humanity, to me. That is the sequence of thought from the first to the third chapter of the Epistle to the Philippians, beginning with the idea of departing and being with Christ, proceeding to the powerful Christological theme about the condescension of the Son of God to sinful humanity (33), reaching its crucial point in the death on the Cross, and in the third chapter concluding with the expectation of the Parousia after faith has previously been depicted as a not apprehending but a being apprehended (34).

There is still to be pointed out a further aspect of the same movement which again, only this time in the sphere of interior spiritual history, reveals the same picture. What we experience chiefly as coming to faith or a coming to Christ is in reality a movement of the church towards me, in virtue of the word of the preacher, of baptism, of my incorporation into the Body of Christ. It is not I who go, but Christ who comes, and in this connexion it is not so much a question of my individual soul's salvation but of the spread of His Kingdom. There is no individual existence in faith but only the being in Christ through membership of the ecclesia. What appeared at first as an inner individual event in the soul is in reality an event in the Kingdom of God, an act of incorporation into the *Politeuma* (35). So also the departing and being with Christ is no merely individual personal happening but only the this-worldly appearance of what from the otherworldly angle is called the Parousia. To die is to be called home by Him the Father, who calls not only me, but His people, humanity, unto Himself.

What creates the greatest difficulty for our conception is the divisibility of time. It is noteworthy that Paul seems to feel no contradiction between the statement about departing and being with Christ in the first chapter and the resurrection as the effect of the Parousia in the third. He harshly juxtaposes the two things with no attempt to harmonize them. The reconciliation of the two ideas from the point of view of time is no problem for faith but only one for thought. It can be solved the moment we become clear that time belongs to the earthly world. Here on earth there is a before and an after and intervals of time which embrace centuries or even millenniums. But on the other side, in the world of the resurrection, in eternity, there are no such divisions of time, of this time which is perishable. The date of death differs for each man, for the day of death belongs to this world. Our day of resurrection is the same for all and yet is not separated from the day of death by intervals of centuries —for these time-intervals are here, not there in the presence of God, where "a thousand years are as a day."

When therefore our death, the departure, can be the way by which Jesus Christ calls us individual men to Himself, or, more correctly, if our death is the this-worldly event in which the other-worldly event, the coming of the Lord, is concealed, should not that perhaps also be true for humanity and human history as a whole? If the coming of the Lord for the individual man happens, as Paul expects, in the earthly experience of departure, of the extinction of life in this world, should not the same for human history as a whole be the earthly appearance of the Parousia? In this connexion it would be indifferent whether the temporal cessation of human history assumed the form of a catastrophic event—e.g. a natural catastrophe of global magnitude, or, as is now thought to be a very real possibility, a natural process unleashed by man himself which within a few seconds would lead to the extinction of all human life—or whether a protracted dying of humanity occurred, for the manner of departure is for the apostle's thought of no concern.

We are well aware that this conception encounters strong intrinsic resistance, for which there is a twofold reason. First, we all live, even though in theory we have abandoned them, on strong chiliastic ideas of a good time coming for man, to be attained somehow or other. It is only with difficulty that we can adjust ourselves to the thought that humanity must have an end, just like the individual man, who must inescapably die. When we are confronted with this outlook it is only then that we perceive how deeply rooted in us all is some form of the belief in progress and how hard it is for us to renounce it. A second point is that the New Testament accustoms us as Christians to entertain a different notion of the end of humanity. The New Testament expectation of an imminent Parousia and end of the world is always bound up with the idea that the returning Lord will find a humanity partly awaiting His advent and partly surprised by it "like a thief in the night" (36).

But this expectation has been deceived not only in the first generation of Christians, who specially cherished it, but again and again. Nay, further: this type of expectation does not think out radically enough, as we have already seen, the thought of an end of history. Rather it makes the attempt at least in one respect to conceive the Parousia as an event within history by thinking of the Day of the Lord as a day of earthly history, viz. as the last day of earthly history, just as the Old Testament creation story similarly describes the day of creation as a first day in cosmic earthly history.

In both ways we must think more radically and take more seriously the thought of the incommensurability between the temporal-earthly and the eternal-heavenly. As little as we can inscribe the day of creation as the first day in cosmic chronology, so little can we inscribe the day of the Parousia as the last day. Between the two there is as little connexion as there is—to dare an analogy—between the world and time of dreams and that of waking life. The moment of waking is not a time point in the world of dreams. It is quite simply its cessation. So is it with the departing and being with Christ. The being with Christ is not the moment immediately after death. For in the eternal world there is no next moment. In death the world of space and time disappears—and it is just this which is the temporal aspect to which corresponds, from the other-worldly point of view, the being with Christ and the future coming of the Lord, both being one and the same.

Or should we perhaps feel that doubts about this analogy arise from our knowledge of the world? Not at all. The history of man began at a point in time several hundred thousand years ago—we know not how or where. Measured against the background of cosmic time it is an infinitely tiny last bit of cosmic history. Regarded from a purely this-worldly point of view, nothing is more probable than that this cosmic episode comes to an end just as it began. From the point of view of faith, this wears a different aspect. By faith we know that history does not end in nothingness, but in the coming of the Kingdom of God as its consummation. This coming of the Kingdom of God has also its preparation within history, just as the advent of the Lord has a preparation within history, in the ecclesia, and the faith of the individual. But this preparation within history is not reflected continuously in the ultimate. Rather, the ultimate comes to it from the beyond, the transcendent, just as the Risen Lord appeared to the disciples from the invisible world of the resurrection, without there being a nexus, an uninterrupted line, from the one to the other. Humanly speaking, nothing more is to be said than that this man has died, has departed this life. From a natural this-worldly angle the cessation of human history is also to be expected. Why should not humanity disappear just as it arose?

Nevertheless we dare to express this only as a possibility, not as a certainty. In fact, we must even, as believers, reckon with the possibility that the Day of the Lord will come while history still proceeds on its course on the earth. Only we should realize that we can form simply no conception of this event, not even of what this coming, seen from the angle of this world (i.e. as an event within history) will imply. We can admit all apocalyptic images only as symbols of the unimaginable and the unknowable. Or should the word of the Psalmist be applicable here: "We shall be as those that dream" (37), as those who awake from an earthly dream into a heavenly reality?

Summa summarum: We know nothing of the how, we know only the fact, and its implication: that it will be the end of history in the Kingdom of God, the judgment and the perfecting of creation in the eternal world.

Chapter Sixteen

THE COMPLETION OF HUMANITY IN THE KINGDOM OF GOD

WE have spoken in several parts of this book from various points of view about the coming of the Kingdom of God into the historical world. We shall deal with that theme no longer. Our present theme is rather the coming of the Kingdom of Glory, which, just because it is the perfect and eternal, cannot fully enter the historical world. We are treating now of the Kingdom of God which marks the end of history. What we may teach about it without exposing ourselves to the criticism of sketching out mere wish-pictures of fantasy would really be an idle, valueless task. At this point, too, we shall remain faithful to the rule hitherto followed, that we have nothing to teach about the future coming of the Lord and His kingdom which does not spring from faith in the Lord Himself. It will consequently be plain that it cannot be a question of either fantasies or wishes.

First, the guiding thread we have just mentioned draws our attention to the fact that in the words of Jesus, though not in the epistles and writings of the apostles, the idea of the *basileia tou theou* is central. The reason is not, as has often been suggested, that the apostles narrowed it down in the interests of the individual Jesus' concern for the Kingdom of God or distorted it in a gnostic sense, and thus were really adopting a different viewpoint from that of Jesus; rather it is that they believed that with Jesus Christ, with His resurrection, the Kingdom of God had already dawned and thus was no longer an object of future expectation. The rule of God is operative in His own Person. For, as the exalted one, He is Lord and King, the heavenly but hidden effective Mediator of the divine rule. What we sing, "Jesus Christ reigns as

King, all is subject to Him," is the confession of primitive Christianity.

The immediate sphere of Christ's reign is the ecclesia, the Body of Christ, over which He reigns as the mind controls the body. Thereby the preaching of Jesus about the Kingdom of God, about the kingly rule of God, is in a certain sense superseded. The theme only indicated in the saying of Jesus, "The Kingdom of God is within you" (1), has now become an explicit main theme, for since the resurrection this kingship of Jesus for the eyes of faith has passed from a hidden to a manifest reality. Alongside this immediate though more restricted sphere of rule, a second more spacious one has become manifest: Jesus Christ has been appointed Lord of all creatures, for to Him is given all power in heaven and upon earth (2). This rule, embracing all things, is indeed yet hidden and the course of life in the world seems not to be influenced by it. But this very rule, still hidden, shall be manifested when He comes to reign in glory (3). For this reason, this theme stands in the foreground although in it is of course implied that of the proclamation of Jesus. That this is so is especially clear from the fact that in Paul what for him is the chief theme—salvation poured out beyond the bounds of the Jewish world—grace, the free gift of God in Christ, is put forward from the theocratic standpoint of the righteousness of God. In Jesus the Crucified God makes effective His righteousness and His kingly will. The Cross is the disclosure of the righteousness of God (4). One fact is particularly plain in this Pauline message—that here it is not a question of the fulfilment of human wishes. The self-seeking "I" must die that the will of God and not human self-will should be realized. It is not a question of happiness but of the realization of the righteous will of God. The whole Pauline teaching of justification by faith alone is directed against the self-honouring of man and has as its purpose the sole honouring of God. And fantasy enters into it just as little as the satisfaction of human wishes; for in the ecclesia the reign of the Holy Ghost is experienced as a reality which is distinct from what is normally called reigning by the fact that it is also a fellowship of the Holy Ghost, the classical sign of which is *Agapé*, self-giving love. This *Agapé* too is truly no fantasy but a living experience by which the reality of faith must be measured, and which also proves itself to be an efficacious operative power (5). The reign of God is manifested as a new life, as the accessibility to the divine and human "thou". In face of these new facts the earlier expectation of the coming kingly Lordship of God recedes somewhat into the background.

But this in no sense means that it is not real and effective in the background. The sayings of Jesus about the coming reign of God are not forgotten or superseded. They are only placed in a new perspective. But we have good reason to lift them out of this background and to reinstate them as a symbol of what the Christian community looks forward to as the fulfilment of human history. It is not good if the Word about the Kingdom of God is simply replaced by that about the Parousia of the Lord, since in that case the understanding of Christ slides all too easily into a false individualism (6). It is especially necessary, when the church and the churches have grown out of the ecclesia, to conceive the hope of mankind not merely in the form of "Fulfilment of the Church", but rather in that of the Kingdom of God. For the primitive community understood itself not as a church but as a Messianic fellowship, which means as a first-fruits of the coming Kingdom of God (7). In order to do justice to precisely what the church meant in calling itself the Body of Christ we must speak about the Kingdom of God, the goal of human history which it awaited.

The end of humanity revealed in Christ, the Kingdom of God, is the fulfilment of what in human history has always somehow been striven after, what it has been sought to realize, but what it could never be and never will be possible to realize as long as we live as sinful men in the bondage of death. Humanity is not simply the sum total of human beings. By learning to know humanity in its history we come to see in ourselves as human beings something other than what we see when we are preoccupied with the individual in isolation. This element of mankind and human history as a whole belongs to God's plan and will just as much as ourselves as individual persons. God wills His people, His humanity, His Kingdom. Therefore the realization of His will is the coming of His Kingdom, the coming of that which brings to its consummation universal humanity. That is the fundamental meaning of the words *Basileia tou theou*, the kingly rule of God. This key-idea of the New Testament means not only the Lordship of God, but His Lordship in a humanity unified and bound together by the realization of His will in His Kingdom.

The main theme of world history is the history of states, whether it be that of kingdoms, or of empires, or of republics and democracies. Humanity has ever tried to realize and manifest its unity through the authority of the state. When occasionally—in the Christian sphere alone has it happened—it has dreamed of a stateless condition as the goal which alone is worth striving for (8), the experiment has revealed more plainly than anything else that the political mode of attaining unity contradicts what is properly human, quite as much as it harmonizes with the human being as *zoon politikon*. No state, no imperium, no democracy, has even distantly realized the end of true human fellowship, if only because every state is a mode of rule and brings into being a minimum of unity only by means of rule—even though it be the delegated rule of democracy—and because rule is precisely what suppresses the element of true community. Further, because each state, even the greatest imperium in world history, is still only a particular body and so finds in other states or empires its limit, its rivals, and enemies. Hence the history of states and empires—whether monarchical or republican—is a history of war and oppression, of disunity and inhumanity. But where, inspired by the dream of human brotherhood, the Marxist programme with its aim of replacing the state by the classless society has been put in operation in recent times, then the opposite is the paradoxical result (9): the dictatorial totalitarian state. In the sphere of history there is no example of the realization of unity through the state because such unity is not compatible with freedom. But what we really want is Lordship plus freedom—and that is the *basileia tou theou.* For where God is Lord—the God who is revealed for us in the Crucified Christ—there is freedom (10). The dictatorship of the Holy Ghost is identical with true brotherhood in the true freedom of the children of God. For here authority is not compulsion, and freedom is not emancipation, but authority is the divine will freely affirmed and freedom is the gift of the Creator recognized as Lord.

Also in the Kingdom of God there are no more particularisms and limits, for all these flow from the will to power of the one who wishes to assert himself and dominate as against the other. The spirit of the Kingdom of God is, on the contrary, the spirit of him who rather suffers wrong than does wrong, the unconditioned will to serve of the Servant of God. The Kingdom of peace and justice is the Messianic Kingdom, and indeed the Kingdom of the Messiah, who is identical with the suffering Servant of God (11). Hence the Kingdom of the Messiah is understandable for us only in the person of the Crucified Lord, who will come again in glory—in the picture language of the Apocalypse, the lion which paradoxically is identical with the lamb (12).

Hence it is appropriate to interpret the Kingdom of God not literally on the analogy of the kingdoms and states of the world, but on that of the ecclesia, of the brotherhood founded on faith in the crucified and risen Christ. It too is concerned with mankind as a whole, is meant to be all-embracing, and constantly reaches out to gather all into its bosom. But, as distinct from the imperium, it is that kingdom which is not built up through compulsion and law, but through the self-bestowing grace of God, and thus is no structure which coheres through force but a community of brothers, no institution but a fellowship of persons, no collective but an organism consisting of free members. The ecclesia of the New Testament is in fact the nearest analogy to the Kingdom of God, but it is more than that: it is the initiation and seed of the latter. For here Jesus Christ reigns as king but His rule is a free gift and a creating of freedom, and the ecclesia is a unity in love embracing all mankind (13).

And yet even it is no more than an earthly historical structure which bears the stamp of earthly fleshly being. Even in the church there are—incomprehensibly but truly so—cleavages, groups which struggle against each other (14). Even there, there is not only the rule of the Holy Ghost, the Spirit of grace and freedom, but also that of law and office, and the more the ecclesia spreads to embrace all mankind the more this hierarchical tendency becomes prominent—law, office, and the subordination of some to others. The ecclesia too, as church, becomes a governmental structure. How should we be surprised at that? For it too is a community of sinful and extremely imperfect men in whom the old Adam has not disappeared and so must be controlled by law.

Above all, the provisional character of the ecclesia is shown in the fact that it stands in opposition to the world, the sphere of unbelief, that it therefore shares in the sufferings of Christ; again in the fact that it operates in the world in a manner which does not spring only from the Spirit but equally from the flesh. This is especially plain where the ecclesia has become the church, and consequently and inevitably the strife breaks out between the two universal structures of humanity, the strife between the emperor and the pope, between the secular and the supposedly spiritual imperium, which yet is far more an imperium of the church than an imperium of the Christ. The tension between the Regnum and the Sacerdotum becomes a main theme of Western Christian history which in a twofold way distorts the idea of the Kingdom of God. For not only the church but also the emperor aspires to realize the divine kingdom, and the caricature of the Regnum Christi which arises from a sacral imperialism (Charlemagne and the Ottos) is not radically different from the secularized priestly rule of the medieval papacy. Both are equally far removed from the Kingdom of God but both are only understandable as a reminiscence of the kingdom proclaimed by Christ. Yet precisely the will to overcome this duality, the determination to achieve a universal theocracy, is what implies the sharpest break with the true kingdom, since in the name of Christ it exercises worldly power and uses to bolster up its worldly authority the insignia of Christ and of the ecclesia—a really terrible *quid pro quo*—and it is still an allusion to the idea of the Kingdom of God (15). For the Kingdom of God is not to be a "church", but humanity in its everyday reality. Nor is it to be a state—in spite of the name kingdom—but an ecclesia, that is, a spiritual brotherhood in the Lord who is the Spirit.

But does the Kingdom of God mean an organized structure with definite characteristics? Does it not rather mean the consummation of the universal human element in its immediate essence, that which makes every man a man, but which is no longer afflicted with the all too human but, rather, liberated to reveal humanity in its truth? Certainly the Kingdom of God is also the perfecting of what humanism of all times has really meant, what stands beyond all historical differences, the element in which men of every race, class and type of culture can understand and affirm themselves, that therefore in which every man understands his fellowman beyond all separations because it is the common element, the essential humanity, not merely a contingent commonalty. The Lord's parables concerning the Kingdom are the classical examples of this essential humanity and enable us to understand the Kingdom as the life in which the purely human is the element through which all coheres, without the need for other bases of coherence—man in his purely human character of community with his fellowcreature, the manner of human living which in every word and deed expresses that which is valid for humanity as a whole.

Yet that is only one aspect of the matter. For not in vain is this ultimate human community called the Kingdom of *God*. In Jesus Christ it has been made plain once for all that the truly human is identical with the truly divine, or more correctly the true humanity exists only where life flows from the self-giving grace and glory of God. For this unity has its source only in God, since only in the Spirit of God is the all too human element of the self-assertive ego overcome. The kingdom of humanity is operative only where God is Lord, where human freedom is rooted in unconditioned dependence on God. Only in Christ can we say: "There is neither male nor female, free nor slave, Greek nor barbarian" (16). This community exists only where all are one in Christ. The unity of the human race, if it exists at all, is not essentially physical, dependent upon ties of blood (17). As a unity of the *humanum* and of *humanitas* it is based on the fact of creation, on the fact that man was made in the image of God. Only where this common origin in creation moulds all and each, is true humanity imparted—and this of course *is* the Kingdom of God. Just as in the Kingdom of God all external distinctions are overcome—one flock and one shepherd—so also all inner divisions; there is current the universal language of love which each understands, whatever his cultural, social, or national origin, whatever his individuality or family history may be. But this love is not something intrinsic to the essence of man; it is that which constitutes the being of God Himself.

We must go still further away from the structural: the Kingdom of God is the humanity in which *the heart* is of central significance. World history, that which stands in the history books, is an ever-continuing violation of the claims of the heart by what is great, what has weight, and counts in society and nation, by what is of functional importance through its efficiency and productive capacity. But the Kingdom of God, although it is the all-embracing, is also the most private, the most secret, the most interior, the vindication of the most vulnerable, of the child's timidity, of that which has not the robustness requisite for world history. Not for nothing is Jesus Christ the discoverer of the child, He who called little children to Himself and promised them, and them alone unconditionally, the Kingdom of Heaven (18). There no status and no office, no V.C., no Nobel prize, is of any avail; there the men who made history are distinguished by nothing as against the anonymous millions; there genius has no privilege as against the *simplex simplicissimus*. There nothing has rank except the heart as God made it, full of trust in Him the Creator, and of confident affection towards the fellow-creature—in short, there comes into his own he who in the world was the unnoticed scullion, most of all because he understands most immediately the being of God, which is nothing other than infinite love (19).

Perhaps there is something of this aspiration in the idea and ideology of the classless society. Of course there stands in the foreground something quite different which, although it is meant as the foundation of the earthly paradise, is precisely what devastates and destroys paradise, namely, justice, understood as perfect equality, the sheer naked absence of differences, an equality which is nothing other than the phantasmagoria of resentment. It is as psychologically understandable that just this wish-dream of perfect equality should fill the minds of the peoples suffering under their present unjust inequalities, as it is clear that this has nothing to do with the true justice of the Kingdom of God. The very demand for equality and the use of it as a criterion is incompatible with brotherly love and childlike humility (20). Of course, equally far from the Kingdom of God is the opposite, the requirement of inequality arising from a privileged *élite*, the exploitation of the advantages springing from natural inequalities of endowment. The Kingdom of God excludes equally the pseudo-justice of egalitarianism and the aristocratic inegalitarianism of an *élite* claiming special privileges. In the Kingdom of God there are no claims, but only love, which, as something which cannot be co-ordinated into a given structure, knows no calculations (21). All claimfulness is overcome because it is realized that complete dependence and freedom, human dignity and divine grace, are not opposites as the autonomous self-centred man supposes. This deepest mistrust, this unending carefulness about oneself in which the sin of the Fall consists (22), is effaced by self-identification with the Crucified, whose death *pro me* strikes at and destroys just this thing which is the root of all evil. The Kingdom of God exists where life springs up from the joyful acceptance of the life which God bestows.

Is the Kingdom of God the fulfilment of the possibilities

inherent in culture? This question brings out the ambiguity of all culture. If culture were nothing other than creative living, the glad and grateful use of the powers implanted by the Creator in the creature, then the ultimate fulfilment of the life of culture would doubtless be identical with the goal of human development and human history. The Kingdom of God is creative living flowing from communion with the Creator. But culture is never definable simply in such terms, nor is it ever predominantly such. It is rather always and primarily something quite different, namely, an anticipatory substitute for the heavenly gift, hence also and fundamentally a harmonic secularization of creative freedom (23). In the realm of culture man creates for himself what causes him to forget that the ultimate reality, the essential humanity is lacking to him. Thus culture is always—or at least in part—a building of that tower of Babel, where men wanted to erect a structure that would reach to the heavens, in order to protect themselves from God and make for themselves a name (24). Hence culture has always a Promethean, Titanic air about it. Only a childlike culture hardly conscious of itself, happily using its divinely bestowed gifts, only the *homo ludens*, unaware of his genius and, if he is aware of it, exercising it as the minstrel of God—only such a one belongs to the Kingdom of God (25).

From this point of view we can see why the New Testament is so uninterested in culture—without, however, negating it. Culture can so easily become a surrogate for the Kingdom of God. So easily, almost inevitably, does it develop into a means for the self-glorification of man, so seldom is it genuinely communicative and, on the contrary, so often is it aristocratic in the sense that it gives rise to a self-conscious *élite*. Hence the history of culture has only an incidental relation to the Kingdom of God, or even a negative one through its modification of the boundaries of the latter or its falsification of standards, its deviation from essentials and its absorption in what is only a substitute. And yet culture in its final term of development belongs also to the Kingdom of God, because it is the product of the formal freedom of the human spirit, since as an expression of freedom it releases man from slavery to his impulses and to the merely utilitarian.

Quite clearly though not so simply is the Kingdom of God related to worship and prayer. In so far as adoration, the bowing of the human spirit in awe in the face of the holy, is the deepest essence of all religion, the Kingdom of God represents the culmination of religious development. For the praise of God and the sense of gratitude to God is the immediate effect of that reign of God which is God's perfect communication of Himself. Inasmuch as adoration is the inmost being of religion, the latter is the expression of the universally human in its inward spiritual sense just as the state or the imperium expresses the outward aspect of humanity. But that is only one—the essential real side of religion. Religion can also represent a means of escape from God, a ready and cheap satisfaction of the divine claim, a payment of tribute, and thus the withdrawal of life from the real ownership and sovereignty of God. Religion expresses not only the inner reality of the holy, but at the same time always its externalization. It localizes the holy, making it administrable, manipulable. It makes man a claimful partner in the affairs of God, instigating him to demand what can only be a free gift of grace. Thus it kills the idea of the servant of God who is free from the law and from the self-righteous attitude of the *homo religiosus* by freely imparted divine love. Hence the Kingdom of God represents the overcoming of religion just as much as its consummation. For it is the Kingdom of Him who was execrated and executed as a criminal offender against religion by religious men, not by any religious men, but by the best of religious men. It is said of the City of God: "I saw no temple therein" (26).

To sum up. The Kingdom of God, of the future reality of which we are assured by faith in the Risen One, is the fulfilment of human history, just as resurrection to eternal life is the fulfilment of human life in its individual personal aspect. But we cannot understand the one apart from the other, for man as person is always at the same time humanity, and humanity as such always implies the individual and personal life. Aristotle calls man the *zoon politikon*; the Bible views him as a being created for the Kingdom of God. There is no fulfilment of the personal individual life possible which does not also imply a fulfilment of humanity in its universal aspect. What the Kingdom of God is, surpasses, like all else that is transcendent and perfect, our knowledge and understanding. But if we hope for it and await it with sure confidence, our expectations are not baseless. The essential character of the Kingdom is disclosed to us in the preaching of Jesus and at least we catch a vision of it too in His Cross and Resurrection. It consists in the kingly reign and sovereignty of God—that is the most vivid symbol by which we can see its relevance to the fundamental patterns of history. But it is also the perfect all-embracing fellowship of humanity, the Kingdom of peace and of that justice in which the self-bestowing grace and the self-illuminating holiness of God are one.

Nearest to it comes what we already learn to know on earth as a foretaste and adumbration of the Kingdom of God: the ecclesia of primitive Christianity, the union and fellowship of those whom Christ has bound to Himself, the breaking forth of the eternal life of God into our temporal sphere. For the sole reason that this breaking forth of the eternal has taken place, and that in Christ, through whom it has taken place and is taking place, the promise of fulfilment lies, can we be confident of its future realization. We do not hope for the latter as a man hopes for the realization of a dream or a wish, but we hope for it with an assurance that is grounded in what has already been given and realized in Christ. The sureness of this hope is in kind and degree exactly the same as that of the faith which is thus expressed: "I am certain that nothing can separate me from the love of God which is in Jesus Christ, Our Lord" (27).

The Kingdom of God comes inasmuch as Jesus comes in His glory. In so far as this happens there comes to historical developing mankind what was from the start its secret meaning and longing and its God-given destiny. It is immanent to man by reason of God's creation; but it is also something hidden from mankind, and universal humanity throughout its history lives in contradiction to it by reason of the rebellion of the autonomous self-seeking man. Not only man as an individual but also mankind in its historical development aims at self-realization, at finding itself, but cannot succeed in its aim. Its God-given goal becomes a cause of dispeace and, in so far as it sets up aims independently, it misses the former, and when it does not set up any aims but lives out its life on a natural plane, then it misses its divine aim all the more and sinks to a subhuman purely natural level. The goal has the character of an unhappy love in the life of humanity; it sets all in motion, yet it is not attained, and what in the historical process in actual fact comes to be is something which in no way corresponds to the divine end.

Thus the end comes to it from above, from the transcendent, from heaven, the world of God, from which Jesus Christ came to earth, He who "came to His own and His own received Him not" (28). This same Jesus Christ, who died for them—not merely for the individual man—on the Cross, was raised up on the third day, and thus became the Firstborn of many brethren, brings in His own Person this fulfilment of His Lordship and His fellowship, this ultimate revelation of humanity and divinity; just as out of His coming in the form of a servant there arose and ever anew arises the ecclesia as a first-fruits of the Kingdom of God, so from His coming in glory there arises the Kingdom of God as the consummation of human history (29).

But between this consummation and its already implanted secret beginnings there lies yet an event which is to make it clear that the consummation cannot simply come to pass as the crown and culmination of a process already begun, but that it requires to be preceded by a moment of purification and separation. Sin which works in history, as in individual lives, as the antithesis of the goal of creation, sin which has constantly checked the growth of the seed of the Kingdom of God, is not merely a matter of imperfection, it is a matter of positive negation which must be destroyed by a divine act of annihilation. A feature of decisive importance would be wanting to any picture of the New Testament expectation of the end which did not include the thought of the final judgment.

Before we pass on to this subject a preliminary question should at least be touched upon, a question which is hardly mentioned in the New Testament but an answer to which is implied wherever the last judgment is spoken of, and no doubt is simply assumed to be known from Jewish tradition: we refer to the resurrection of the godless to judgment.

We have urgent reason to pose this question, because we based belief in the resurrection exclusively and unequivocally on communion with Christ. How then stands it with those who have either never met Christ or have denied Him? What does death mean for him whom Christ has never awakened to life?

We recall here what was said in Chapter Eleven about Christian thoughts on immortality. "With whomsoever God speaks—be it in anger or in grace—the same is certainly immortal." Not because the human soul is divinely charged with the potentiality of eternal life does it fail to perish in death, but because God's intention with every man is an eternal one—for that reason none is annihilated in death. It is not thus easy to escape the judgment of God. Even the heathen have had some intimation of this. But the New Testament unambiguously shows every man as encountering, on the other side of the threshold of death, the God who judges. He summons everyone to appear before the judgment seat of Christ (30). There is no possibility of escaping Him through a dissolution into nothingness, for whosoever is human cannot eternally evade Christ.

By the fact that the moment of judgment precedes that of consummation we are made aware of something which might easily be overlooked through the strict correlation of person and fellowship. It is indeed a question of the Kingdom and of universal humanity at the same time as of the individual; but one enters the Kingdom only as an individual, one is excluded from it only as an individual. In this matter there are no collectives which count, neither the church nor marriage

disaster threatened as certain in the case of disobedience (2). Generally speaking, the judgments of God, which the prophets announce, concern the people as a whole and also heathen nations as a whole; the judgment of God has a collective non-individualized character, although individual judgments are not excluded, and from a certain point of time collective punishment is recognized as something contrary to the divine will (3). More and more judgment, which had previously been a menace of corporate disaster, takes on the character of discrimination, crisis. The just are separated from the unjust: the curse and punishment strike down only the latter. In fact a process of divine judgment comes to be conceived in which God exercises His activity as a Judge, ascertaining with precision the guilt of the individual and making judgment accordingly: this is especially the case in connexion with the expectation of a dual resurrection, some to eternal life, others to eternal damnation.

In the New Testament these thoughts are in part accepted, in part deeply modified. The man who is considered to be righteous according to generally accepted standards is more gravely condemned, in so far as he considers himself righteous, than is the man who is generally despised as a sinner and who knows himself to be such. "Publicans and sinners will enter the Kingdom of Heaven" before the rigidly pious and self-righteous Pharisee (4). God's pronouncement of judgment is no longer merely analytical, that is, made in strict accord with the discovered state of affairs, but synthetic; that is, one which creates a new condition of things through the free pardon of the sinner. But even this—no longer judicial but regal—pronouncement of God, this gracious pardon, can be revoked when the pardoned sinner does not for his own part adopt an attitude of forgiveness towards his fellow-men (5). On the other hand, the discrimination of right and wrong becomes at certain points so sharp and penetrating that the disciples anxiously inquire of the Lord: "Who then can be saved?"—to which Jesus replies: "With men this is impossible but with God all things are possible" (6).

In Paul we find a theology of judgment which seems curiously self-contradictory. On the one hand he carries to its logical conclusion, by his doctrine of the justification of the sinner through grace alone, Jesus' paradoxical reversion of standards. No longer is the actual conduct or condition of a man the ultimate criterion, but solely and exclusively forgiving Grace, mysteriously justifying the sinner and imparting to him newness of life. The one test then becomes—the existence of simple faith corresponding to free grace, the resignation of all claimfulness and attempts at self-justification, total self-surrender to the pardoning mercy of God, which lays the foundations of new life. But this doctrine of justification—which in spite of Albert Schweitzer is the *centrum Paulinum*—is completed by a conception of judgment which seems to be logically incompatible with it, the traditional, straightforward, rational idea of judgment according to works (7). Union with Christ by faith does not therefore shield a man from the judgment which takes place according to the criteria universally accepted in the thought of everyman, as the basis of judgment.

In John a new thought emerges into the foreground which in net result is at one with the Paulinian doctrine of justification: the discrimination of judgment is already implied in the attitude of faith. Whosoever believes in Christ is not judged; for Christ "came not to judge but to save" (8). But as in Paul so in John there exists alongside this main thought a secondary one—which therefore easily becomes the prey of literary criticism—a thought which gives value to the traditional conception of judgment as the last judgment for all mankind. In the Revelation of John, in accordance with the general tendency of the work, judgment is made concrete and particular in a series of dramatic acts, of terrible times of visitation, while on the other hand the classical criterion of faith in Christ, and the sincerity of the works to which it gives rise, is sharpened and underlined.

It was necessary here to take cognizance of the manifold variety in the New Testament witness before seeking to clarify our thoughts about the meaning of Christian teaching on the last judgment. But in contrast to this variety of testimony it is necessary to emphasize, as the one consistent and basic factor implied through it all, the conviction that the conception of judgment flows necessarily from a recognition of the holiness of God. God is He who takes His Will in absolute seriousness, He who is not mocked (9). As union with the divine Will spells salvation, so resistance to it spells disaster.

In the thought of judgment there appears the original divinely constituted connexion of obedience and life. To be with God, in harmony with God, is life, to be against Him is death. The God who reveals Himself to us in Scripture is not light *and* darkness, life *and* death, good *and* evil, like many gods of heathen mythologies; He does not occupy an attitude of indifference "beyond good and evil" (10) because His will has a distinct and determinate aim which excludes its opposite. Even the justification of the sinner would be entirely misunderstood if it were interpreted as implying something beyond good and ill. It means rather—and for this reason it discloses paradoxically the righteousness of God—the expression and effect of the fact that God Himself, by His gracious free gift, realizes His will, in view of the fact that its realization by sinful man has become impossible. From this point of view, evil is not neutralized but concentrated at one point—that of the self-affirmation of the self-justifying man who trusts in his own unaided efforts. The opposite of this attitude is the surrender of this "self-glorying"—unconditional trust in the life-imparting grace of God. Even in this doctrine of the justification of the sinner it is still the holiness of God, identified with His graciously pardoning love, on which the thought of judgment rests. God is nowhere and never neutral, resting in an attitude of indifference with regard to the antithesis holy-unholy, resistance to God and obedience to God: He carries through the one in opposition to the other, and He carries it through against all resistance by means of the process of discrimination and crisis—the process of judgment.

This non-neutral positive purposefulness is so consistently and piercingly the Biblical idea of God that we cannot be surprised that the thought of judgment penetrates unequivocally every section and layer of Holy Scripture. Everywhere the objective fact of judgment stands firm and clear, its when, how, and why is disclosed only in the course of revealing sacred history. Even John does not take his stand over and beyond the thought of judgment; the fact is rather that he transfers judgment to the sphere of the "now already", and does so because "now already" the "yes" or "no" to Christ is decided. Likewise, in the case of the other witnesses to revelation, Old Testament prophets and apostles, who speak of imminent judgment, indeed in the words of the Lord Himself, judgment is but the full manifestation of what is already a secret fact—in which connexion of course God alone knows how at any given time it stands with each individual, whereas men powerfully deceive themselves. Therefore the last judgment is a disclosure in which man becomes exposed to the searching light of God (11).

The fact that a last judgment is in question does not imply a denial that there already exist judgments of God. Rather the latter are being carried out unceasingly, both in the life of individuals and in the history of nations and of humanity as a whole. In this sense Schiller's dictum, "World-history is world-judgment" (12), is completely correct; only we must not forget, in recognizing the fact, that such judgments betray their provisional character inasmuch as those who are the instruments of them involve themselves in new wrong in the very process of executing them, and so make a fresh judgment necessary. The French Revolution was the judgment on the *ancien régime*; Napoleon the judgment on the degenerate revolution, the Holy Alliance the judgment on Napoleon, the revolutions of '48 the judgment on the Holy Alliance, and so on up to our own times. The character of these judgments which arise within the historical process is such as to make ever new judgments necessary.

It is illegitimate to conclude from this: therefore there must be a last, an absolute judgment, however obvious this inference may be. In any event, such a logical inference is not the basis of the Christian belief. Rather the Christian belief in the last judgment, like every other doctrine of the Christian faith, is founded solely upon revelation. Jesus Christ is the revelation of the Holy God, of the God who wills His purposes unconditionally, and hence, with the ultimate realization of His will, terminates the state of affairs in which obedience and opposition to Him mingle confusedly. Hence the exposure of human character must be the counterpart of His own final and full self-revelation in the Parousia. As within the historical process the event of Christ brings about crisis and judgment, so also human spirits are discriminated in the light of Christ. There is no neutrality in face of Christ. The idea of Antichrist which we have already discussed calls attention to this aspect of the movement of history, viz. that neutrality becomes ever less possible, that with increasing clearness the spirits of men are separated by the judgment of Christ. And yet within the framework of history itself a final discrimination is as little possible as is a final conquest of evil. But this temporary stage of confusion must—as a result of the initiative of God, not of men—one day have an end, and will be ended by the advent of Christ in glory. For the two factors—the intermingling of good and evil and the full realization of the divine will—cannot co-exist together, since each is the negation of the other. Hence in the New Testament witness the expectation of the Parousia is everywhere indissolubly linked with the expectation of judgment. Judgment must not only reveal the state of man but also the fact that resistance to God means ruin, obedience to God life and peace (13), and that man cannot dwell partly in the one and partly in the other.

Just as the resurrection puts an end to death, so judgment terminates the state of confusion and obscurity, of inconclusiveness. Judgment spells ultimate decision, and thus ultimate discrimination. For this reason it is understandable why judgment is not only an object of fear but also of hope, as already in the Old Testament we see how God the Judge is identical with God the Saviour and how in one breath God can be praised for judgment and salvation. For the obscurity of the provisional stage, the condition in which the Lordship of Christ and that of Antichrist co-exist, is intolerable. If we may express ourselves in such anthropomorphic terms, it is intolerable for God also in the long run; that He permits the provisional stage of inconclusiveness to last so long is an indication of His patience and long-suffering, and can be interpreted by faith only on the hypothesis that God wills to create opportunities for penitence (14).

Thus the long-suffering of God is the category under which world history falls (15): world history is possible only because God is long-suffering. But by a kind of false anthropomorphism this thought must not be so interpreted as if God would one day tear the threads of patience. As little as the expression "the wrath of God" may be understood in a psychological affective sense, but is meant to imply a strict objective necessity, so also the conception of long-suffering. That one day saturation point will be reached, and it will be necessary to terminate the provisional period, is not rooted in the fact that God will eventually have had enough of it but in the fact that God wills not to leave His eternal plan of salvation unfulfilled, and that therefore in accordance with strict divine necessity the provisional must one day (we know not when) be superseded by the *definitivum*. The vague surmise or intuition—a surmise widespread among many peoples who know nothing of the Christian revelation—that one day all secrets must be disclosed, that a time of final retribution and reckoning must come, is thus in harmony with the divine will as it is revealed in Christ.

The judgment of God is represented to us in the Bible, even by Jesus Himself, and by Him with particular force and vividness, under the figure of a court of judgment and an actual visible separation. We must all appear before the judgment seat of Christ. The figurative character of this expression is obvious; nothing further is needed but that the divine light should pierce man's being so that what is hidden—like the internal parts of the body under X-rays—becomes visible. This again is a metaphor implying the full disclosure of what has hitherto been concealed. "It comes to light"—that is the essence of judgment. It is revealed—not for God:

for how could anything have ever been concealed from Him?—but for ourselves. We shall stand naked and exposed, according to the truth of our being, with no concealing raiment. No dossier, no protocol will be needed. It does no harm if we visualize judgment as an action, but this figurative conception is not essential: the sole decisive thing is the fact of manifestation.

But judgment not only implies a manifestation of what is hidden in man; it is also a matter of crisis and separation. Nowhere is this division of the ones from the others so vividly and graphically represented as in Jesus' parable of the Last Judgment (16), where there takes place a visible separation of the sheep from the goats, the blessed from the accursed, and an allocation of the former to eternal life, of the latter to eternal perdition. It would contradict the whole Gospel tradition about Jesus to refer to the severity of the later church this conception—so odious to the modern man—of an ultimate discrimination and, by contrast, fearlessly to present the preaching of Jesus as being wholly concerned with the religion of love (17). Not only in this impressively clear and unmistakable parable but in many others has Jesus spoken of this final decisive division at the Last Judgment (18). This most solemn of all points of view that can be put before us men belongs to the preaching of Jesus just as much as to that of all His disciples.

How could it be otherwise? God's self-revelation in the Bible is God's call to decision. It permits no neutrality, no indifference. It is a question of deciding for or against God. But again this decision is not a matter of choosing, like Hercules at the parting of the ways, between two possibilities. That is precisely what it is not. God's revelation means that God claims us for His own. It is not to be left to man's free choice to decide whether he will say "yes" or "no". But it is said to him: You belong to God. Man is not placed in the position of an arbiter in the *liberum arbitrium indifferentiæ*—precisely this freedom called indifference does not exist for him. God confronts man with the unequivocal demand that he should recognize and endorse the prior decision which

God has already made concerning him by electing man to belong to Himself. But man must not be compelled to make this recognition, he must perform such an act in freedom. Only the man already emancipated from God in a species of false independence (19), only the autonomous man supposes that such freedom is inadequate, only *he* imagines freedom to consist essentially in the *liberum arbitrium indifferentiæ*, and then, on realizing the impossibility of this, lapses inevitably into a deterministic denial of freedom. But freedom before God consists in the fact that man is to make his own, and assent to, the divine decision that he belongs eternally to God. But in this connexion he should realize that it is not for him a matter of free choice how he shall decide.

It is only this which makes the decision a really serious one—that to man is entrusted, of man is expected, merely the echo, the subsequent completion, of a decision which God has already made about him and for him. Man's freedom is thus set within the limits of personal responsibility, man's decision cannot be a first but only a second word, an answer to the primal divine Word which claims him unconditionally. But that this limitation of his freedom is not something which, if he so wishes, he can overlook, ignore, or dispute, but rather that he would pay dearly for such presumption, that it would in fact be ruinous to him—just *that* is the essential meaning of judgment, of the ultimate, both inescapable and finally valid, manifestation of the truth that it is God's decision, not man's, which is the decisive and irrefragable test, disposing with sovereign authority of man's destiny, determining his salvation or perdition, his life or death, indeed his eternal life or eternal death. Only this thought of *judgment* gives to the thought of *responsibility* its ultimate seriousness, and thus makes clear the relationship between God and man. Apart from the prospect of divine judgment, man may repeatedly misunderstand his freedom as freedom in irresponsibility, as absolute indetermination, and such a misunderstanding of his own being spells his own sin and death. But these implications are only revealed through judgment. If judgment is disposed of in free speculation, then the path is clear for self-misunderstanding; in fact, the denial of judgment is already a decision in the sense of radical misunderstanding, stemming from the presumptuous opinion that only absolute freedom is real freedom. Such an interpretation of freedom is, however, tantamount to a negation of responsibility.

It is nowhere so clear as at this point to what an extent man's thoughts of the future determine his present. For here it is not a question of the fortuitous content of a provisional present; it is a question of the meaning of human life itself. Whether man claims to be himself the controller of his ultimate destiny or whether in regard to ultimate realities he realizes himself to be bound in responsibility, depends on whether he is or is not aware of final judgment. Atheistic existentialism is the philosophy of freedom in the sense of absolute indetermination. That is really a tautology. For to interpret one's existence apart from God means to interpret one's freedom as indeterminacy. But whosoever is aware of his freedom as bound by responsibility is aware at the same time of the fact of the last judgment. Without the conception of judgment all talk of responsibility is idle chatter.

Thus in our thoughts about judgment it emerges clearly how far we recognize God seriously as God, and man as man. If there is no last judgment, it means that God does not take His own will seriously: then God is for us no more than a theoretical hypothesis, a regulative idea necessary for the construction of a unified view of the world. In that case He is not the God of revelation, the Lord God who wills us for Himself, who wills to manifest in us His sovereign excellence as Creator, and therewith our true humanity. On theoretical speculative lines we may well have an idea of God to which judgment is not integral; but such a God is not the God who reveals Himself as the living One and who in revelation makes Himself known to us as the Lord.

Yet in the repugnance to the traditional interpretation of judgment, with its antithesis of the blessed and the accursed —so familiar to us in medieval art, especially the plastic sculpture of cathedral doors—there comes to expression a highly significant insight even though it be perhaps only by way of dim surmise. This static symmetry picturing the two opposites, apparently in complete conformity with the words of Jesus about a last universal judgment, is somehow essentially false. While the picture-symbol shows inevitably this symmetry, the intention of the words of Jesus is quite different. The picture suggests: there are these two alternatives, the one and the other, the salvation of the blessed, the damnation of the accursed; but the Word of Jesus is a summons calling for decision, a Word exhorting to penitence and promising grace. In contrast to the plastic representation, the living Word just does not know this symmetry—notice the linguistically unsymmetrical treatment of those on the left hand and those on the right. The fundamental intention of the Word of Jesus is utterly asymmetrical and anti-static. It is a dynamic Word, a Word implying God's movement towards us with the aim of determining our movement towards Him. The meaning is not: these *are* the two realities. Rather it is: come forth from perdition into salvation. The criterion on the basis of which judgment is passed is not calculated to awaken a sense of security in the pious and of fear in the impious (20), but, on the contrary, to arouse every listener to put to himself the question: am I perhaps among the lost? and also to inspire in everyone the hope—for me too there is the possibility of salvation. For the criterion according to which the sentence is decreed is, simply and solely, quite unequivocal mercy on those who need it. But the criterion is not so presented to us as to suggest that man himself can make the judgment and say: I am among the saved; it is rather that this very judgment is the exclusive prerogative of the divine Judge of the world. Those who are saved do not realize the fact: those who suppose that they are, are not. The point therefore is in any event to shatter the self-assurance, the self-glorying, the obsessional persuasion of the pious, and to leave open for all the possibility of salvation.

But this is the fundamental tendency of the whole evangelical message. It is expressed above all in the tremendous asymmetry of the New Testament preaching, in a lack of logic which must be the despair of all those who make logic the ultimate test of truth, in the fact that we find, alongside the proclamation of judgment implying a twofold issue of world history, a declaration of universal atonement suggesting the opposite. This contradiction has not normally been understood by the church and its theologians because they have striven to attain the ideal of firm doctrine—not to say hard and fast doctrine.

In the attempt to overcome this contradiction, church teachers have almost always chosen one of two possibilities. Some have adopted the teaching of a dual issue of history as it finds expression most plainly in the thought of an ultimate separation of good and evil through judgment and have fitted in the other aspect of the kerygma—universal redemption—by a slight toning down of their chosen doctrine; others, on the contrary, have made the kerygma of universalism the norm and have modified it in such a way as to make room for the thought of judgment. The first solution, when pushed to logical extremes, leads to the doctrine of dual predestination; the second, if consistently emphasized, to so-called *apokastasis* —or the doctrine of universalism.

After speaking of judgment it is necessary to give a hearing to this other element in the New Testament message.

The divine will revealed in Jesus Christ is *Eu*angelion—good tidings of great joy. God wills life and not death, salvation and not perdition. God is light and not darkness. Certainly the world lies in the power of the evil one, and the man who makes himself God is God's enemy, defying God even though he is not aware of it. But into this world which lives in contradiction to God the Son of God has been sent as Saviour, not Judge, not as the King who destroys the rebels but as the King who allows resistance to work itself out in fury against Himself, who takes upon Himself the curse which follows sin as thunder follows the lightning flash, and in so doing imparts a new meaning to the conception of the righteousness of God. For this righteousness of God is pardoning Grace, which is paradoxically called the righteousness of God because in it the revelation of God's will to establish His

Kingdom, the Kingdom of love, comes to complete expression and realization. The righteousness which God *requires*, expressed in the law, has not led to the attainment of this goal. But the righteousness which God *bestows* does lead to its attainment, because its sole ground lies in Almighty God Himself and is dependent on no human achievement.

It is therefore not surprising that the doctrine of forgiving Grace—the doctrine of justification—finds its crown in a proclamation of universal redemption (21). God wills that all men should be saved and come to the knowledge of the truth. "For it pleased the Father that He, Christ, should reconcile all to Himself through the blood of His Cross, whether it be things on earth or things in heaven" (22). "To Him, Christ, has He given a name that is above every name, that at the name of Jesus every knee should bow, and every tongue confess that Jesus Christ is Lord to the honour of God the Father" (23). That is the revealed Will of God and the plan for the world which He discloses, a plan of universal salvation, of gathering all things into Christ (24). We hear not one word in the Bible of a dual plan, a plan of salvation and its polar opposite. The Will of God has but one point, it is unambiguous and positive. It has one aim, not two.

All this is essentially nothing other than the explication of the Biblical thought of God. God is the Lord—therefore He wills that all should be interpenetrated by His Lordship, His honour, his excellence. God is love, therefore He wills to impart Himself to all creatures. God is omnipotent, therefore there can be nothing ultimately to check the realization of His Will. How should the feeble creature in its defiance of God, its "no" to God, show itself to be stronger than God? Must God be content with a situation in which He can indeed bestow His life upon those who open themselves to His sovereign rule or grace but, as regards those who finally resist Him, is obliged to accept a second-best solution—viz. their elimination? Might not hell be considered to be a confession of a merely partial, an imperfect victory?

Thus it is understandable that the aim not to obscure this unmistakable ground-tone of Biblical revelation by any subordinate harmonies leads to the attempt to qualify all affirmations about the last judgment by making the latter an interim affair after which alone that which is truly the ultimate will come (25). Hence the expressions by which the New Testament emphasizes apparently the finality of the last judgment and of the damnation of the reprobate are so interpreted as to impart to judgment the character of a transitional stage, of a pedagogic cleansing process. *Aionios* does not mean eternal, but only eschatological; the inextinguishable fire, the worm that dieth not, the *apoleia*, the destruction, the second death, etc., all these quite unequivocal expressions in themselves are subjected to such a protracted process of exegetical chemistry that they lose the definiteness of their ultimate character. The means of this exegetical chemistry do not stand the test of conscientious examination; we have here evasion rather than exegesis.

What then is our conclusion to be—the word concerning judgment and separation, heaven *and* hell, or the message of universal redemption? Both aspects remain juxtaposed in their harsh incompatibility. We cannot even assign them to their respective witnesses. They stand in the same epistle, in fact in the very same chapter. And the one, by its very absoluteness, logically excludes the other. Which of them is the ultimately valid point of view?

Our answer is: both voices are the Word of God (26). But God's Word—and this we must repeat over and over again to the point of satiety—is a Word of challenge, not of doctrine. Its implication is not: There are . . . As little as the Word of judgment is correctly understood when it is understood in the sense of "There are", so little is the word of universal redemption. The sentence which begins with "There are" is a theoretical sentence making me a spectator, an observer of a certain state of affairs. But the divine Word refuses to tolerate spectators and observers; it is just this customary theoretical outlook of the neutral observer from which it snatches us. It gives us therefore no satisfying information, but it draws us into the heart of a struggle and confronts us with the necessity of a decision, and indeed a decision of a particular kind, a decision in which the act of deciding is taken out of our hands and we are invited to recognize a decision already made about us.

The Word of Scripture is truth but not, as all other truth aims at being, a truth representing an objective condition of things, but formative, subjective, personal, truth which makes me true by making me aware of God in the sovereignty of His love, truth which claims me and moves out to meet me (27), truth in its twofold personal movement: God's movement towards me, the aim of which is to inspire my movement towards Him. To wish to think objectively about God shows a lack of reverence and makes impossible what is the chief thing aimed at: trust in His love.

We must listen to the voice which speaks of world judgment as to the voice of God Himself, in order that we may fear Him; we must listen to the voice which speaks of universal redemption as to the voice of God Himself, in order that we may love Him (28). Only through this indissoluble duality do we grasp the duality of God's being which yet is one: His holiness and His love. All symmetrical, logically satisfying knowledge of God is death-bringing. Hence the criterion of all genuine theology is this—does it lead to the cry "God be merciful to me a sinner!" and, beyond it, to the exclamation: "Thanks be to God, who giveth us the victory through Jesus Christ Our Lord."

Chapter Eighteen

THE END OF ALL THINGS: THE CONSUMMATION

IT is tempting to the Christian thinker, when he draws near to this last and culminating point of Christian doctrine, to lay down his pen and, instead of expounding the ultimate glorification of God in the consummation of the created world (*Doxò-logie*) (1), to hand over to the worshipping and singing church, since obviously hymn and liturgy are far more adapted to perform this doxology. And yet he must not succumb to this natural impulse if he is not in the last resort to be disobedient to his mission. For just this theme raises so many and difficult questions that he must hold on to the very end and not fear the reproach of making into a problem what can really only be the matter for hymns of praise and faith. For after all it is not he who raises the problems, they press upon everyone who withdraws from the atmosphere of worship into the world where the cold light of reason requires us to come to terms with it. It is, above all, in this concluding section, where questions threaten to tangle themselves into an inextricable skein, that we shall only succeed in mastering our task if we rigorously adhere to the rule so far followed, viz. that we are in the last analysis obliged to accept only the contents of Christian revelation itself and not isolated Biblical formulae.

There is nothing easier, and also nothing more unprofitable, than to sketch out a glorious Biblical finale such as has been done time and time again by strictly Biblicist theologians, with the result that we possess dozens or hundreds of such doctrinal schemes claiming to delineate the end of the world, and to follow precisely Holy Scripture, yet all mutually contradictory and evading the questions which a thinking man of to-day cannot fail to raise. The uselessness of such

Biblicist-fundamentalist or orthodox-transitionalist eschatology is at no point so plain as at this culmination. Only a thoughtfulness which sincerely faces the problems raised can hope to perform the service which is expected of theology here above all.

I

On the very threshold of our subject we are confronted by the thesis of those modern critics who insist on an existentialist interpretation of the New Testament: the thesis that all cosmic-eschatological statements of the New Testament form no part of the essential contents of the kerygma but belong merely to the mythical forms in which it is clothed—forms which spring from gnostic redemption myths. In spite of the fact that this thesis bears to some extent a modern stamp, it is at bottom only a new variation of the old theme with which for the last half century the Ritschlian school has familiarized us; that faith has nothing to do with judgments of being but only with judgments of value, and that therefore statements about the world in general do not fall within its scope. After the Christian church has experienced the kind of impoverishment of belief which results from this thesis, it will do well not to let itself be fooled a second time by such axioms.

The thesis alludes in particular to the two passages which have always been the main texts for the New Testament doctrine of the cosmic significance of the Christian faith, and especially for the doctrine of a world-consummation in and through Christ—the two "deutero-Pauline" statements of Colossians 1: 13–23 and Ephesians 1: 9–23. It is supposed that they are based on a gnostic hymn which has simply been worked over in Christian terms (2). Without allowing ourselves to become involved in the subtle but essentially purely hypothetical arguments of such exegesis, we would prefer to put the decisive question, which is independent of such exegetical results: what place has a cosmological affirmation in the economy of the Christian faith? Does the fact that we believe in Jesus Christ as the ultimate personal revelation of God imply anything as to the whence and whither of the world?

The answer to this question is already contained in the confession that Jesus Christ is the revealer of the Creator-God (3). The Gospel of Jesus Christ disintegrates into senselessly disconnected parts if the strand concerning belief in the creation is detached from the web of the whole. The God revealed in Jesus Christ is no other than the Creator of the world, "the Creator of heaven and earth". But the special feature which distinguishes the Christian from the Jewish or any other philosophical-theistic creation belief is this—that it recognizes in Jesus Christ the Logos in a twofold sense as the Logos by whom and the Logos to whom the world was created. In Jesus Christ we own both the ground and the goal of creation, the God who is both the whence of my life and of the life of the world and also the whither of my life and of the life of the world. This is not *only* the statement of the "deutero-Pauline" letters, but stands already quite unmistakably in the First Epistle to the Corinthians (4). The Bible as a whole knows no revelation of God the Redeemer which is not at the same time a revelation of God the Creator. The passages in Colossians and Ephesians only expound with particular clarity and special detail what the confession of the Kyrios Christos includes right from the start. As man in the Mosaic creation story is represented as the crown of creation, so the express image of God (5), Jesus Christ, in whom and to whom He was created, is the corner-stone, the One in whom everything must cohere, because everything from the very beginning was built towards Him and radiated from Him. Even if we had no knowledge of Colossians and Ephesians, we should still know that in Jesus Christ "the mystery of His Will has been declared to us, to gather up all into Him, in heaven and upon earth" (6). As the Prologue to St. John's Gospel states, the objectively necessary implication of the Christian faith is: the Will of God revealed to us in Jesus Christ as the world-ground and the world-origin is also disclosed to us in Him as the world-goal and the world-end.

It may at first sight seem strange to us that, in the two classical texts to which we have referred, the confession of faith in Him who forgives our sins so boldly expands into a confession of faith in Him as the ground and goal of the world. One forthwith inquires: What has this intimately personal event, the forgiveness of sins, to do with the origin and end of creation? It is well that this cosmic expansion allows us to discern something of the offensiveness which the rational man finds in the Gospel message generally. It is certainly not only the modern man who feels committed to modern scientific knowledge and the modern scientific view of the world, who appears to himself to be struck in the face by the New Testament kerygma, and it is certainly not only the cosmological element in the economy of the creed which thus scandalizes him. Rather this cosmological enlargement merely brings out the fundamental offence which the rational man terms the fantastic extravagance of the Christian Faith and which consists essentially in the fact that God is called "Father", "my Father".

The mythical element begins for the untheologically-minded man not only where the affirmation of faith receives this cosmic expansion, but much earlier, where the believer speaks of the Lord of the world as "Thou", as of Him "who names thee by thy name." Worldly lay people know far better than theologians buried in their exegetical problems that myth begins at the point where the Lord of the world is supposed to address me, and I Him, as "thou". A God who acts, a God who forgives sins, is no less mythical for the modern man than the God who in Jesus Christ unfolds to us His world-plan. The crucial cause of offence is: the God who speaks with us. When that has once been understood, then the attempt to make the Gospel intelligible to the man of to-day by means of de-cosmologization, i.e. by the elimination of the cosmic dimensions from the Gospel statement of faith, strikes us as somewhat childish, as an idea emanating from the theological classroom. In a word, the myth consists in the assumption of the living God, "the God of Abraham, Isaac and Jacob as opposed to the God of the philosophers"

(Pascal). The cosmic enlargement of the creed, which is in question, if once the fundamental cause of offence—that the Lord of the world is He who addresses me as "thou"—is overcome, has at most the importance of drawing our attention to a scandal which is already implicated in the message of forgiveness of sins.

Nevertheless, it is justifiable to ask the question why the apostle brings into such close connexion the fact of atonement or forgiveness of sins and those two other facts—the creation of the world and its consummation—as we see is the case in these two classical texts. How can we understand this connexion as fundamental, as grounded in the nature of things?

If we could appreciate the necessity of this nexus, then we need no longer be worried about gnostic prototypes, nor even be impressed by the existence of such prototypes. In truth, this nexus is vital and essential. For sin is that which obscures our view both of our origin and our end. And if I know neither my whence nor my whither, I have no understanding of my being at all. The point at issue is not a purely cosmological question, a question of scientific curiosity, but rather a question of whether I recognize God as my whence—my Creator—and my whither, my destiny. But sin clouds my vision of both aspects; in fact it is, in the last resort, the denial of God as the ground of my being, the assertion of a freedom which is incompatible with dependence on God. If, however, I disown my creation by God, then also the world as the context of my being, as that without which I am not and cannot be, is unintelligible; indeed, the world itself becomes my place of origin, my substitute for God, my idol. The effect of the denial of God as my original ground is that I become enslaved to the world, and my destiny at the same time is lost. Man in his illusion of freedom is always at one and the same time enslaved to the world, immersed in the world, and mastered by the world. He becomes necessarily entangled in its revolving course, he can then understand his being only as a "being unto death". Sin and the fact of darkened origins and darkened destiny are one.

But forgiveness of sins, which we apprehend and believe through faith in Jesus Christ, the Crucified and Risen Lord, as God's word and deed, discloses to our view both our origin and our end. Not only that: human existence, wrenched out of its place in God's scheme of salvation, is once again fitted into the same. By faith in Him we are "rescued from the power of darkness and translated into the Kingdom of the Son of His love" (7). Enslavement to the creature is cancelled, freedom from the bondage of the world is again restored precisely through our dependence on God the Creator, and eternal life is revealed to us as our goal. Thus the revelation of Christ effects both things—the redemption of creation and the prospect of its ultimate perfection. In Jesus Christ, the Revealer and Mediator of reconciliation, the initiating word of creation and the promising word of consummation are heard, harmonized in a unity.

As already stated, the difference between the Old and the New Testament doctrine of creation consists in the fact that only in Jesus Christ do we apprehend the Word of whence—the ground of creation—as identical with the Word of whither—the goal of creation, and that as the one revelation of the Son of God. The creation is understood in the light of its end, and the end for which the world was created can be no other than the goal of human history: "Christ, the hope of glory" (8).

At the beginning of this work (pp. 32 f.) we saw how differently related, in non-Christian and Christian thought, are cosmos and history. The man of myth religions wholly assimilates himself and his history to the cosmic process, he can understand history only as part and parcel of cosmic cyclical revolutions. Something similar takes place in the thought of modern humanity, so alien to Christian belief. It too views man and his history as a tiny and insignificant part of the cosmic process. Of course modern man has given up the idea of cosmic circularity; it has ceased to exist for him ever since the Christian discovery of history (9), but he has no substitute for its metaphysical implications in so far as the belief in progress has been lost to him. Thus he is driven despairingly into nihilism. Thus the cosmic process in which man is engulfed is meaninglessness. The pre-Christian man tried to escape from this nothingness, which began to threaten him in proportion as myth decayed, by means of the philosophy of timelessness. In so doing he rescued his higher self, in virtue of the idea of immortality, but therewith surrendered the element of history and the ultimate significance of the history of mankind (10). Hence we recognize three fundamental possibilities: history engulfed in the cosmos—nihilism; the deliverance of the ego from the cosmos at the price of surrendering history; the inclusion of the cosmos in history through Christian faith.

Before we investigate more precisely this latter, let us examine a supposedly fourth possibility, claimed by theological existentialism—that of a historical faith detached from cosmic implications. Here, as we have already seen, faith in the action of God in Jesus Christ, the Word of atonement proper to the New Testament kerygma, is consciously and sharply divorced from the cosmic dimensions which the New Testament claims for it. What is asserted is faith in the God who forgives my sin in Jesus Christ. Both a backward glance upon creation and a forward look towards world consummation are repudiated as so much gnostic mythology, as a broadening of scope which both obscures the central New Testament kerygma and is also unacceptable to the modern man. The latter point will concern us in a moment. We ask immediately: what are we to think of this faith in itself? I believe in the forgiveness of sins—but I can have no hope in the future, no knowledge of the ultimate destiny of the world. Is it not clear that a conception of history thus detached from cosmic implications necessarily either comes under the judgment that it signifies nothing in the cosmic process, or else is secretly related to an idealistic system of timelessness in such a way that, behind the resignation of eschatological futurism, there persists the idea of immortality? In other words: if it is *not* the Creator and Lord of the world who forgives my sin in Jesus Christ, what can this event of forgiveness mean? With whom have I to do in this forgiveness which Christ mediates?

In what relation stands the God who acts at this point to the cosmic process in which I am involved? But if the God who forgives my sins in Jesus Christ is truly the Lord of the world, as Biblical faith always claims, how then should this fact of forgiveness not be anchored in the origin and end of creation? In point of fact, therefore, it is not really a question of a fourth possibility here, in addition to the nihilistic, the idealistic, and the cosmic dimensions of the Christian hypothesis, but only of a vacillation about relating the forgiveness of sins to one of these three alternatives. This means, however, that this so-called existentialist interpretation of the New Testament must finally decide whether in the last resort it is to be assimilated to nihilism or idealism or whether it is to remain Christian by admitting those cosmic implications.

But is the latter a possibility for men of the modern scientific era? Do the presuppositions of the modern scientific view of the world permit such an inclusion of the cosmic in the historical process?

Once again we would clarify the issue. First possibility: the assimilation of history to the cosmos, which means either the heathen mythology of eternal recurrence or nihilism. Second possibility: the negation of the reality both of the cosmic and the historical process—absolute idealism. Third possibility: the inclusion of the cosmic in the historical process, through Christian faith, implying a unity in the revelation of the ground of creation, the end of creation, and the fact of redemption. The question now is whether this third possibility is at all feasible for the man who accepts the world-picture presented by modern science. We must be clear from the start that what is at stake here is nothing less than the Christian faith in its entirety. If this inclusion of the cosmic in the historical is not possible, in other words, if Jesus Christ is not the *world* goal, then the Christian faith collapses; it can only hover uncertainly between nihilism and idealism until it is absorbed by one or the other tendency. At this point it is really a question of all or nothing, not of an appendix to Christian doctrine which could eventually be maintained or dropped. So much the more serious is the question whether a decisive negative must or need not be the consequence of the modern world-view.

In fact, when we speak of man as the inhabitant of this cosmos with its astronomical proportions, if the individual life is meant, which is but a speck of dust on the earth seen as a speck of dust, in a universe where the diameter of the earth's yearly course around the sun represents only a hair's breadth, a microscopic fragment measured against cosmic standards, then no significance can be ascribed to him. Seen in the light of the objective world-picture evoked by cosmology, man is a *quantité invisible et négligeable.* This means to say that for a type of thought which considers the objective world, the universe as known to natural science, to be the final reality, man with all his faith in God imparting meaning to his life is swallowed up and lost. Within such a world-view even the encounter with a God who forgives sins has only the significance of a beautiful illusion.

Not so for the idealist. For him the enormous magnitude of the universe which science has been discovering since Copernicus has nothing terrifying about it. He feels that he is not in the slightest degree threatened by the fact that as a result man has been continuously dwindling to vanishing point. For he realizes—what Kant called the second Copernican revolution—that for man as subject, the universe with its huge proportions is a mere appearance—perhaps even an illusion. The thinking subject is not menaced by the quantum of the world, nor in the slightest impressed, for it is of course this very capacity for thought which enables man to measure and weigh the world; the subject transcends the object, even though the object be the immeasurable universe. But this second Copernican revolution, which Kant claimed as his own discovery but which nevertheless the philosophy of the Vedanta had completed already three thousand years previously, and which in unbroken continuity has persisted until to-day in the philosophy of Hinduism—such a philosophy of timelessness and the immortality of the human spirit pays dearly for its metaphysical salvation of man through its flight into the sphere of timelessness and its surrender of the historical.

The naïve apocalyptic anthropocentricism of the Judaic world-view, which is bound up with a theocentric faith, gathers the cosmos into history by means of the thought of a cosmic catastrophic *dénouement*, when "the stars will fall" and "the sun and moon lose their light", etc.—this particular connexion between the end of the cosmos and the end of history is not in fact acceptable to us. But what we described as the cosmic implications of the Christian faith point us to a solution of quite a different kind, distinguishable equally from materialist positivist objectivism, from idealist subjectivism (with its surrender of time and history), as also from the dualism of a naïvely anthropocentric world-view and theocentric faith. We shall define this New Testament solution as the theanthropocentric one. The world is not a subjective illusion, nor does it merely exist for me; it exists through and unto the Logos of the Creator—and Saviour—God.

He, the personal Logos of creation, has been incarnated and revealed in Jesus Christ the Redeemer, and He is also the personal Logos inhering in world-consummation. The world was created in Him, through Him and unto Him. The world must be envisaged neither from the standpoint of its ultimate objectivity—which would imply an idolization of the world—nor from that of its subjectivity—which would imply an idolization of the ego—but from the standpoint of the divine Logos, who became man in Jesus Christ. It is a theanthropocentric world. But this theanthropocentricism is not a third philosophical possibility in addition to objectivism and subjectivism, it is identical with the revelation of God in the God-Man and is therefore only possible as an insight springing from faith in revelation.

The God who created the world out of nothing can revoke it into nothingness: "Heaven and earth must become what they were before their creation" (P. Gerhard)—thus writes the pious poet, in the spirit of Scripture. The world is no entity in and for itself, no *absolutum*, as materialism imagines, nor is it a mere appearance or illusion (*maya*), as idealism posits, but the creation of God. It is what and how God wills it to be, it exists so long as God permits it to exist. What we call laws of nature are so many formulæ pointing to the Will of the divine Creator and Preserver.

As the truth was: God spake and it was done, God commanded and it stood fast, so the truth will be: He speaks and it is no more there. But just as little as we can conceive the act of creation from the standpoint of our existence in this world—Fichte is right a thousand times in asserting the philosophical absurdity of the idea of creation—but can apprehend the act of creation only in so far as through the Word of revelation we are carried beyond the limits of the world and as it were from God's point of view, and hearing by faith the fiat of God's creative word, see the world spring forth out of this word—so also by such means alone can we apprehend the end and consummation of creation. But apocalypticism endeavours by fantasy to view the end of the world from within the world, and thereby loses itself in fanciful speculation.

But the message of the Matthean apocalypse is not fanciful apocalypticism but strict revelational theology: "Heaven and earth shall pass away, but my words shall not pass away" (11). The very existence of the cosmos—mathematically speaking—is a function of the Word. Not of the rationalistic logos accessible to unaided human thought, but of the revealed divine Word of the Creator and Redeemer. From that as its living Centre the entire cosmos radiates in a theanthropocentric manner. Not the individual human being, but humanity redeemed in the God-Man Jesus Christ, is the end of the whole cosmos in its unimaginable magnitude. From the point of view of materialistic objectivism this assertion is a delusion, a monstrous over-estimation of man. From the point of view of idealistic subjectivism it is a half-truth, since it does not adequately emphasize the unconditional priority of mind over matter. But it represents the truth which flows of necessity from Biblical revelation: the theanthropocentric faith in the eternal plan of creation and redemption revealed in the man Jesus Christ.

What repercussions has the world-view of the modern scientific man upon the theanthropocentric faith of New Testament Christianity? The answer can only be: none whatever. In so far as science remains science and does not exceed the limits of its own relativity and attempt to become a scientific outlook, in so far as it remains aware of that mystery which it can never pierce—the co-existence of subject and object in man, who lives in time as an indissoluble unity of body and spirit—and this means as long as, in a self-critical manner, it realizes the limits of its own type of knowledge, it will allow the pronouncement of faith to the effect that the world was created by God through the Son and for the Son, so that in Him all temporal existence should reach its completion and crown, as a pronouncement which lies entirely outside the sphere of its own competence and which it can neither confirm nor deny. The critical scholar, however, who remembers that he himself is not merely a scientist but at the same time a responsible man needing love and striving with passionate earnestness to discover the meaning of his own existence, will as a plain human being turn his attention to this testimony of faith, which particularly emphasizes that it springs from a source beyond the limits of human knowledge, and will do so realizing that it affects him as an ordinary human being and not as the possessor of a scientific outlook.

And the critical philosopher, who is conscious of dwelling in the dangerous zone where the thinker's points of view tend to harden themselves into absolute metaphysical systems, will recognize in this confession of the Logos revealed in the God-Man Jesus Christ something essentially different from a philosophy, something which can answer the inexorable demand of the *Logon didonai*, the call to render a reasonable account of itself, only by pointing to a Logos to be accepted as something given—a Logos which speaks with its own intrinsic authority and which itself calls to account all human logoi and philosophies. Perhaps even when he has begun to doubt the ultimate and unimpeachable authority of his own system of thought, and to suspect that the reason which is the instrument of that thought *is* not a master but *has* a master, he will appreciate a little the necessary connexion between faith in God the Creator and the eschatology of world-consummation.

II

What do we mean by the theanthropocentric character of the Christian affirmation of faith and of the Biblical testimony? We have come to formulate this idea in asking the question from what point of view the cosmic can be brought into integral connexion with the historical. First of all, we would establish the negative point that this cannot happen in an objectively naturalist, materialistic or positivistic philosophy for which the objective is the absolute. For objectivism the historical is subsumed in the cosmic, for subjectivism both the cosmic and the historical are engulfed in the timeless eternity of spirit. The integration of the cosmic with the historical takes place solely in the religion whose centre is faith in that which has happened once, and once for all, in history—the event of Jesus Christ. There we find it expressed in the New Testament faith-testimony that Jesus Christ, the revelation of our whence—and of the whence of our world—is at the same time the revelation of our whither and of the whither of the world. We find that this affirmation coheres in closest connexion with the testimony to the redemption from sin effected in Jesus Christ and to His foundation of the church as a fellowship of the redeemed and a sphere in which world-consummation is awaited. And we do not merely find this connexion as a fortuitous circumstance, but through faith we appreciate its necessary and essential character. How could it be otherwise than that the God who in Jesus Christ reveals to us our eternal election also reveals to us in Him the goal and perfection of the creative process?

Not a philosophical speculation but the Word of Him who judges us and forgives our sin is the foundation of the doctrine of the summing-up of all things in Christ, the Head of the church, the ground and meaning of creation. And now we understand why philosophy, which takes its point of departure in an objectivized or a subjectivized world, cannot attain such an integration of the cosmic with the historical. As man's thought it is always necessarily either cosmos-centric or ego-centric. In both cases alike history loses ultimate value either through the impersonality of the cosmos or the timelessness of pure spirit. Only where in the once-for-all historical revelation the living God Himself appoints the God-Man as the meaning of the cosmos, by revealing Himself as the Creator and Saviour, the Origin and End of history, only there is history illuminated as that for the sake of which the cosmos exists. But there we have to do not with man but with the God-Man, not with history as made by man, but with history as made by God. That is the God who from the beginning of creation wills to communicate Himself to the world and to glorify Himself in the world, and purposes the true fulfilment of the creative process by His self-communication to man and self-glorification in man, and who wills that the world in its inconceivable heights and depths should be co-ordinated to this *telos* and attain in this *telos* both its end and perfection.

III

The theme of the end of the world, which so powerfully agitates apocalypticists, is no detached independent theme in the structure of the Christian faith. For these apocalyptic imaginings of an end of the world spring, of course, as has been shown above (pp. 131 f.), from the fact that this world consummation is not conceived radically enough as the ultimate break-up of this whole world of time. We can no more represent to ourselves the end of the world than we can imagine the creation of the world out of nothing. All pictures of apocalyptic catastrophes which have been formed in ancient and in most recent times, and in terms of which the Biblical discourse of the end of the world is expressed, still move on the plane of the created world. But the end of the world signifies an event which can only be compared with creation out of nothingness; and what the Bible is really concerned about is not this negative aspect of ultimate dissolution but the positive consummation in eternity, which can only take place through the destruction of this present world-order; for "the form of this world passeth away" (12).

Only at one point does the negative aspect become an independently emphasized theme: the end means the annihilation of "hostile powers".

Does this talk of such powers belong merely to the mythical world-view of antiquity or does it point to a reality which exists independently of changing world-views? For the typically modern man the living God, the God who acts and speaks, is just as much a piece of outworn myth as these powers of which the Bible speaks. Might not this be an indication that faith in this living God who has revealed Himself in history, in Jesus Christ, implies also a belief in the existence of negative powers? We have shown elsewhere (13) why Christian faith cannot surrender the conception of a supra-personal Satanic power. Evil, opposition to God in the world, is of course directly known to us only as human evil; but a deeper awareness of the power of evil drives us to assume the existence of a supra-personal active centre from which radiates the energies manifest in temptation and seduction. Human sin as the usurpation of a freedom which bursts the limits of creaturely order, and which is therefore a snatching at the being of God Himself, has the effect of bringing us into a bondage to the world, the description or interpretation of which is incomplete without the presupposition of supra-personal negative powers.

We may not simply understand Biblical statements concerning the power of darkness on the basis of universal primitive demonology, because by that means we shall most certainly misunderstand them. There is more insight into spiritual realities implied in those expressions than our enlightened understanding can do justice to. The revolt against God which we term sin and seek to explain to ourselves on the lines of theological-anthropological concepts, has an aspect which eludes description by such formulæ—the aspect of participation in a supra-personal movement of rebellion which alone gives to human sin its irrational depth, its inevitability, its character of slavery or subjection. The purely rationalistic psychological interpretation of the text "Whosoever committeth sin is the slave of sin" (14), consisting in the supposition that the formation of bad habits leads to vice, is utterly inadequate to explain the central feature of sin, which is revolt. That precisely this revolt leads to slavery is a reality which cannot be grasped by the concept of habit. At this point the analysis of sin is confronted by the implications of the "dæmonic", which it is impossible to understand on purely psychological or even collective psychological lines.

The decisive point in the Biblical conception of sin is that it implies an active positive negation, not in the old sense of evil as a passive negative, a mere absence of good, a mistake. But after that has been said and sufficiently emphasized, the other point must also be made which, if made first, would be devastatingly misleading: sin is also sheer nothingness. If God is life and sin a deviation from life in God, then sin is necessarily a lapse into the non-existent. In all sin this grasping at the void, this servitude to what is vanity and emptiness, is a characteristic feature. So also emancipation, the revolt of the creature against the Creator, is the attempt to seize a mere non-existent freedom; likewise the surrender to the lusts of the world, in spite of all satiation by lust, is always also a straining after a will-o'-the-wisp, an illusory image of what is nothing. Sin never really satisfies; behind all saturation and intoxication with pleasure yawns the void. Nay, more: it is as though this very emptiness effected an essential impulse to sin, like the suction effect of the vacuum, the very attraction of nothingness—the magnetic power of death. Flight from being—a general formula for the attractive power of nothingness in sin and death. But nothingness presenting itself as something, as the positive, is the form of manifestation of the dæmonic-Satanical. The latter reigns solely in virtue of this deceiving appearance. In this sense it is correct to say that sin is error: it consists in the illusion that nothing is something, in the illusion that outside the sphere of dependence on God there is freedom, that the abolition of creaturely limitations would mean equality with God, divine being, divine freedom. All sin has its root in this attempt to capture a deceptive freedom, a void presenting itself as something positive. But that this nothingness has power not only to entice but to bind and chain, that it surrounds itself with a pseudo-numinous splendour and can provide for itself a vesture of pseudo-numinous majesty—that is the moment in which the void stands forth most clearly as power, and indeed as a supra-personal positive power.

This dæmonic-Satanic ground-tone belongs essentially to historical existence even though it is not everywhere manifested in the historical process. It has the closest connexion with being unto death. It is like a continuous and deep organ bourdon, above which the historical life that we know moves, and which unceasingly reverberates through other harmonies, at times drowning everything else, and remaining impervious to all human influences—just as much as physical death—not even apparently affected by that radical though concealed revolution which faith accomplishes at the heart of interior personal life. Faith knows indeed that the judgment of annihilation has already been spoken over these negative powers by the atonement effected through the Cross (15), that from the point of view of divine transcendence they are already robbed of their harmful effects: but within historical existence that unique atoning event has not manifested its full operation. The powers of darkness and death are unbroken in their actual effectiveness, and therefore they set specific limits to all renewals of life which the Spirit of God achieves within history: the tares which the enemy sows grow together with the wheat of God (see above, p. 80) until the harvest (16).

For this reason the advent of Christ in glory is primarily a negation of this negation, the destruction of these powers, the elimination of this bass continuo, which as such belongs to the very texture of historical life. It is noteworthy that in the Bible the most immediate effect of the coming of the world of the Resurrection is represented as the conquest of "the *last* enemy" (17): the repeal of the law of death, the final disappearance of the being unto death, which even in the life renewed by Christ, while being covered by that newness of life, still was and remained beneath the covering, an unimpaired reality. This obviously deepest zone in the experience of separation from God and from life is pierced only by the full manifestation of Christ in His glory, by the passing away of the form of this world. Transience is the very mark of the structure of this world, which is destined to pass away. One might almost say that this is the mathematically exact formula of the negation of the negation: the passing away of that which passes away, the death of death.

Faith in Jesus Christ, the Crucified and Risen Lord, means faith in the God who wills to accomplish the abolition of all negations; that is to say, not only salvation *from* the power of darkness, but also the ultimate removal of the latter. As already in the historical message and work of Jesus this struggle against the dominion of powers hostile to God is no subordinate feature but the very heart and soul of the kerygma, the desire to de-mythologize which can only spring from a theology of rationalistic enlightenment, so also the emancipation of human existence from the dominion of these powers, which above all determine the form of this world, is a central and indispensable aspect of Christ's future coming in glory. It is not in itself the consummation, but its underlying and necessary presupposition.

IV

World-consummation as the goal of redemption through Jesus Christ, and as the cosmic scope of the completion of human history in the Kingdom of God, is only slightly indicated in the New Testament witness. The cosmic element in Scripture is always only the framework and the setting of the history of mankind as a whole. Of course we hear of "a new heaven and a new earth". But nothing is said as to what and in what manner this new heaven and new earth are to be, except that "righteousness will dwell there" (18). The negative point is sharp and definite—that "the form of this world passeth away", that death and transience will no longer be (19). But, apart from what directly concerns the new life of man and humanity, the positive side is left almost completely vague. Obviously we need to know nothing beyond the fact that even in eternity there will be a world. For this presupposition is implied in the creaturely status of human existence, even of the perfected eternal humanity which has become wholly like the Christ.

In this connexion the dictum of F. C. Oetinger has often been quoted with approval: "The end of the ways of God is corporeality." In fact this saying enshrines a decisive Biblical "motif", namely, that even the consummation does not mean the cancellation of creatureliness, of the dialogue between Creator and creature, but rather its perfecting. The dictum of Oetinger is meant as a counterblast to the philosophy of timelessness, to the idealism of the Leibnitz epoch. For the precise aim of this philosophy is to dissolve the confrontation of Creator and creature in an ultimate unity. It sees in creatureliness as such, in finitude, in non-divinity, the ground of all evil. The philosophy of timelessness envisages as the goal not fellowship but unity (20). It is monistic even when its monism is not so nakedly expressed as is the case in the philosophy of India which specifically defines itself as *A-dvaita*, as non-duality. Its eschatology therefore can consist in nothing else but the overcoming of duality, of the encounter between Creator and creature.

As against this whole philosophical doctrine of monistic spirituality, the dictum of Oetinger concerning corporeality as the end of the ways of God expresses the decisive characteristic of the whole fundamentally Biblical outlook. Creation is no error, not something which must vanish when God shall be all in all. On the contrary, God wills the creature to exist in contradistinction to Himself. And bodiliness is just the mark of the creature existing in his characteristic difference. Hence it is so important that the conception of humanity, as perfected in the world of the resurrection, should include the aspect of corporeality through the paradoxical idea of the spiritual body (cf. p. 149). In any event it is true of humanity, as Oetinger says, that the perfect is still the corporeal. The end can never mean the dissolution of the individual life in God. That Paul's "so that God may be all in all" (21) may not be so interpreted is shown by the decisive importance of the concept of the spiritual body as the typical mode of being of resurrected humanity.

On the other hand, we cannot regard as Biblically founded Oetinger's view that the perfected world will be very like the earthly world we know (22). For "the form of this world passeth away", heaven and earth will pass away. But what the new heaven and the new earth will be, of that we have no surmise. It must suffice us to know that even in that unearthly plane there will be a world, a whither for our creaturely life, but one in which God's glory is manifested in perfection. Childishly naïve is the supposition that the blessed have their dwelling-place above the stars of heaven ("where the pious shall come when they depart hence in peace . . ." P. Gerhard). To speculate about the heavenly dwelling-places is an idle occupation of fantasy for which the witnesses to Jesus Christ give us no inducement.

On the other hand, the *time*-aspect of the consummation is a direct concern of our eternal hope, firstly, because what we know as time is transience and, secondly, because eternity if interpreted as timelessness belongs to that philosophy which bears a merely negative relation to the historical. We already realize, however, where the solution lies according to Biblical thought: in the conception of the present as time shot through with eternity. Consummation is the perfect present of God. The Biblical symbol for that is the "vision of God face to face" (23). It is, of course, a complete misinterpretation of the Pauline statement if this vision is understood as an expression of an objectivization of the time-world (24). The context in which it appears should guard us against such an error. For the phrase about the face-to-face vision stands in the chapter which has been called the New Testament Song of Songs, whose theme is *Agapé*. This is based not upon an objectivization of the time-world but exclusively upon the idea of the present as transformed by the perfection of communion between personal spirits, the idea of a unity constituted by a fellowship between persons such as overcomes transiency, and which must be the ultimate expression of a doctrine of consummation. We have already (25) gained some insight into the connexion on the one hand between the present and love; on the other, between eternity and love. But the idea of the vision face to face symbolizes the fact that even this eternal plenitude of God's present, this perfect life in His love, is still a personal encounter in which God gives and man receives. For the phrase stands in closest connexion with the passage about knowledge which here below is partial and fragmentary, and there is a mode of knowledge which in reality consists in a being known. Through it too there doubtless echoes something of the original Hebraic sense of knowing which implies the communion of persons.

In this phrase is comprehended a whole theory of knowledge. Our human earthly mode of knowing is always accomplished in an act of our ego, in the subject-object tension. This very fact makes perfect personal communion impossible. For it renders God the object and our knowledge of Him fragmentary. For all knowledge of the object is necessarily imperfect: every apprehension of the object is partial. As long as God is the object of our knowledge it is just impossible to know Him, since He becomes depersonalized and viewed from within our finite perspectives. Rather, true knowledge of God consists in His self-communication—which is identical with love—and which apprehends us instead of our apprehending Him. True knowledge of God is fused with love of God, and there is in fact no knowing Him but only a being known. "If anyone loves God, he is known of Him" (26). At this point the doctrine of justification by grace alone becomes a doctrine of the knowledge of God: we possess the truth as we possess life and righteousness, only as constituted of God and by the appointing of His love. In human language there can be found no more perfect exsymbolic character and understood as a description of an objective event, the idea of this eternal cult must awake in us the feeling of boredom and an impoverishment of life—an impression which even the sublime poet of the *Divina Commedia* was not wholly able to escape when he passed from the description of the Inferno and Purgatorio to that of the Paradiso.

V

A last point remains to be made, one which stands in some degree of opposition to what we have said about theanthropocentricism. "When all things have been subjected to Him, then the Son Himself will subject Himself to Him who has put all things under His feet, that God may be all in all" (32). We might describe this as eschatological subordinationism. But this thought of subordination must never be set in opposition to the *homousios* of the Trinitarian doctrine. It is not of course a question of subordination of being—an inequality of being—but rather a question of subordination in regard to office and work. The Son is appointed by the Father to the fulfilment of a particular office, and with the accomplishment of that office His work of mediation is completed and immediacy must prevail. Scripture is absolutely consistent here, for it never speaks of any decision or counsel or election made by the Son. The subject of counsel is always God alone. But the Son is He through whom the Father sets in operation, and carries into effect, His counsels. And that applies equally to the counsel of creation and to the counsels of redemption and consummation. Everywhere in these matters the instrumental *dia* is used, never the *hypo* relating to the subject. The world is created not *by* but *through* the agency of the Son. It is the Son who is sent by the Father—a reversal of this order is of course never in question, but that fact is highly significant. The creation of the world and humanity is orientated towards the Son, who as Head of the fellowship He has founded is to be the Lord and the Crown of creation—the *kephale* of the *Ankephalaiosis* and the *Caput* of the *recapitulationis*. All that is the theanthropic work. All is co-ordinated symbolic character and understood as a description of an objective event, the idea of this eternal cult must awake in us the feeling of boredom and an impoverishment of life—an impression which even the sublime poet of the *Divina Commedia* was not wholly able to escape when he passed from the description of the Inferno and Purgatorio to that of the Paradiso.

V

A last point remains to be made, one which stands in some degree of opposition to what we have said about theanthropocentricism. "When all things have been subjected to Him, then the Son Himself will subject Himself to Him who has put all things under His feet, that God may be all in all" (32). We might describe this as eschatological subordinationism. But this thought of subordination must never be set in opposition to the *homousios* of the Trinitarian doctrine. It is not of course a question of subordination of being—an inequality of being—but rather a question of subordination in regard to office and work. The Son is appointed by the Father to the fulfilment of a particular office, and with the accomplishment of that office His work of mediation is completed and immediacy must prevail. Scripture is absolutely consistent here, for it never speaks of any decision or counsel or election made by the Son. The subject of counsel is always God alone. But the Son is He through whom the Father sets in operation, and carries into effect, His counsels. And that applies equally to the counsel of creation and to the counsels of redemption and consummation. Everywhere in these matters the instrumental *dia* is used, never the *hypo* relating to the subject. The world is created not *by* but *through* the agency of the Son. It is the Son who is sent by the Father—a reversal of this order is of course never in question, but that fact is highly significant. The creation of the world and humanity is orientated towards the Son, who as Head of the fellowship He has founded is to be the Lord and the Crown of creation—the *kephale* of the *Ankephalaiosis* and the *Caput* of the *recapitulationis*. All that is the theanthropic work. All is co-ordinated characteristic of the Biblical conception of the goal, but also the lack of all erotic symbols for the ultimate and highest bliss.

It is certainly tempting to interpret the symbol of marriage on erotic lines, as medieval mysticism—and still more unrestrainedly the non-Christian mysticism of Asia—has done (30). In the New Testament the feature is completely missing. The reason for this is not the sense that emotional-affective elements should be repressed: in the description of the earthly ecclesia expressions of strong and passionate joy and rapture are not lacking. The reason is rather that erotic bliss implies fusion of personalities, whereas heavenly bliss means a fellowship of persons in mutual encounter. Personal life fulfils in communion rather than union, in the confrontation of persons rather than their merging. Just as the prophets protest passionately against the association of cult and eros—although in the Old Testament there is no ascetic proscription of sexuality—so the erotic must not be used as a symbol of world-consummation. Even for the saints in bliss God still remains the wholly other, the transcendently holy, separated from the creature by the note of distance, to be venerated as the Ineffable and the Highest, and further, fellowship with God can never be interpreted in a purely individualistic way, it is always at the same time through and through social. The erotic is in its very essence a mystery of the individual and private universe—something withdrawn from public and social life. The marriage feast, on the other hand, is the most appropriate symbol of this joyful fellowship, which is stamped with the character of publicity and sociality.

Equally as a symbol of consummation in the Kingdom of God we find the use of the practice of adoration and cultic worship (31). The goal of world history, not merely human history, is the perfect praise of God, in which not merely men but all creatures can participate. A fundamental feature of Biblical teaching is that God seeks to be glorified not only by man but by all creatures. This again has only the value of a symbol for something in itself inconceivable. Divested of its pression of the life of eternity as consisting in the eternal plenitude of God's love, graciously bestowed, than in these verses of 1 Corinthians.

In the traditional doctrine of the church, the expression which stands in the foreground as symbolizing the life of heavenly consummation is that of blessedness, or the beatific vision. But this corresponds much more to the natural human desire for happiness than to anything in the New Testament witness. In New Testament Greek, however, there is not even a word which could be translated "beatific": the idea of beatification does not exist in the New Testament (27). The reason for this is that the consummation, seen from the divine angle, is directed not towards the happiness of man but exclusively towards the realization of the divine will, of God's rule in His Kingdom, of God's purpose in creation and plan for the end (28). Certainly the achievement of this purpose involves as a corollary the achievement of the end of mankind and the end of the historical process. To use once again our key word, Christian eschatology is theanthropocentric. God wills to be glorified in His creation and, above all, in that creature who is able to respond to his "thou" by a spontaneously uttered "thou", for only so can His glory be realized as self-communication in love.

But this theo-centricism, just because it is also the*anthropo*centric, includes the realization of the human desire for life and happiness. In this fulfilment of God's purpose man is not the loser, because the God-Man is the centre and goal of the divine counsels. Hence the perfected end of creation is represented by the symbol of a marriage or festive meal. Again, the New Testament message is called Eu-angelion—good tidings of great joy. This joy consists not merely in the negation of negations, in deliverance from death and sorrow, but includes also the sense of fulfilment of life. "The Kingdom of God is joy and peace in the Holy Ghost" (29). For joy is the obvious accompaniment of fulfilled vocation. The man who has attained the goal whereby the whole purpose of his being is fulfilled cannot be other than happy. Yet not only is the lack of a special word for beatification upon an objectivization of the time-world but exclusively upon the idea of the present as transformed by the perfection of communion between personal spirits, the idea of a unity constituted by a fellowship between persons such as overcomes transiency, and which must be the ultimate expression of a doctrine of consummation. We have already (25) gained some insight into the connexion on the one hand between the present and love; on the other, between eternity and love. But the idea of the vision face to face symbolizes the fact that even this eternal plenitude of God's present, this perfect life in His love, is still a personal encounter in which God gives and man receives. For the phrase stands in closest connexion with the passage about knowledge which here below is partial and fragmentary, and there is a mode of knowledge which in reality consists in a being known. Through it too there doubtless echoes something of the original Hebraic sense of knowing which implies the communion of persons.

In this phrase is comprehended a whole theory of knowledge. Our human earthly mode of knowing is always accomplished in an act of our ego, in the subject-object tension. This very fact makes perfect personal communion impossible. For it renders God the object and our knowledge of Him fragmentary. For all knowledge of the object is necessarily imperfect: every apprehension of the object is partial. As long as God is the object of our knowledge it is just impossible to know Him, since He becomes depersonalized and viewed from within our finite perspectives. Rather, true knowledge of God consists in His self-communication—which is identical with love—and which apprehends us instead of our apprehending Him. True knowledge of God is fused with love of God, and there is in fact no knowing Him but only a being known. "If anyone loves God, he is known of Him" (26). At this point the doctrine of justification by grace alone becomes a doctrine of the knowledge of God: we possess the truth as we possess life and righteousness, only as constituted of God and by the appointing of His love. In human language there can be found no more perfect exthrough the Son and towards the Son as its end—*by* the Father.

But in the end this work must serve the glorification of the Father. Yes, in the Son also and through the Son, the Father wills to glorify Himself. The real object of the *gloria* is the Father—*gloria patris*. The Son is the principle of the divinely human; but the divinely human is not in itself the ultimate. "So that God may be all in all." But that may only be said after the work of creation and redemption has been unequivocally related to the Son. Theanthropocentricism is necessary in order to determine the inter-relation of history and cosmos. If the "God all in all" were emphasized prematurely, it would lead necessarily to pantheism, which means the dissolution of the historical in the cosmic. Only after the historical meaning of the cosmos has been fulfilled, only after the powers of this world have been subjugated to the Son, may the final Word be spoken. Jesus Christ is indeed not only the Head of the church, but also of the cosmos; but Jesus Christ also *has* as His head: God (33).

Yet again this eschatological subordinationism must not be understood to mean that ultimately the aspect of divine self-glorification will be placed higher than that of divine self-impartation—holiness will transcend love. The high-priestly prayer leaves no doubt about the fact that in the same way the love of God, which is the ground and aim of the sending of the Son by the Father, leads equally to the same thought of ultimate subordination. "I have made known to them Thy Name, that the love wherewith Thou hast loved me, may be in them." Despite the unassailable *homousios to patri*, the Trinity is not three-pronged but one-pronged. It is always and everywhere a question of the one God who appoints to the Son His position as Head of the church and of the cosmos, and who therefore is Himself the Head of the Son. Theanthropocentricism flows ultimately into theocentricism. The Father is the whence and whither not only of the creature but also of the Son. This is not to define the Son as a created being. For He is not created by the Will of the Father, but eternally begotten of the being of the

Father. God has given Him "to have life in Himself" (34). He is the One loved of the Father eternally before the foundation of the world, the One who had the Father's glory before the world was (35). Only in Him are we too beloved and elected, only through Him have we part in the eternal consummation. But the subordination of the Son to the Father after the completion of His work in creation and redemption expresses the point that all, even the work of the Father which is in fact founded and completed in the Son, has not its eternal ground in a changeless being but finds its ultimate goal in the Father alone.

Postscript instead of Foreword:

THE PRESENT THEOLOGICAL SITUATION

THE theme of Christ as the hope of the world has been chosen as the principal subject of debate at th next meeting of the World Council of Churches at Evanston.

The choice of theme shows both insight and courage. Insight, because the problem of hope is in fact the essential problem of our time. A church which has no clear and definite message to give on this point has nothing to say at all. For that reason the choice is also a proof of courage, for who would be prepared to guarantee that the church will find such a message? One solution would of course be easy: the simple repetition of Biblical-liturgical and eschatological formulæ sanctified by church custom. But the utter hopelessness of the world of to-day will not be helped thereby. Nor even would it be of service to the church, to believing Christians. For no amount of skill can patch up the tear which rends Christendom and which arises from the fact that for some groups the repetition of traditional formulæ represents a confession, of the ultimate truth of which they believe themselves to be convinced, while others are honest enough to admit that such a repetition of the ancient formulæ is not calculated to silence the doubts and questionings of the modern man. Christendom itself consists of men who share in the questionings of their time, men who can do no other than take note of the changes which modern knowledge has introduced into our picture of the world, and who may even take an active part in this process whereby the advance of science modifies our outlook. Thank God we have not yet to deal with a Christian church whose members consist only of the ignorant and of men who live in an outmoded world-view. But that certain Biblical apocalyptic conceptions are incompatible, whether we like it or not, with this new world-view imposed upon us is obvious. Thus the church is faced with the task of so formulating its hope that it does not confront man with the choice: either science or faith. Where this alternative emerges, it has again and again become clear that theology has neglected one of its principal tasks, which is to formulate the New Testament faith in such terms as to show that it is not bound up with the outlook of a former age but is essentially independent of all changes in our conception of the universe.

Questions arising from the scientific world-view form only one group among the many which agitate the modern man and apparently constitute for him an obstacle in the way of his accepting in faith the Christian message as the church delivers it. The one fundamental task of the theologian is so to understand the Gospel that it answers the questions of men of every "present age". If he does not do this, if he ignores the questions of the man of to-day, then he is ignoring the living man himself and failing to capture his attention. What is the use of preaching the Gospel if it does not reach those to whom the church owes the good news?

The World Council of Churches has appointed a group of men, well known through their work as thinkers in the service of the church, to prepare a message from the church on the theme: "Christ the hope of the world." I myself have had the honour to belong to this group, although circumstances were such as to prevent me from taking part in their discussions except on a single occasion. But from this one ten-day meeting I received the impression that such a theological document as was aimed at cannot achieve the task which is especially required of the modern church: it is unable to penetrate sufficiently deeply into the questions which cause a tension between the modern man and the message of hope in Christ as to succeed in proclaiming convincingly the Biblical word to our modern age. The commission of this group of research-theologians is so much the more difficult to execute, because the necessary preparatory work on the theological side has not been done at all. It is one of the curious features of the theological-ecclesiastical situation that precisely the eschatological question, the question as to the substance of the Christian hope, has during the last two centuries, when so much that is decisive on other theological questions has been accomplished, remained almost completely outside the scope of the debate. It is as though no one had the courage, or felt the inner impulse, to attack this subject with the necessary energy.

One cannot easily over-estimate the contribution which Karl Barth and his co-operators in a narrower and broader sense have made. I think I may say so much, although I myself belong to the circle of those who, at least in the wider sense, may be reckoned among his coadjutors and have been not wholly without a share in the revolution which has switched theology over from the general theme of religion to the particular theme of the Bible—the revelation of God in Jesus Christ. But if we ask what this theology has so far achieved—my own included—for the interpretation of the Christian hope and a new formulation of eschatology, then one must confess with shame and astonishment that at this point a great lacuna is visible. Apart from the very meritorious work of Paul Althaus, which at least in its more recent editions is not uninfluenced by the new orientation of theology, practically nothing of any great significance has been achieved in this field. This is so much the more strange because in the early years of this theological landslide, which was connected with the appearance of Karl Barth's *Commentary on the Epistle to the Romans*, the key-word "eschatology" was of frequent occurrence and formed an integral part of the programme thus inaugurated. But it soon became clear —especially through the critical examination which the work of Folke Holmström, *The Eschatological Thought of To-day*, required—that the type of eschatological teaching which is represented under the title "The Resurrection of the Dead" in Karl Barth's short commentary on 1 Corinthians could do justice neither to the New Testament witness nor to the problems of the modern man.

Then in recent years something of great significance took place. One of the leading New Testament critics of to-day, Rudolf Bultmann, who from the start had belonged to the wider circle of Barth's co-operators and had made the catchword "eschatological" his very own, came forward with a theological programme which was enthusiastically welcomed by some because it at last took serious account of the questions of the modern man, but on the other hand was violently rejected both by the exponents of Biblical-fundamentalist theology and by those of Biblical theology in the Barthian sense, because they could only understand it to imply a surrender of the most central elements in the Biblical Gospel. Bultmann's hypothesis of de-mythologization concerned, above all, New Testament eschatology, and the "interpretation" of it resulted virtually in its elimination. What in Bultmann's view remains over as eschatology is no longer a hope in an eternal future, but merely a new self-understanding for present-day man, arrived at through ultimate decision, and which therefore can only be termed "eschatological" in a sense quite other than that of the New Testament "eschatological"—having reference to the last things. In this re-interpretation the dimension of the future has quite simply fallen out of the New Testament kerygma. While Bultmann, with his distinction between chronicle and sacred history, at least takes the trouble to set the Christian self-understanding of modern man in essential connexion with the saving fact of Jesus Christ—a fact of the past—so that past and present become one in faith, the future is represented only in the sense that man by faith is liberated to create his future, but not in the sense that he hopes for a promised future action of God, a final redemption in the future, a life beyond the grave and a fulfilment of history beyond death. The theology of Bultmann therefore amounts to a faith without hope.

It is thus evident that this theology cannot be accepted as a valid interpretation of the New Testament kerygma. For the interpretation and that which is to be interpreted should at least in essentials resemble each other. A kerygma without hope for the future is certainly not the message of the New Testament, neither that of the Synoptic Gospels, nor yet that of Paul or John. But this does not prevent the fact that the work of Bultmann accomplishes a necessary service for Christian theology—otherwise it would be hard to explain why it has been taken so seriously by German theology as a whole. It has had the effect of a breath of fresh air blowing into a theological situation petrified by orthodoxy. Barthian objectivism showed itself to be dangerous in two respects. Firstly, it was unable to hinder the movement of confessional orthodoxy, and, secondly, it failed to answer adequately the doubts of the modern man. Both weaknesses are rooted in this very one-sided emphasis on the objective aspect of things. The insight of Sören Kierkegaard, attained through his struggle with the Hegelianism and church orthodoxy of his time, that truth is subjective, was overlooked by Barth because his vision was focused exclusively on the overcoming of Schleiermacher's subjectivism, of a false theology of experience. The warnings which some of us have for long been issuing just in this respect were lost in the wind, or suspected as so much synergistic semi-pelagian heresy; for, in the stress of the crisis in which the church was then involved, it was felt that successful endurance could only come from the utmost possible massive objectivity of faith. But once again, as so often before, the extreme swing of the pendulum of reaction has only served to call forth a reaction from the other side—and this has taken the form of Bultmann's subjective existentialist interpretation.

In one sense this hypothesis is thoroughly justified. If theology does not succeed in so shaping the statement of faith that faith is apprehended as a new understanding of life and a transformation of life, then it has neglected its most essential task. It was this which, at the commencement of the theological revolt in the 'twenties, by the renewal of Kierkegaard's questionings, gave such momentum to the new movement in theology. But soon this renaissance was deflected into a one-sided objectivism and at one stroke lost thereby its dual effectiveness: its power to quicken church life and its missionary impulse. But those who recognized the danger of this objectivism and held fast to Kierkegaard's principle that "truth is subjective", in order by so doing to serve the cause of church renewal and the work of evangelization, were branded as mediatorial theologians. The importance which objectivism had won in the struggle for survival of the confessional church did not permit this corrective to exercise its due effect. This objectivist defensive theology led, on the one hand, to confessionalism, and on the other to an isolation of theology over against the world, which in truth was not what the church needed—far too isolated as it already was from the world.

For this reason the assumptions of Bultmann were felt, with some justification, to be a liberating force. Here the attempt was once more made to address the man of to-day, preoccupied as he is with questions which he cannot avoid asking. The aim which has always characterized broad-minded or liberal theology—not to lose sight of contemporary thought—was here approached from a new angle. In this connexion, men could not fail to see that this time it was not a question of the old liberalism which substituted timeless truths for the revelation of salvation in Biblical history, but of a theology which took seriously the saving history, the kerygma of the revelation of God in Jesus Christ, as a unique historical event. Therefore, too, the theology which took as its point of departure the New Testament witness to Christ could not help paying serious attention to this new advance—if only for the reason that during the struggle of the church Bultmann had stood unequivocally and bravely on the right side in line with those who had set their face against the destruction of the Christian church by the people's totalitarian state. Especially the younger generation hailed Bultmann in the correct realization that the objectivism so appropriate for the time of crisis in the church was inadequate for the post-war epoch with its quite different mentality and urgent evangelistic task. Bultmann succeeded in producing something like a theological upheaval, at least in Germany. The effect of theological objectivism had obviously already passed its climax, in spite of the fact that at just the right time it had availed to secure all the strategical ecclesiastical and theological strong points and to hold them up to the present. It will not be possible to check the new and opposing swing of the pendulum by any sort of boycott on the part of church authorities.

Perhaps this new reaction might have been prevented had the programme of objectivist theology not been so rigidly adhered to and had the exigencies of the critical church situation been emphasized as its practical justification. The false security of this objectivism was the reason why the new reaction assumed such a very radical or extreme character. The existentialist interpretation will have to decide sooner or later whether it is to purge itself of the mythological remnants (1) which it still conceals and cast in its lot with a philosophical existentialism which from the outset ignores the datum of a saving history, or whether it is prepared to recognize that existentialist interpretation must be something other than mere elimination. And this matter will be decided above all at the point which forms the problem of our time: the hope of the future. Up to now, as we have already suggested, Bultmann's new existentialist interpretation of the kerygma involves an elimination of the dimension of the future. If it persists in this elimination, it will result inevitably in a dissolution of the Christian faith, since, in this form, it will not be able to escape the consistent "de-kerygmatization" (the new catchword already coined by F. Buris) which is already being demanded by extreme liberals. Hence the decisive question to-day is the attitude adopted towards New Testament eschatology. If we cannot succeed in formulating the New Testament hope of the future in such a way as does justice to the reasonable demands of existentialists, and especially so as not to bring it into conflict with the modern scientific view of the universe, then the lapse into a boundless liberalism which has lost all connexion with the sacred-historical revelational faith of the Bible is unavoidable, and the maintenance of the Biblical faith will be committed to the keeping of an already sufficiently precarious fundamentalism.

That is the point at which our own study enters the field of discussion. Instead of continuing the already interminable and to some extent fruitless debate about the rights and wrongs of Bultmann's hypothesis, it develops the theme by daring the attempt to give an interpretation of Biblical eschatology as the hope of the future and eternal, which is as completely dissociated from the ancient view of the world as it is faithful to the Biblical testimony to this hope. This outline of an eschatology claims to be as definite and penetrating an existentialist interpretation (2) of the New Testament witness, as it holds fast by integrity of theological thinking to the Pauline and New Testament hope of the future. Its basis is the new orientation of temporal existence in its three dimensions, past, present and future, which takes place through the unique event of the Christ. From this recognition there flows on the one hand the impossibility of detaching the aspect of future expectancy from the Christian faith without destroying its total structure and meaning, and on the other hand the non-essential character of all Jewish apocalyptic and Gnostic mythical elements, which are reconcilable neither with the modern world-view nor with the central features of the New Testament kerygma. Such an interpretation of the primitive Christian hope is based on the insight that the revelation of God in the Son of God and the Son of Man, Jesus Christ, sets history above the cosmos without necessarily surrendering the cosmic implications to the process of de-cosmologization. I am as certain that this is the right path as I do not doubt that this outline takes us only one step forward along it, and that in detail there are consequently to be found in it many imperfections and probably mistakes also. But I may hope that thereby I have occupied the position transcending both objectivism and subjectivism which I postulated fifteen years ago in my brochure *Truth as Encounter* ("*Wahrheit als Begegnung*").

It remains to be seen whether existentialist subjectivism has already so hardened into a dogmatic scepticism as to reject this attempt right from the start as so much mythology, or whether it is still sufficiently alert and sensitive as to accept the criticism which is here addressed to its elimination of hope in a future consummation. It will also be seen whether theological objectivism has already developed into a church orthodoxy which neither needs nor is capable of receiving any corrective, or whether it has retained sufficient of its original Kierkegaardian subjectivity as to be willing to accompany us along this path which leads to the New Testament, i.e. to theological-existentialist, eschatology.

But this eschatological study was not attempted primarily in view of the theological situation, but arose on the one hand from the crying need of church life; on the other, from the exigencies of a type of thought which was conscious of its obligations towards the message of the Bible. It rests upon the conviction that a church which has nothing to teach concerning the future and the life of the world to come is bankrupt. Co-operation in the work of the ecumenical commission made this theological task undertaken by an individual seem so much the more urgent. Since my first visit to the Far East (1949–50) I have worked unremittingly at this most thorny problem of the final volume of my *Dogmatics*, promised seven years ago already, but again and again I felt obliged to pause, since I could not satisfy myself that I was doing justice to the twofold postulate of loyalty to the Bible and the needs of the present hour. For this, no doubt, the great personal sorrow was needed which came to me last summer through the tragic experience of losing my son in the railway accident of Bevers, and as a direct result of which this theological problem became for me a burning issue of personal life. The matter was clinched by a circumstance which compelled me to publish this concluding section of the last volume of my *Dogmatics* before the publication of the work as a whole: I refer to my appointment which took place in February, 1952, to the International Christian University of Tokio, in which I recognize something more than a call of men. But it was impossible to produce as a whole the final volume of my *Dogmatics* before the autumn of this year, when my work in the Far East is to begin. Thus to the first excursus, which took shape as a small book, *The Misunderstanding of the Church*, in the summer of 1951, there is now added this second one as a further preparation to the concluding volume of my *Dogmatics*, which I shall not be able properly to take in hand until after my return from Tokio in three years' time.

This outline of an eschatology is not only the product of a theology which is concerned to express, in terms of contemporary thought and without substantially modifying it, what the apostles proclaimed to their day and generation as the great abiding hope, but is also, quite as much, the fruit of the wrestlings of a simple believing Christian who, assailed by the sorrowful experience of death, has sought the consolation of the Gospel. In this process he came to realize that the Gospel offers no comfort to the individual which is not at the same time a promise for the future of mankind as a whole. This unity of the personal with the universally human—the *leitmotif* which runs like a thread through my theology as a whole—is, together with what is expressed in the title, viz. the indissoluble unity of what faith now enjoys and what it hopes for as the future and eternal consummation, the chief content of this work. May it thus serve the purpose of inducing modern humanity, so bankrupt of hope, to turn to the Gospel and to its great promise for the future, which offers the only solution to the hopeless position of the world to-day. May it above all in some degree accomplish the most direct service which a theological work should perform, that of helping the preacher of the Gospel to proclaim to modern humanity this great hope.

In conclusion, it still remains for me to thank the new director of the Zwingli publishing house, Mr. Otto Salomon, for his counsel, and my friend Pastor H. U. Spycher, of Neuhausen, for the fact that he has relieved me of the work of supervising the printing and correcting proofs at a time when I am already beginning my journey to the Far East.

ZÜRICH,
August, 1953.

NOTES

CHAPTER TWO

(1) John Baillie, *The Belief in Progress*, 1950, furnishes an excellent guide to the history of the idea of progress. See also *The Idea of Progress, an Inquiry into its Origin and Growth*, by J. B. Bury, 1920.

(2) Baillie draws attention particularly to Lucretius, who in his *De Rerum Natura* reflects on the superiority of Græco-Roman culture to the barbaric cultures of the surrounding world and of former times. Cf. also C. Cochrane, *Christianity and Classical Culture*, a study of thought and action from Augustus to Augustine.

(3) I have developed these thoughts in the essay *Das Einmalige und der Existenzcharakter* (1929, Blätter für deutsche Philosophie) in counter-action to Ernst Cassirer's *Philosophie der symbolischen Formen.* Recently such ideas have been most powerfully expounded in O. Cullmann's *Christ and Time*, 1946, clearly without knowledge of my own work.

(4) So much may be said because it is not Judaism but Christianity which has shaped the thought of Western Europe. For the relation between the two, see below, p. 34.

(5) Cf. Baillie *op. cit.*, p. 108ff, where he quotes from Bury: "What Saint Pierre did was to combine Bacon's and Descartes' belief that increase in knowledge was the secret of moral and social progress with Fontanelle's belief in the inevitability of the former."

(6) E. Hirsch, *Die Reich-Gottes-Begriffe des neueren europäischen Denkens*, 1921, Ferner ; E. von Sydow, *Der Gedanke des Ideal-Reiches von Kant bis Hegel*, 1914.

(7) Most clearly in Schleiermacher's *Entwurf eines Systems der Sittenlehre.*

(8) The teaching about the succession of religious metaphysical and scientific stages of thought can be interpreted in Aug. Comte's system as a connecting link between idealistic and naturalistic evolution. Comte's positivism is still impregnated by Christian humanistic values, as can be seen from his *Religion de l'Humanité*. Nor is Spencer a pure naturalist. In his idea of differentiation there persist unconscious idealistic-theological remnants.

(9) Among those who never allowed themselves to be dazzled by the belief in progress belong especially the two great historians of the middle of the century, Leopold von Ranke and Jacob Burckhardt. In what follows, cf. the penetrating criticism of the belief in progress made by Reinhold Niebuhr, *Faith and History*, 1951, and his studies in American history, *The Irony of American History*, 1952.

(10) Cf. my *Revelation and Reason*, p. 379 (German edn.).

(11) Cf. Aldous Huxley's novel of the future, *Brave New World*, which has for its theme totalitarian human selection.

CHAPTER THREE

(1) Luther still uses the word 'future' exclusively in the theological eschatological sense: the advent of the Kingdom of God, of the Lord. According to the

oral information given me by a great Indo-Germanic and Semitic scholar, J. Hausheer, such a connotation of the idea of the future occurs, outside the Christian West, only in Avestic Persia, i.e. in the field of another eschatological religion.

(2) *Glaubenslehre*, § 159.

(3) *Kritik*, etc., Part I, Book II, § 2.

(4) Martin Kähler, *Die Bedeutung der letzten Dinge*, Dogm. Zeitfragen II, p. 496.

(5) *Glaubenslehre*, Introduction, § 11.

(6) It occurs of course as a historical reality in the great fanatics who "made history".

CHAPTER FOUR

(1) Cf. Glasenapp, *Die fünf grossen Religionen*, 1951.

(2) Cf. Weizsäcker, *Geschichte der Natur*, 1948.

(3) I have developed this whole sequence of ideas in my essay *Das Einmalige und der Existenzcharakter*, 1929.

(4) A causal connection between Israel's revelation through history and that of Zarathustra has become most improbable since the date of Zarathustra has been moved back to about 1000.

(5) Zarathustrianism has no doubt direct historical successors, but they all belong to the type of cyclical heathen religions.

(6) This vagueness in the conception of the eschatological goal of history was recognized also by Calvin, the great exegete of the Old Testament, *Institutio* II, 11: *de differentia testamentorum.*

(7) Luke 3: 1.

(8) John 1: 14.

(9) The meaning of this *eph hapax* is plainly appreciated in Rom. 6: 10; 1 Pet. 3: 18; Heb. 7: 27, 9: 28.

(10) Niels Ferré has misunderstood in his otherwise very estimable book, *The Christian Understanding of God*, 1951, p. 173, my idea of uniqueness as I developed it in 1927 in my work *The Mediator*. The uniqueness of the revelation of atonement does not preclude the idea that this revelation must be repeatedly purified and ever renewed by the Holy Spirit.

(11) That is an insight which has passed into general currency through Rickert's work, *Die Grenzen der naturwissenschaftlichen Begriffsbildung*, 1896. Cf. also, on this point, Collingwood, *The Idea of History*, 1946, about Rickert.

(12) Cullmann gives an account of how that has happened, p. 13.

(13) Mohammed claims only to be a prophet, the Buddha plays no part as a personality in his own teaching.

(14) Heb. 7: 27; Phil. 2: 6ff; Isa. 53.

(15) Rom. 1: 5; 16: 26.

(16) Rom. 5: 12ff.; 1 Cor. 15: 45ff.

(17) Precisely this sense of the absolutely historical, as of the absolutely human, distinguishes it from Judaism and its derivative, Islam.

(18) The physicist v. Weisäcker, on the other hand, calls the absence of the historical in nature an optical illusion resulting from the smallness of our time-span. Again, he calls the law of entropy (the second main law of thermodynamics), which teaches the irreversibility of natural processes, the law of the historicity of nature; *op. cit.*, p. 16.

(19) This danger is obvious in Spengler, but even in so great a historian as Toynbee the tendency to discover laws is evident to a degree that is dangerous for pure history.

(20) Cf. G. Schrenk, *Die Geschichtsanschauung des Apostels Paulus auf dem Hintergrund seines Zeitalters*, Jahrb. d. theol. Schule Bethel, 1932; Wendland, *Geschichtsanschauung und Geschichtsbewusstsein im Neuen Testament*, 1938; Delling, *Das Zeitverständnis des Neuen Testaments*, 1940.

CHAPTER FIVE

(1) *Les Données Immediates de la Conscience*, 1889.
(2) 1916.
(3) 1927.
(4) K. Heim, *Zeit und Ewigkeit*, in *Glaube und Leben*, 1928; W. Schmidt, *Zeit und Ewigkeit*, 1927; E. Brunner, *Das Einmalige und der Existenzcharakter*, 1929.
(5) O. Cullmann, *Christ and Time*, 1946.
(6) Cullmann, *op. cit.*, p. 55 (German edn.).
(7) Heim, *op. cit.*, p. 555.
(8) Cullmann, *op. cit.*, p. 42 (German edn.).
(9) Augustine, *Confessions*, XI: 15.
(10) Bergson, *op. cit.*, and *Evolution créatrice.*
(11) I understand from personal talks that the idea of the inclusion of the eternal within the time series is an essential element in the theology of H. H. Farmer, of Cambridge.
(12) If I am not mistaken, the idea of the "once-for-all" as the category of Christian revelation was used for the first time in my book, *The Mediator*, 1927, pp. 84, 129ff. (German edn.).
(13) In spite of Cullmann, the thought of the pre-temporal exists in the New Testament; cf. 1 Cor. 2: 7.
(14) Ps. 139: 16.
(15) Rom. 6: 11.
(16) Rom. 8: 38ff.
(17) Rom. 7: 25.
(18) John 3: 36, 6: 40, 47, 54.
(19) John 11: 26.
(20) Col. 3: 3.
(21) 1 John 4: 8.
(22) 1 Cor. 13: 13.
(23) 1 John 4: 15.
(24) Gal. 5: 6.
(25) 1 Cor. 12: 31.
(26) Rom. 5: 5.
(27) *Confessions*, XI: 15.
(28) Cullmann, *op. cit.*, p. 55 (German edn.).
(29) Cullmann, *op. cit.*, p. 39–41 (German edn.).
(30) Cullmann, *op. cit.*, p. 41 (German edn.).
(31) Ps. 90: 4.
(32) Gunkel, *Schöpfung und Chaos in Urzeit und Endzeit*, 1895.
(33) 1 Cor. 15: 45.
(34) 1 Cor. 8: 6.
(35) For the following, cf. *The Christian Doctrine of God*, Dogm. I, pp. 323ff. (German edn.).
(36) Gal. 4: 4; Eph. 1: 10. In the former text this expression denotes the historical revelation of Christ, in the latter the goal of saving history.
(37) *Dogmatik*, I, p. 150.
(38) Rom. 8: 31.

(39) John 17: 24.
(40) Rom. 5: 5.
(41) 1 Cor. 13: 13.
(42) Heim, *op. cit.*, p. 558.

CHAPTER SIX

(1) W. Kümmel, *Verheissung und Erfüllung*, 1945; the same, *Kirchenbegriff und Geschichtsbewusstsein in der Urgemeinde und bei Jesus*, 1943.
(2) Cf. my *Misunderstanding of the Church*, 1951.
(3) C. H. Dodd, *The Apostolic Preaching and its Developments*, 1936.
(4) *History of the Research into the Life of Jesus.*
(5) Ed. Schweizer, *Gemeinde nach dem Neuen Testament* (Theol. Stud. ed. Barth, No. 26); Cullmann, *op. cit.*; Kümmel, *op. cit.*
(6) Bultmann, *Neuen Testament und Mythologie*, in *Kerygma und Mythus*, ed. Barthsch, 1951.
(7) This is especially emphasized by Ed. Schweizer, *op. cit.*
(8) Rom. 12: 1.
(9) Gal. 5: 18.
(10) Rev. 21: 5.
(11) 1 Cor. 3: 9; 1 Thess. 3: 2.
(12) 2 Cor. 5: 17.
(13) Mark 2: 5.
(14) John 3: 3.
(15) Cf. on this point my *Misunderstanding of the Church.*

CHAPTER SEVEN

(1) 1 Cor. 1: 5; Eph. 4: 15.
(2) Eph. 4: 13.
(3) Acts 2: 41.
(4) Matt. 28: 19; Mark 16: 15.
(5) Col. 3: 3.
(6) Gal. 5: 22.
(7) Cf. Richard Niebuhr, *The Kingdom of God in America*, 1937, and my small essay, *Die denkwürdige Geschichte der Mayflower Pilgerväter*, 1920.
(8) *De Civitate Dei*, XX, 7, 9.
(9) Although he opposes the Utopian socialism of his predecessors and sets over against it his own scientific socialism, he is a typical Utopian and Chiliast in so far as he views history in the light of the vision of an ultimate condition of humanity (H. Barth, *Wahrheit und Ideologie*, 1945, p. 145). This ultimate condition—that of a classless society—is the one in which society "produces man in the whole richness of his being—the richly developed, deeply wise man which is its abiding product." (Marx Engels.)
(10) 1 Cor. 15: 58.
(11) *Confessio Augustana*, art. 17.
(12) *Confessio Helvetica posterior*, cap. 11.

(13) Gottfried Keller's justly famous poem *Faith of Spring*, of course, falls under this judgment also:

> The song of universal peace,
> Of the ultimate felicity of man,
> Of the golden age when some time
> Dreams will be realized on this earth.

In spite of his adjuration:

> Whoever gave up that hope
> Cheated by lying fear
> Would be better unborn,
> For already he lives in the grave.

(14) Richard Niebuhr, *The Kingdom of God in America*, is absolutely right in the opinion that the best things in American culture and society can be traced back to the stream of Christian idealism which flowed into the American continent in the seventeenth century.

(15) Cf. the article "Communism" in the *Prot. Realenzykl.*, X, 657. The Christian communist settlements which still exist to-day live only as a result of their complete isolation from the world.

(16) Matt. 13: 24ff.

CHAPTER EIGHT

(1) Matt. 24: 21ff.

(2) The unspirituality of technocracy dominates not only the communistic totalitarian state but also prevails in the democratic West. But up to the present the still living will to freedom and respect for human dignity prevents the extreme consequences of this development. If the process of secularization in thought should go further, however, even the democratic West would necessarily become assimilated to the totalitarian West.

(3) 2 Cor. 11: 14.

CHAPTER NINE

(1) The denial of any essential meaning in life and the challenge to give life meaning through free personal decision is the basic thought of the existentialism of J. P. Sartre. But even Heidegger's *Eigentlichkeit* is not essentially different unless one understands *Sein und Zeit* in purely formal terms as R. Bultmann obviously does.

"A life first becomes independent when it owes its essence to itself." "My life has its ground necessarily outside itself so long as it is not its own creator." (Marx Engels, III, 124.)

(2) "The more man commits to God, the less he holds for himself" (Marx Engels, III, 83). The system of Marxian philosophy is obviously: To man's real dependence on the forces of society in the pre-communist state, corresponds faith in God as the ideal or ideological projection of this condition of things and that God is the invention of his own brain: men who are thus enslaved by a power really alien to them imagine this oppressive force to be the trickery of the so-called World-Spirit.

(3) 2 Cor. 4: 6.

(4) 2 Cor. 4: 14; Phil. 1: 23.
(5) John 19: 5.
(6) John 18: 36.
(7) Cf. the development of this thesis in the work of the biologist Leconte du Nouy, *Die Bestimmung des Menschen*, 1948.
(8) 1 John 3: 2.
(9) 1 Cor. 8: 6; Col. 1: 16ff. See the concluding chapter of this book.
(10) 2 Cor. 5: 7.
(11) Rom. 5: 5.
(12) Rom. 8: 39.

CHAPTER TEN

(1) 1 Cor. 15: 17.
(2) Reinhold Niebuhr is certainly right when, in opposition to the romantic tendency to idealize the Christian Middle Ages, he constantly stresses the relativity of all such judgments with regard to the history of ideas. In spite of that, a sentence like the above is simply indisputable.
(3) Cf. the truly apocalyptic prophecy in *Die Fröhliche Wissenschaft*, Book V, No. 343.
(4) Cf. K. Löwith, *Nietzsche und die Philosophie der ewigen Wiederkehr des Gleichen*, 1935.
(5) Cf. my anthropology in *Man In Revolt.*
(6) H. Thielicke, *Tod und Leben.* Unfortunately this extremely significant essay has not yet met with the attention it deserves.
(7) So already in his first novel, *La Nausée*, and still more openly in the play *Lucifer and the Lord.*
(8) 1 Cor. 15: 32.
(9) Cf. the collection of essays by ex-Communist authors under the title *The God Who Failed.*
(10) There is no doubt a sort of Buddhistic nihilism which, for example, in modern Japan finds literary expression. But as far as I can see it is characterized by the fact that it is always bound up with religious mysticism and thus plainly distinguishes itself from the crass nihilism which has developed in the West from Russian antecedents.

CHAPTER ELEVEN

(1) Cf., above all, the classical work of F. A. Lange, *Geschichte des Materialismus.* Further, P. Apel, *Die Ueberwindung des Materialismus*, 1909; von Weizsäcker, *Zum Weltbild der Physik*, 1943.
(2) L. Busse, *Geist und Körper*, 1911; K. Heim, *Die Wandlungen im naturwissenschaftlichen Weltbild*, 1951.
(3) Cf. N. Söderblom, *La vie future d'apres le Mazdéisme à la lumière des croyances parallèles dans les autres religions*, 1901.
(4) Cf. the controversy between Carl Stange and Paul Althaus concerning the doctrine of immortality in Luther. Stange, *Zur Auslegung der Aussagen Luthers über die Unsterblichkeit der Seele*, and *Luther und das fünfte Laterankonzil*, 1928. Althaus, *Luther und das fünfte Laterankonzil*, 1928; *Unsterblichkeit und ewiges Leben bei Luther*, 1930. In addition, Stange, *Das Ende aller Dinge*, 1930; Althaus, *Die letzten Dinge*, 4th edition, 1933.

(5) Above, p. 93.
(6) Rom. 6: 23.
(7) Ps. 90: 7.
(8) 1 Cor. 15: 26.
(9) Col. 3: 3.
(10) 1 Tim. 6: 16.
(11) John 1: 2; 1 John 1: 1.
(12) That is the content of Kierkegaard's *Philosophical Fragments.*
(13) Luther, *Werke*, 43, 481, 32ff. (*Weimarer Ausg.*).
(14) Cf. my *Man In Revolt*, pp. 164ff. (German edn.).

CHAPTER TWELVE

(1) 1 Cor. 2: 2.
(2) 1 Cor. 11: 24.
(3) Rom. 3: 25.
(4) The idealistic doctrine of the divinely immortal self is the most sublime form of this evasion. (Brunner here encloses in inverted commas the word *kneifen*—a slang duelling term, meaning to shirk an engagement to fight a duel. *Tr.*)
(5) So Calvin, *Institutio*, III, 2, 7.
(6) Rom. 6: 8; Col. 3: 3; Gal. 2: 21.
(7) Rom. 6: 4.
(8) Bultmann, *Kerygma und Mythos*, I, p. 46.
(9) A. Schweitzer, *Die Mystik des Apostels Paulus*, 1930.
(10) This unity of immediacy and mediation is particularly clear in Gal. 2: 19–21.
(11) See my *Misunderstanding of the Church*, pp. 53ff. (German edn.).
(12) John 3: 36; 6: 47; 11: 25.
(13) 1 Cor. 15: 31.
(14) 1 Cor. 15: 55ff.
(15) Phil. 1: 21.
(16) 1 John 3: 14.
(17) Col. 3: 3, 4.

CHAPTER THIRTEEN

(1) The discussion of this problem raised by R. Bultmann is now in essentials summarized in the two volumes *Kerygma und Mythos*, published by Bartsch, 1951–52.
(2) 1944.
(3) Bultmann, *ibid.*, I, p. 18.
(4) Cf. my *Christian Doctrine of God*, Dogm. I, pp. 255ff. (German edn.).
(5) Thus recently in the outstanding work of Paul Tillich, *Systematic Theology*, 1951.
(6) Between the scientific world-view of the nineteenth and that of the twentieth centuries the great difference is that the nineteenth century taught the infinity of time and space, the twentieth century their finitude. The scientific myth of endless space and time—like that of the absolute object and absolute causality—has been exploded. Cf. in this matter von Weizsäcker, *Zum Weltbild der Physik*, and Karl Heim, *Die Wandlungen im Naturwissenschaftlichen Weltbild*, 1951.
(7) R. Prenter in *Kerygma und Mythus*, Vol. II, p. 74.

(8) So Albert Schweitzer in *Die Weltanschauung der Indischen Denker*, 1935.
(9) So F. Buri in *Kerygma und Mythus*, II, pp. 85ff. The new catchword and linguistic monstrosity is "*De-Kerygmatization*".
(10) Matt. 24: 29.
(11) 1 Thess. 4: 17.
(12) Cf., for example, in this respect the monograph *Jesus kommt wieder*, G. Wasserzug, Beatenberg, 1952.
(13) Mark 13: 32.
(14) Matt. 24: 14.
(15) *Christ and Time*, pp. 122ff. (German edn.).
(16) This thought occupies a very important place in the work of the two Blumhardts and, especially, in that of Johann Christoph.
(17) Cf., for example, the report on the ecumenical conference of Zetten, *Hoffnung in der Bibel*—Ecumenical Studies, No. 5, p. 16: "What the English said seemed to the continentals pure gnosis or Platonism, while the continentals seemed to the English to be pure apocalypticists."
(18) Especially has F. Holmström's *Das eschatologische Denken der Gegenwart* addressed this criticism towards the Platonizing eschatology of earlier dialectical theology and that of Paul Althaus in its earlier stages, and thus exercised a salutary influence on theological development.
(19) *History of the Research into the Life of Jesus*, p. 407 (German edn.).
(20) Bultmann, *op. cit.*, p. 205.
(21) 2 Cor. 5: 7.

CHAPTER FOURTEEN

(1) John 1: 14.
(2) Jer. 31: 31.
(3) Matt. 11: 3.
(4) 1 Pet. 1: 3.
(5) 1 Cor. 15: 17.
(6) 1 John 3: 2.
(7) 1 Cor. 13: 12.
(8) 1 Thess. 4: 17.
(9) Matt. 26: 64.
(10) Matt. 24: 27.
(11) Heb. 13: 8.
(12) Rev. 1: 8.

CHAPTER FIFTEEN

(1) Matt. 22: 32.
(2) Matt. 28: 20.
(3) Matt. 18: 20.
(4) Bultmann, *op. cit.*, I, p. 46. The objections which K. Barth raises to Bultmann's subjectivism (KD, III, 2, pp. 531ff.) have by no means been overcome by the "kritische Prüfung der Haupteinwände Barths gegen Bultmann", *Kerygma und Mythos*, II, pp. 113ff. On the other hand, I can see no clarification of the discussion in K. Barth's *Rudolf Bultmann, Ein Versuch ihn zu verstehen*, 1952, but only an obscuring of the situation.
(5) *Op. cit.*, I, p. 20.
(6) Cf. K. Heim, *Weltschöpfung und Weltende*, 1952.

(7) Cf. G. Spoerri, *Das Inkoordinable*, 1929.
(8) John 20: 25.
(9) Luke 24: 13ff.; Acts 9: 3ff.
(10) Cf. Ellwein, *Vom Neuen Leben*, 1925. The attempt to bring out the Lutheran restraint (the *novitas vitæ*) in its full New Testament value is made in A. Nygren's *Romerbrief Kommentar*, 1951, especially in his exegesis of Rom. 7.
(11) Rom. 8: 29.
(12) 1 John 3: 2.
(13) 2 Cor. 3: 18.
(14) Rom. 8: 2.
(15) 1 John 3: 14.
(16) Rom. 8: 11.
(17) 1 Cor. 15: 31.
(18) Gal. 2: 20.
(19) Rom. 8: 38.
(20) Cf. above, p. 111.
(21) Phil. 1: 21.
(22) Phil. 1: 23.
(23) 1 Cor. 15: 55ff.
(24) Matt. 22: 32.
(25) Isa. 43: 1.
(26) 1 Cor. 15: 44ff.
(27) *Op. cit.*, I, p. 20.
(28) Matt. 8: 11.
(29) Phil. 3: 20. "For the Kingdom of which we are a colony is in heaven and from thence we await also the Saviour, the Lord Christ."
(30) Rom. 6: 23.
(31) Col. 1: 13.
(32) Phil. 3: 12.
(33) Phil. 2: 6ff.
(34) Cf. G. Bornkamm, *Evangelium und Mythos* in *Die Zeichen der Zeit*, 1951, I, pp. 1–15: "The new story of the Christ in which I am included, both in its ground and goal altogether transcends the history and interpretation of my life," p. 13.
(35) Phil. 3: 20.
(36) Matt. 24: 43; Rev. 3: 3.
(37) Ps. 126: 1.

CHAPTER SIXTEEN

(1) Luke 17: 21.
(2) Matt. 28: 18.
(3) Cf. Cullmann, *Königsherrschaft Christi und Kirche im Neuen Testament*, 1941.
(4) Rom. 3: 25.
(5) Gal. 5: 6.
(6) It is this which the two Blumhardts and the religious socialism of Kutter and Ragaz inspired by them rightly criticize in a Lutheranism which is one-sidedly Pauline, and, moreover, Pauline in a Lutheran sense, and what in different fashion A. Schlatter insisted on, when he again and again demanded that Paul should not take precedence over Matthew.
(7) Cf. my *Misunderstanding of the Church*, 1951.
(8) Anarchism has its roots already in medieval mysticism and in the Chiliastic sects. Cf. Benz, *Ecclesia spiritualis*, 1943.
(9) It is always insufficiently understood that the development from

Marxism to Stalinism through Lenin is unavoidable, and is rooted in the nature of the case, as soon as, like Lenin, one takes seriously the immediate realization of socialism or communism.

(10) 2 Cor. 3: 17.

(11) Only quite recently has it been recognized that this unity is the vital centre of the Synoptic reports concerning Jesus. See above all the article of Jeremias, "*pais theou*", Servant of God, in the *Theol. Wörterbuch zum Neuen Testament*, v, 655–713. Further, the commentaries of Schniewind on Matthew and Mark, and Ch. Maurer, *Knecht Gottes und Sohn Gottes im Passionsbericht des Markusevangeliums*, 1953, pp. 1–38.

(12) Rev. 5: 5, 6.

(13) Eph. 4: 4–16.

(14) 1 Cor. 1: 10.

(15) The same point applies to theocracy on a Reformed basis, whether it be that of Geneva or of Zürich or of Cromwell or of the Puritan New England states. How serious the Reformed attempt to embody the Kingdom of God can be appears nowhere more clearly than in Bucer's *De Regno Christi*, 1557.

(16) Gal. 3: 28; Col. 3: 11.

(17) On the most recent state of biological anthropology cf. B. Bavink, *Ergebnisse und Probleme der Naturwissenschaften*, pp. 559ff.; A. Neuberg, *Das Weltbild der Biologie*, 1942; K. Heim, *Weltschöpfung und Weltende*, 1952, pp. 36–69.

(18) Matt. 19: 14; 18: 3.

(19) This aspect of the Kingdom of God is wonderfully brought out in H. Kutter's *Bilderbuch Gottes*.

(20) As the modern idea of freedom is bound up with atheism as such, so the modern rationalistic idea of equality is bound up with a denial of the doctrine of creation.

(21) Cf. G. Spoerri, *Das Inkoordinable*.

(22) Gen. 3: 1.

(23) Cf. my Gifford Lectures, *Christianity and Civilization*, 1948. I: "The Problem of Creativity," pp. 142ff.

(24) Gen. 11: 1ff.

(25) Cf. Huizinga, *Homo ludens*, 1939, and also the fine remarks of K. Barth about Mozart in *Die Protestantische Theologie im 19. Jahrhundert*, 1947, pp. 53ff.

(26) Rev. 21: 22.

(27) Rom. 8: 38.

(28) John 1: 11.

(29) The Bible does not say "mankind", but either "creation" (ktisis) or the "world" (cosmos). "So God loved the world" (John 3: 16).

(30) Rom. 14: 10 ; 2 Cor. 5: 10.

CHAPTER SEVENTEEN

(1) Rev. 20: 14.

(2) Deut. 30: 15ff.

(3) Jer. 31: 29ff.; Ezek. 18: 2ff.

(4) Matt. 21: 31.

(5) Matt. 18: 23ff.

(6) Matt. 19: 25ff.

(7) Rom. 2: 6; 2 Cor. 5: 10; Gal. 6: 7.

(8) John 3: 17ff.; 8: 15.

(9) Gal. 6: 7.

(10) This outlook usual in polytheistic heathendom, and which is most sharply opposed in the Old Testament and New Testament alike, has recently been represented by the neo-gnostic school of C. G. Jung.

(11) 2 Cor. 5: 10.

(12) In the poem *Resignation.*

(13) Rom. 2: 6ff.

(14) Rom. 2: 4.

(15) Cf. my *Christian Doctrine of God*, Dogm. I, p. 296 (German edn.).

(16) Matt. 25 : 31–46.

(17) In his book, *Das Christentum und die Angst*, O. Pfister shows clearly that this contrast between church Christianity and Jesus is not tenable: but he is himself on the whole inclined to adopt the view, because he is unable to see any connexion between fear and love.

(18) The parables of Jesus should be read from this point of view, and it will be astonishing to see how they all express the thought of judgment.

(19) It is very remarkable how Fichte in his first *Ethik* (1798) in vain tries to derive responsibility from freedom. Pure freedom, freedom *sans phrase*, can only consist with an atheistic system, as, for example, in N. Hartmann or, more massively, in J. P. Sartre.

(20) This is overlooked by the criticism of Pfister. In the teaching of Jesus fear is not an independent motive, but only a means to lead to trust. But when judgment is understood under the category of "There is", then there is left only naked fear.

(21) Cf. W. Michaelis, *Versöhnung des Alls*, 1950.

(22) Col. 1: 20.

(23) Phil. 2: 9ff.

(24) Eph. 1: 9ff.

(25) Thus consistently in Michaelis. The following quotations are from his book.

(26) His misunderstanding of my position is to be explained by his failure to grasp this paradoxical juxtaposition of consummation at the Last Judgment and universal redemption—a point of view already represented in these precise terms in my *Dogmatics.* I have now tried to formulate it still more unmistakably.

(27) This title of my book contains in itself a theological programme which, as it seems to me, has not been adequately dealt with. See below, pp. 217ff.

(28) This insurmountable dualism of the love and fear of God, which has its ground in the holiness and love of God, is expressed with the inspiration of genius in Luther's *Katechismus-Auslegung der Zehn Gebote.*

CHAPTER EIGHTEEN

(1) The Lutheran A. von Oettingen describes the concluding chapter of his Dogmatics as "Doxo-logy".

(2) Bultmann, *op. cit.*, I, p. 16. E. Käsemann, *Eine urchristliche Taufliturgie in Festschrift für R. Bultmann*, 1949. In addition, Ch. Maurer, *Der Hymnus von Epheser I*, "Evg. Theologie", 1951, pp. 151–72.

(3) *Christian Doctrine of God*, Dogm. I, pp. 323–381 (German edn.).

(4) 1 Cor. 8: 6.

(5) Rom. 8: 29.

(6) Eph. 1: 9.

(7) Col. 1: 13.

(8) Col. 1: 27.

(9) As is known, Nietzsche tried to renew it, but in vain. Cf. Löwith, *op. cit.*

(10) No doubt idealism in the Western world can hardly any longer be

described as a spiritual power. But it is all the more so in the East. Cf. the, in its way, magnificent work of Radakrishnan, *The Community of the Spirit*, 1952, which, in proud self-consciousness, seeks to show that the age-old philosophy of the Vedanta is the truth behind all religions and philosophies.

(11) Matt. 24: 35.

(12) 1 Cor. 7: 31.

(13) Cf. my *Christian Doctrine of Creation and Redemption*, Dogm. II, pp. 153–171 (German edn.).

(14) John 8: 34.

(15) Col. 2: 14ff.

(16) Matt. 13: 30.

(17) 1 Cor. 15: 26.

(18) 2 Pet. 3: 13.

(19) Rev. 21: 4.

(20) The title of the already mentioned book of Radakrishnan should accordingly be expressed as *The Unity of the Spirit*. Community is an unconscious borrowing from Christianity.

(21) 1 Cor. 15: 28.

(22) The same applies to E. Thurneysen, *Ausführungen über Christus und die Zukunft*, *Zwischen den Zeiten*, 1931, p. 209: "These woods, these fields . . . will be the stage of redemption."

(23) 1 Cor. 13: 12.

(24) Bultmann, *op. cit.*, II, p. 205.

(25) Above, p. 51.

(26) 1 Cor. 8: 3.

(27) The "Blessed are" of the Beatitudes does not refer to the condition of heavenly beatitude. Cf. Schniewind, *Das Evangelium nach Matthäus*, p. 40.

(28) This makes clear how impossible is S. Freud's derivation of religion (Christian) from the unsatisfied desire for happiness. Cf. his *Future of an Illusion*.

(29) Rom. 14: 17.

(30) It is significant that medieval erotic-mystical description of the ultimate consummation could not help but base itself upon the allegorical exegesis of the Old Testament Song of Songs. The latter, however, is not intended in reality to bear this mystical allegorical interpretation, but to be understood quite naturally as a love lyric. The most famous example of this medievalist interpretation is to be found in Bernard of Clairvaux's *Sermons on the Song of Songs*.

(31) Cf. the vision of the heavenly adoration of God in the Book of Revelation, e.g. 5: 11ff.

(32) 1 Cor. 15: 28.

(33) 1 Cor. 11: 3.

(34) John 5: 26.

(35) John 17: 24.

POSTSCRIPT

(1) Bultmann, *op. cit.*, I, 48.

(2) As is known, Bultmann lays great stress on the importance of the distinction between "*existentiell*" and "existential". If this were not amalgamated with his uncritical acceptance of Heidegger's philosophy, one might adopt the distinction. Hence for my part I would prefer to remain faithful to Kierkegaard's "*existentiell*", especially as I have never shared in the development from Kierkegaard to Heidegger, nor do I now propose to share in it, particularly as Heidegger to-day is himself developing on quite other lines.